FIRESIDE

INDEPENDENT VIDEO

A Complete Guide to the Physics, Operation, and Application of the New Television for the Student, The Artist, and for Community TV

by Ken Marsh

designed and illustrated
by David Holzman

technical consultant,
Morton Schiff

FIRESIDE

A Fireside Book
Published by Simon and Schuster
New York

A Fireside Book
Published by Simon & Schuster
A Division of Gulf & Western Corporation
Simon & Schuster Building
Rockefeller Center
1230 Avenue of the Americas
New York, New York 10020
FIRESIDE and colophon are trademarks
of Simon & Schuster

Previously Published by Straight Arrow Books
Manufactured in the United States of America

1 2 3 4 5 6 7 8 9 10

Library of Congress Cataloging in Publication Data

Marsh, Ken.
  Independent video.

  (A Fireside book)
  Bibliography: p.
  Includes index.
  1. Television. I. Title.
[TK6640.M37 1980]   621.388   80-12256
ISBN 0-671-21887-5

To Duf and Elaine and Morgan

We wish to acknowledge and thank all those who have helped in putting together *Independent Video*:

To those who opened themselves for periodic brain pickings; thanks to Mark Brownstone, Don Hood, Chuck Kennedy, John La Valle, Richard Marsh, Ray Merry, Carolyn Sachs of the New York State Commission on Cable TV, Bob Sample of the Cable TV Information Center, and to the people at Adwar Video, CTL Electronics, Professional Video Techniques, and especially Jack Goldman at Technisphere Corporation.

To those who participated in the numerous readings and re-readings of the manuscript to ensure technical veracity; thanks to Mark Anderson, Ellis Richardson, Mike Kutcher of IBM, and especially to John Godfrey of the Television Laboratory at WNET/13 for the definitive and final reading.

Thanks to Rhonda Avidon for her wizardry with a compositor, Kay Zentall for copyediting and proofreading, and Sherri Holzman for her help to David. A special thanks to the New York State Council on the Arts for their support and encouragement, and to Alan Gordon for starting us off.

A super special thanks to Margaret Wolf, the editor, for her skill and precision in bringing it all together.

PREFACE

I recently had the pleasure of a visit from the distinguished Japanese television engineer and designer Shuya Abe. Since he was the co-inventor of the Paik-Abe video synthesizer, I put on the video cassette of a recent program which I had produced which includes some works created with the synthesizer. Mr. Abe immediately went to the set, sat cross-legged in front of it, and watched the program with a serene half-smile, his face no more than fifteen inches from the screen. I was struck by this expression; it pleased me to imagine something like it illuminating Bernard Berenson's face as he contemplated a Botticelli, or Toscanini's as he read a Beethoven score. He knew, profoundly, just what he was looking at.

This book should help us all move closer to that blissful state. By all, I mean those primarily interested in the extraordinary potential of video as an informational tool which can effect social change, as well as those drawn to it as an artistic medium. Ken Marsh, an ex-painter with a deep social conscience, is one of the hardy few who could claim, if he cared to, to be an authentic video pioneer. He is supremely well qualified to write a book that combines a strikingly clear exposition of the physics and electronics of the medium with practical procedures for the videomaker.

In a period when the "video movement" is pausing to re-assess its accomplishments and its aims, shelving its most utopian fantasies and examining its own esthetics, this is a most timely and valuable contribution.

Russell Connor

Russell Connor

CONTENTS

LIST OF ILLUSTRATIONS

Television is now in our homes for its third decade. For most of that time it has predominantly been a medium for news and entertainment supported by advertising. Program production is big business. As a government regulatory agency, the Federal Communications Commission (FCC) guards over broadcast TV—setting technical standards, making airwave allocations, licensing, and censoring. Until recently, very few people from outside the commercial television industry have had any opportunity to know and use the tools of TV making and broadcasting.

Recording and playing back TV via magnetic tape (videotape) was introduced by Ampex in 1955, and until 1968, other than in the industry, video tape recorders (VTRs) were used only by military, scientific, industrial, and educational institutions for closed-circuit TV operations. In 1968, a low-cost, easily operated, portable videotape recording/playback system was brought out by the electronics industry of Japan. The equipment, like previous closed-circuit systems of much greater cost, did not meet broadcast standards. However, teachers, artists, psychotherapists, journalists, and just people began to produce and show their own tapes —TV shows. Schools, video theatres, cable TV systems, and even living rooms became places to go to see a different kind of TV. Since that time, relatively inexpensive and simple to use TV equipment has become still more versatile and widely available.

This book is a video handbook: It explains video technology and tells you what equipment is available and how to use it. You need not necessarily read this book sequentially—go where your interests take you and allow new interests to emerge and lead you back and forth between practical experience and the book. The information is here for you when *you* want it and need to know it.

The greater the understanding the more of us have of our media of communications, the more effectively we can know and share our world, I think.

K.M.
Woodstock, New York

THE BIG WORKS

INTRODUCTION

THE UNIVERSE

The Universe is comprised of substance and energy. Substance is matter which has size and mass. It can also have color; be solid, liquid, or gaseous; feel sticky or slippery, etc. Energy is the mover of matter; and all forms of energy are derived from matter. Video systems are based on the laws of matter-energy conversion. The forms of energy operative in video technology are **electrical, magnetic, electromagnetic propagation,** and **mechanical.**

ELECTRICAL ENERGY
POWER TO THE CIRCUITS

Matter is made up of **atoms**, which contain particles: **protons** and **electrons**. Protons lie within an atom's center, or **nucleus**; and electrons, spinning on their axes, circle the nucleus. Both these particles carry an electric charge: the proton a positive charge, the electron a negative one. The number of protons and electrons is equal in a neutral atom.

A charge is surrounded by a **field**, the area in which the charge is active. When fields meet, charges that are opposite attract, charges that are alike repel. Thus, protons and electrons attract each other. Under some circumstances, electrons can be freed from the attraction of protons and made to flow through **conductors**—certain materials such as copper wire.

Putting a positive charge at one end of a wire and a negative charge at the other end creates a **potential difference**. Utilizing this difference, we can generate the flow of electrons called **electric current**. Think of a waterfall. Due to gravity, water falls from a high point to a low one. For the purposes of this book we shall say that electrons flow from negative to positive. The direction of flow is from an excess of electrons to a paucity—a smaller number—of electrons. The negative charge is excess and the positive is paucity.

This movement of electrons produces energy which we are able to utilize—electricity. Electricity provides the power for video circuitry, and this electrical energy can also be coded and used to carry information.

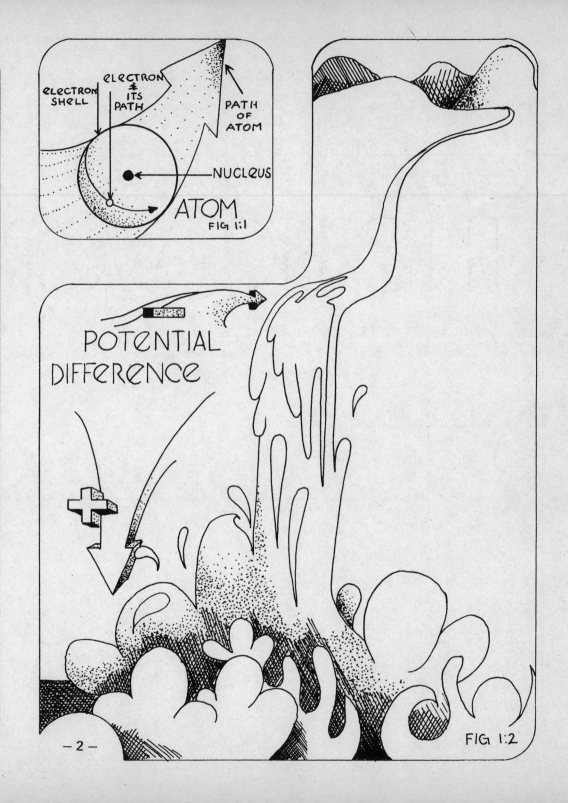

ELECTRON SHELL — ELECTRON & ITS PATH — PATH OF ATOM — NUCLEUS

ATOM
FIG 1:1

POTENTIAL DIFFERENCE

FIG 1:2

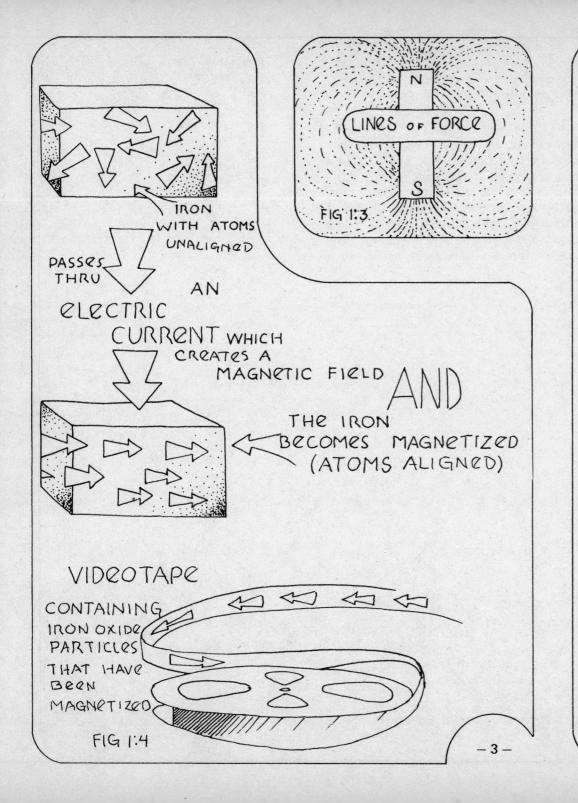

IRON WITH ATOMS UNALIGNED

PASSES THRU AN ELECTRIC CURRENT WHICH CREATES A MAGNETIC FIELD AND

THE IRON BECOMES MAGNETIZED (ATOMS ALIGNED)

VIDEOTAPE

CONTAINING IRON OXIDE PARTICLES THAT HAVE BEEN MAGNETIZED

FIG 1:4

FIG 1:3

LINES OF FORCE

N

S

MAGNETISM
THE VIDEO MEMORY

Magnetic forces are the partners of electrical forces. A spinning electron creates a magnetic field, and in turn, this magnetic field can generate electricity. A magnetic field consists of **lines of force**. If the lines of force are intersected by a wire, electrons will flow through that wire.

To understand lines of force, let's look at an atom of iron which is itself a tiny magnet. The spin direction of any electron can be to the left or the right. If, as in the iron atom, the majority are spinning in the same direction, their magnetic fields are aligned. Science's theoretical model ascribes north and south poles to each electron's axis. The lines of force flow from the north, and loop to the south. As with charges, opposite poles attract and like poles repel. When two magents are put together with their north poles upward, the lines of force will repel; turn one magnet upside down and the lines of force will attract. To generate electric current in a wire with a magnet, the wire must intersect the loop of the lines of force.

The atoms of a piece of iron are not necessarily aligned. If, with an electric current, we create a magnetic field and expose the iron to it, the iron will become magnetized. Even after taking away the external field the iron will remain a magnet—meaning that many of its atoms will be aligned.

Videotape is coated with iron oxide particles arranged by magnetic forces in coded patterns to store information.

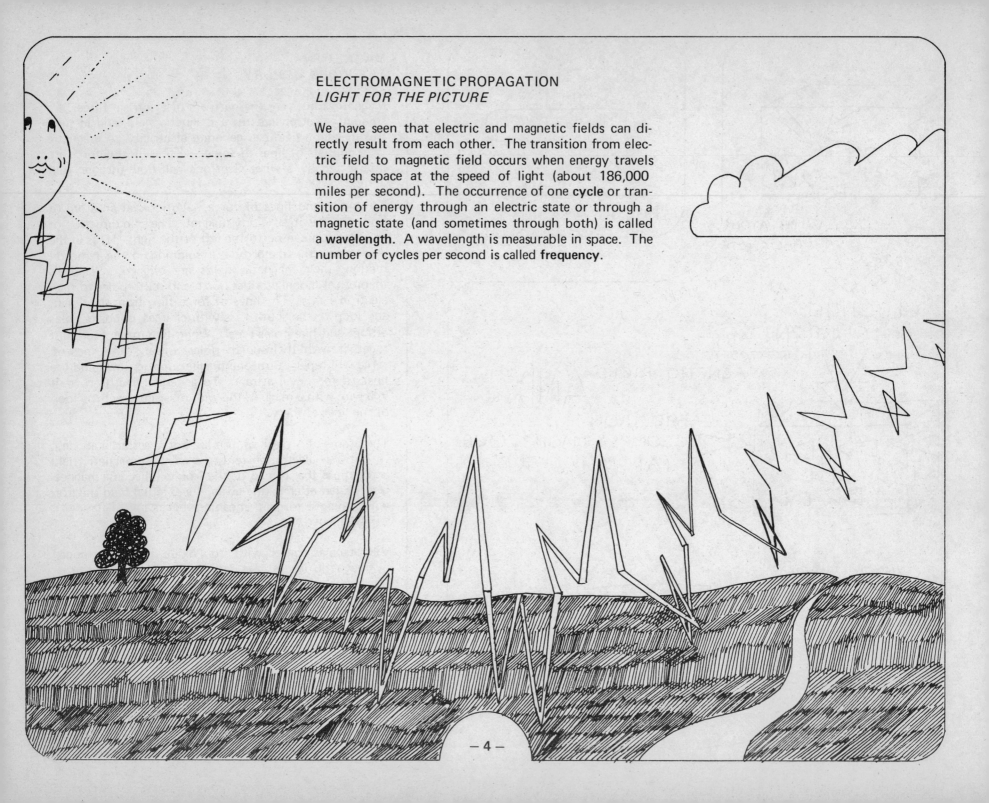

ELECTROMAGNETIC PROPAGATION
LIGHT FOR THE PICTURE

We have seen that electric and magnetic fields can directly result from each other. The transition from electric field to magnetic field occurs when energy travels through space at the speed of light (about 186,000 miles per second). The occurrence of one **cycle** or transition of energy through an electric state or through a magnetic state (and sometimes through both) is called a **wavelength**. A wavelength is measurable in space. The number of cycles per second is called **frequency**.

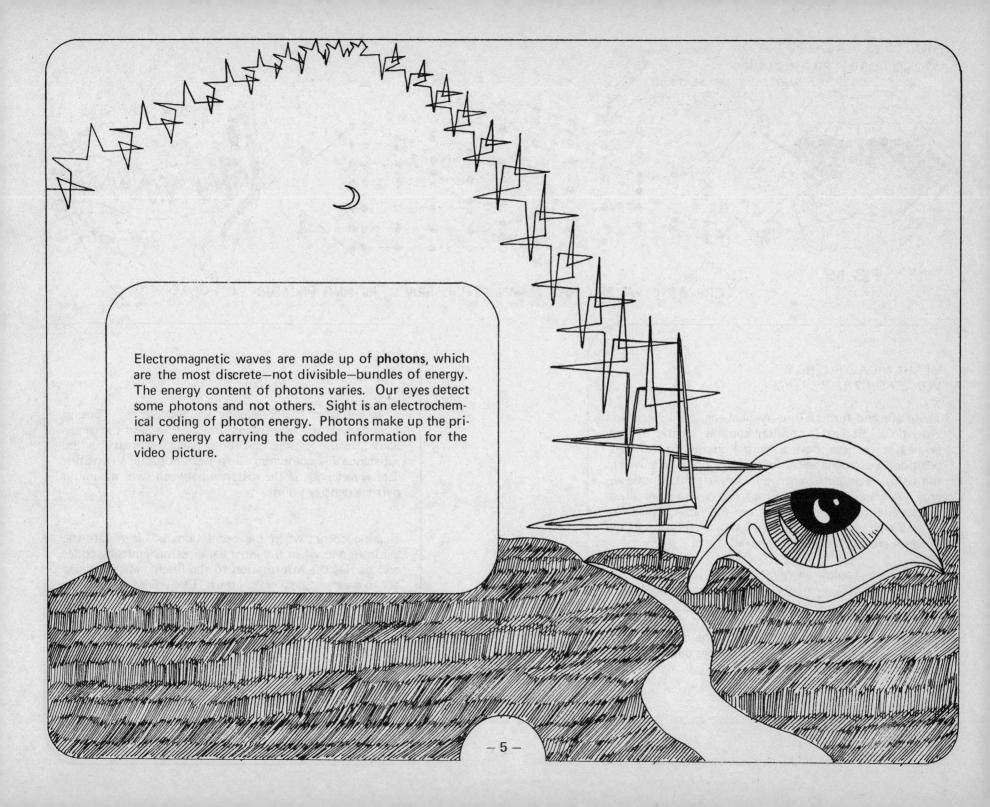

Electromagnetic waves are made up of **photons**, which are the most discrete—not divisible—bundles of energy. The energy content of photons varies. Our eyes detect some photons and not others. Sight is an electrochemical coding of photon energy. Photons make up the primary energy carrying the coded information for the video picture.

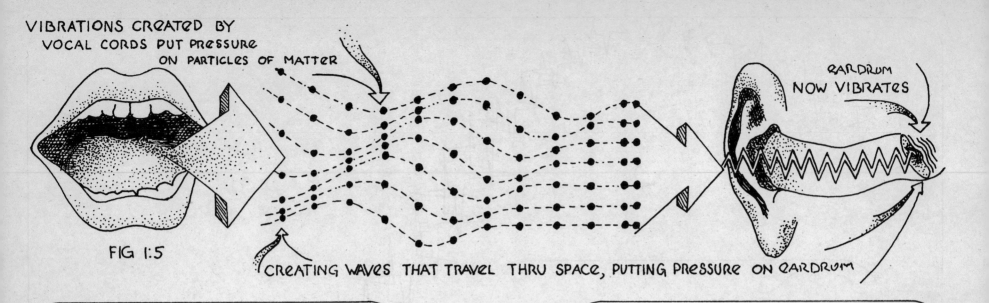

VIBRATIONS CREATED BY
VOCAL CORDS PUT PRESSURE
ON PARTICLES OF MATTER

FIG 1:5

EARDRUM
NOW VIBRATES

CREATING WAVES THAT TRAVEL THRU SPACE, PUTTING PRESSURE ON EARDRUM

MECHANICAL ENERGY
VOICE FOR THE PICTURE

There are two forms of mechanical energy: kinetic and potential. Bodies in motion contain **kinetic energy**. Bodies at rest can have **potential energy** due to their position in a gravitational field. As a body falls within the field, its potential energy is converted to kinetic energy. A glass on the edge of a table is in a state of potential energy. When it falls from the table it picks up kinetic energy. Generally, things that go bump in the universe are mechanically energized.

Sound is mechanical energy. A sound puts pressure on a substance, moving that substance's particles momentarily. As the particles are moved, they cause shifting of their neighboring particles and so on down the line. This action is called a **sound wave**. The density of the substance through which a sound moves determines the sound's speed of travel.

A sound wave has frequency and wavelength. Sound frequency is the number of times per second the generated pressure causes maximum particle density in the substance (as compared to its normal particle density). The wavelength is the distance between two maximum particle density points.

Hearing occurs when the oscillations of air vibrate the eardrum and when the inner ear electrochemically codes and carries the information to the brain. Microphones act like ears. Speakers' outputs, like voices, cause pressure changes in their surroundings. Energy in speakers is changed from electrical to magnetic to mechanical.

WORKING THE BIG WORKS

TRANSDUCTION
INFORMATION CONSERVATION

Matter moving in certain ways is energy, and energy at rest is matter. What's important is that the two can convert back and forth. Akin to matter-energy conversion is **transduction**, or the conversion of one form of energy to another.

Lighting a stick of dynamite is a good example of matter-energy conversion. Matter is changed in an extreme way and converted to energy to perform some kind of work, like move mountains. Seeing, on the other hand, is an example of transduction. The eye is a transducer which detects light's energy—photons. The lens of the eye focuses incoming photons onto detectors within the eye. Focusing acts to place the photons at the points in the eye which correspond to the points from which they are reflected in the field of vision. The detectors—rods and cones—receive the electromagnetic energy of the photons, and the rod and cone electrons are moved.

A stick of dynamite works to move mountains. The eye works to receive light information and transmit it to the brain. The eye acts to conserve energy information, not utilize the energy to do work.

Looking closely at the eye, we can see what a transducer is. The lens alone is not a transducer; it influences the light, but cannot change it to another form. The rods and cones, however, detect and interact with light's energy and therefore perform transduction. If we proceeded back along the optic nerve, into the brain where the information is processed, we could find a number of other transductions occurring.

Any complete "package" that changes energy from one form to another is a transducer. The retina, iris, lens, rods, and cones make up one transducer. We will see later that the vidicon, the video camera's light-sensing circuit, is a transducer of light energy to electrical energy. Whenever the process of energy-to-signal-to-energy exists, we can be sure that transduction is at work. Lest we forget, information is coded energy.

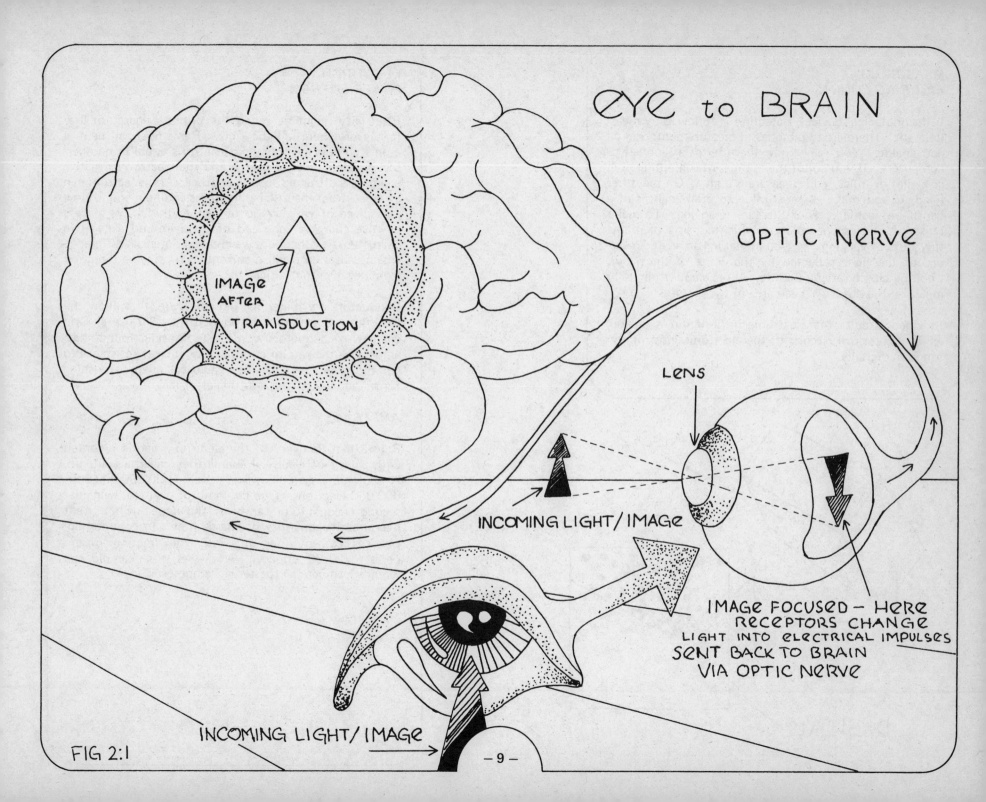

eye to BRAIN

OPTIC NERVE

IMAGE AFTER TRANSDUCTION

LENS

INCOMING LIGHT/IMAGE

IMAGE FOCUSED - HERE RECEPTORS CHANGE LIGHT INTO ELECTRICAL IMPULSES SENT BACK TO BRAIN VIA OPTIC NERVE

INCOMING LIGHT/IMAGE

FIG 2:1

MEASURING
FIGURING COUNTS

In technological devices, detection is followed by measurement. There are two modes of measurement: **digital** and **analog**. You may know these terms as applied to computers. If you count the number of something such as cycles or miles, your measure is digital. On the other hand, if you make a statistical or overall analysis of a density of activity, your measure is analog. To make sense of a newspaper picture which consists of many tiny dots of varying size, you are taking an analog measure of the light reflected by the white of the paper. Looking closely at the picture, you can count (digitally measure) the dots in a given area of the picture.

In video circuits the electronic information is analog, while the control circuits of the electronic information function digitally.

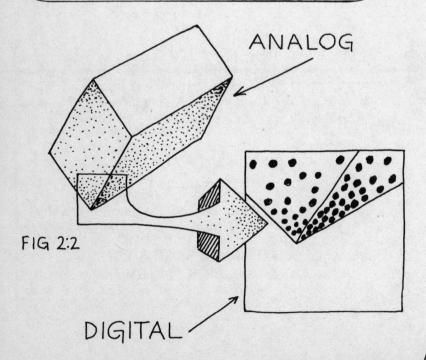

ANALOG

DIGITAL

FIG 2:2

ELECTRICITY
POWER ENERGY

Electricity might be called the primary energy of life. It is everywhere, all the time. Remember, all neutral atoms contain protons and electrons equal in number; the proton's positive charge and the electron's negative charge are attracted to one another. And, electrons can be freed from their places in atoms and be made to flow in a piece of wire. Also remember that if we place a positive charge at one end of the wire and a negative charge at the other end, we create a potential difference which causes an electric current to run in the direction from negative to positive.

Conductors are materials, like the wire, that allow the free flow of electrons through them. To use electric current in conductors we need to consider four things: amperage—the rate of current flow; ohms—resistance to current flow; voltage—the electrical charge's pushing force; and watts—the resulting electrical power.

AMPERAGE

Before the discovery of the electron, scientists worked with a unit of electrical charge they called a **coulomb**. A coulomb is actually made up of 6,000,000,000,000, 000,000 electrons. One coulomb of charge flowing per second is equal to one **ampere**: the amperage of current measures the quantity of charge flow. In common appliances, current flows at a rate from fractions of amperes to 20–30 amperes. A TV set, for example, can require 1 ampere; a toaster, 12 amperes.

OHMS—RESISTANCE

We must accept that electrons moving in any medium give off heat and lose energy. This phenomenon is called **resistance**. Every material has an intrinsic resistivity, which is measured per cubic centimeter of the material (ohms per centimeter). The larger the diameter of a cross section of the material, the lower its actual resistance.

The filaments in lightbulbs are made of tungsten because its particular resistivity and high melting temperature permit the extreme heat necessary to produce light. In the vacuum of the bulb, heat boils off the tungsten's electrons which in movement convert to electromagnetic energy, photons of visible light (see this section, page 39). A unit of electrical resistance is called an **ohm**. The resistance of no. 12 household wiring is about 1.6 ohms per 1,000 feet; of a wire for a clothes dryer, .644 ohms per 1,000 feet.

VOLTAGE

Besides amperes, which measure the amount of charge flowing per second, and ohms, which measure the resistance, there are **volts**, which represent the pushing force of the charge, somewhat akin to water pressure in a plumbing system. Voltage levels are usually fixed in the source of current. Flashlight batteries are 1.5 volts; chargeable batteries for both cars and portable video systems, 12 volts (see **VIDEOWORKS**, page 115). Household current in the United States is set at 110–120 volts AC (alternating current, which we shall soon discuss). In Europe, current operates at 220–240 volts AC.

WATTAGE

A **watt** is a unit of electrical power or heat-generating energy. Wattage is calculated by multiplying the voltage by the amperage. In other words, the pushing force multiplied by the amount of current flow per second equals the electrical power. Interestingly, horsepower is a unit of mechanical energy. About 760 watts of electrical power is equal to one horsepower of mechanical energy. Mechanical energy is often used to generate electrical power, and in fact, the amount of power we can obtain is dependent on the amount of mechanical energy used to generate it.

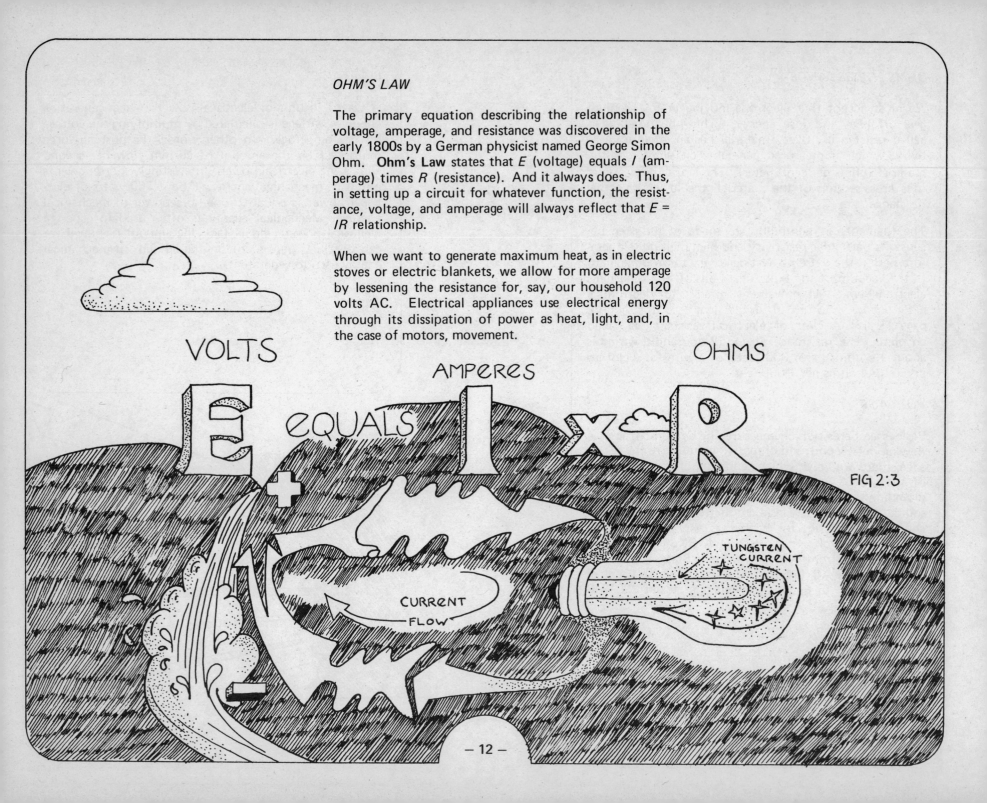

OHM'S LAW

The primary equation describing the relationship of voltage, amperage, and resistance was discovered in the early 1800s by a German physicist named George Simon Ohm. **Ohm's Law** states that *E* (voltage) equals *I* (amperage) times *R* (resistance). And it always does. Thus, in setting up a circuit for whatever function, the resistance, voltage, and amperage will always reflect that *E = IR* relationship.

When we want to generate maximum heat, as in electric stoves or electric blankets, we allow for more amperage by lessening the resistance for, say, our household 120 volts AC. Electrical appliances use electrical energy through its dissipation of power as heat, light, and, in the case of motors, movement.

VOLTS

AMPERES

OHMS

E EQUALS I x R

FIG 2:3

+

−

CURRENT FLOW

TUNGSTEN CURRENT

When we are concerned with an electrical signal conserving a bit of information that it has encoded, as in a video camera or record deck, we need to be aware of the $E = IR$ relationship so as not to cause any unwanted changes in our signal as it is carried through various circuits.

CIRCUITS

A simple circuit: Using the lightbulb, remember the tungsten filament is a resistor which heats up, boils off electrons, and thereby gives light. Let's say we have a 60-watt bulb, one designed for optimum lighting when consuming 60 watts of power. The standard household current is 120 volts AC. Remember, wattage is voltage times amperage. To find the amperage, divide the 60 watts by the 120 volts; you'll get .5 amperes. With I

(the .5 amperes), and E (the 120 volts), we can now solve for R, resistance in ohms; thus, 240 ohms. If $E = IR$, then our solution for R is equal to $E \div I$.

For comparison, take a 15-watt bulb and divide that by 120 volts; you'll get .125 amperes. Using $R = E \div I$ again, E (120 volts) divided by I (.125 amperes) equals R (960 ohms). Note that for a given voltage, the lower the resistance the higher the amperage, and the higher the amperage the higher the wattage. In other words, the lower the resistance, the greater the flow; and the greater the flow, the more power consumed.

It's important to note that without resistance we could not use electric current; it would run away with itself. The generated power would burn up the conductor through which it flowed. There must be resistors.

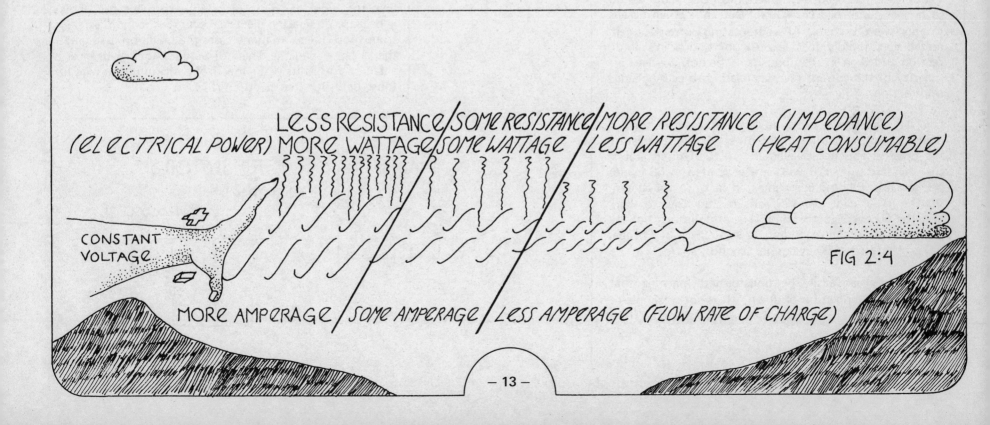

LESS RESISTANCE / SOME RESISTANCE / MORE RESISTANCE (IMPEDANCE)
(ELECTRICAL POWER) MORE WATTAGE / SOME WATTAGE / LESS WATTAGE (HEAT CONSUMABLE)

CONSTANT VOLTAGE

FIG 2:4

MORE AMPERAGE / SOME AMPERAGE / LESS AMPERAGE (FLOW RATE OF CHARGE)

SERIES AND PARALLEL CONNECTIONS

Resistors can be lined up either in **series** or **parallel** (see fig. 2:5). A series connection divides the voltage of a system among its resistors. If three resistors have the same resistances, the voltage across each of them will be 1/3 the total voltage of the system. If the resistances are different, each will have a voltage across it in proportion to its size, and the sum of all three will equal the total voltage of the system.

A parallel connection is one in which every resistor is provided with the full voltage of the system; resistors are not interconnected and therefore do not split the voltage among them.

ALTERNATING CURRENT AND 60 CYCLES PER SECOND

Though AC has been mentioned, most of the discussion so far has concerned **DC—Direct Current**—which travels in only one direction. **AC—Alternating Current**—is generated very rapidly from a zero point, first in one direction and then in the opposite. The positive-negative polarity of the current reverses itself with every change of direction.

One AC cycle is the occurrence of current generated in one direction and then in the other, or the reversal of the positive and negative poles. In the United States, the standard 110–120 volts are generated at 60 cycles per second. Electric companies, in fact, do not guarantee the AC level at 110–120 volts, but do strive to maintain the 60 cycles per second. The establishment of the 60-cycles-per-second standard is arbitrary. In Europe, AC is generated at 50 cycles per second.

AC voltages can easily be **transformed**—meaning that they can be stepped up or down. (It is not so simple to transform DC.) The lines that carry electricity from

generating stations to users are generally very long and therefore have high resistances which can lead to the dissipation of power and loss of voltage. Large-diameter wire which provides less resistance can be used, but it is very expensive.

Remember that wattage (power) is voltage times amperage. Let's say we generate 2,000 watts at 120 volts AC. Remember, power dissipation comes from high amperage. The amperage in this case is 16.7 amperes. Utilizing a transformer, we can step up the voltage by a factor of 10 to give us 1,200 volts; the amperage will drop to 1.7 amperes, thereby reducing the loss of power. The process then can be reversed at substations which will step down the voltage and distribute electricity to users at the desired lower voltage.

Electrical energy cannot be transmitted without some power loss. You may notice while driving under power lines that your car radio picks up excessive static. This is because dissipating electrical energy is radiating freely from those lines. In many cases the radiation is so great that a law called the Theft of Service Act has been enacted to forbid us plain folk from sticking up a wire in those fields for free electricity.

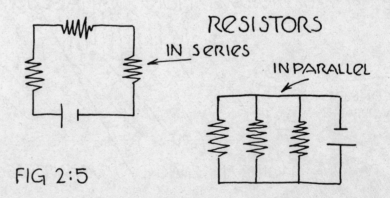

RESISTORS

IN series

IN PARALLEL

FIG 2:5

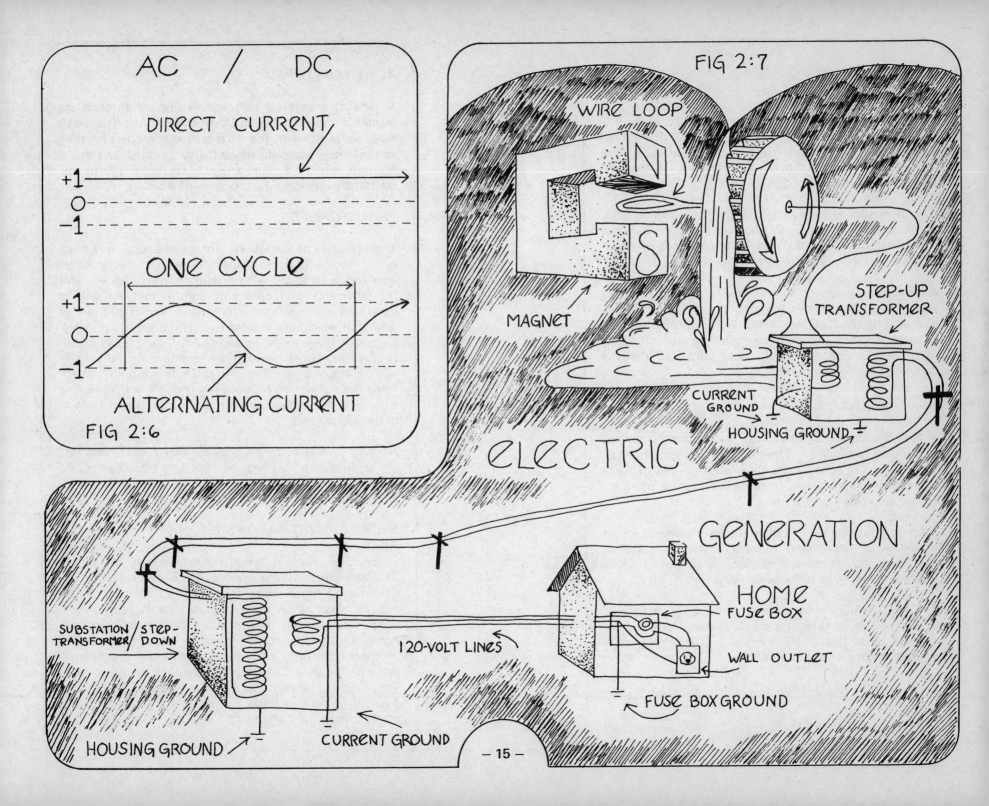

AC / DC

DIRECT CURRENT

+1
0
–1

ONE CYCLE

+1
0
–1

ALTERNATING CURRENT

FIG 2:6

FIG 2:7

WIRE LOOP

N
S

MAGNET

STEP-UP TRANSFORMER

CURRENT GROUND

HOUSING GROUND

ELECTRIC

GENERATION

SUBSTATION / STEP-DOWN TRANSFORMER

HOUSING GROUND

CURRENT GROUND

120-VOLT LINES

HOME FUSE BOX

WALL OUTLET

FUSE BOX GROUND

ELECTRIC MOTORS

A simple motor consists of a C-shaped magnet with a wire loop placed between its poles (see fig. 2:8). Remember (see **THE BIG WORKS**, page   3) that a moving wire cutting across a magnetic field's lines of force produces an electric current in that wire. Either the magnet or the wire can be in motion.

Two things to note: 1) the stronger the magnetic field, the higher the voltage; 2) the faster the motion, the higher the voltage. Also, current moving in a wire generates a magnetic field around that wire.

As we supply current to the loop, the magnetic field produced interacts with the magnetic field of the magnet, causing the loop to rotate. We need only attach a shaft to the loop and we have an electric motor, so long as current is supplied. In this case, electrical energy is converted to mechanical energy.

GENERATORS

A generator is similar to a motor except that no current is supplied to the loop. The shaft is rotated mechanically, moving the loop across the magnet's lines of force and thereby producing a current which can be transmitted by wire (see fig. 2:7).

Electric companies use either steam-driven engines or falling water from dams to turn generators. Atomic power plants use nuclear reactors to generate heat to produce steam to turn the generators.

The magnets used in large generators are not permanent magnets. They are electromagnets powered by a current which enables them to reach a greater number of **gauss**—units of magnetic field strength.

AC GENERATORS

A side of a rotating loop moves upward through the magnet's lines of force and then downward. As a loop's side moves upward, the current flows in one direction; as that side moves downward, the current flows in the opposite direction. The generated current is alternating, constantly changing the direction of flow.

TRANSFORMERS

The principle of **induction**—storage of energy in a magnetic field—is basic to transformers. If one end of an iron rod is wrapped with a wire coil carrying AC, and the other end is wrapped with another coil, AC will be generated in the second coil. If the second coil in this simple transformer has fewer turns than the primary coil, the voltage in the second coil will be stepped down. If there are more turns in the second coil, the voltage will be stepped up. The iron rod acts as a path, intensifying the magnetism produced by the AC in the primary coil. The rod's magnetism then induces current to flow in the second coil.

Another, more common, transformer model does not use an iron rod. Instead, two coils are placed alongside each other; their proximity allows the magnetism to cross over from the primary to the secondary coil.

SHORT CIRCUITS AND FUSES

So-called zipcord—common household wire for lamps, TVs, etc—contains two separately insulated wire strands. Each strand is connected to a prong of the plug. Short circuits occur when the two wire strands touch. This contact cancels out the wires' resistances and things get hot fast. In order to minimize the damage and danger of short-circuiting, fuses are used to break the flow of current. Fuses are made with wire that has a low melting point. They exist as a sort of weak link in a conductive path, and can break if there are any shorts or excesses of current in the path.

ELECTRIC MOTOR   FIG 2:8

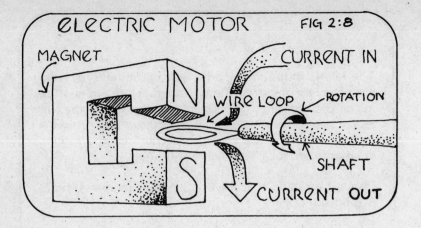

MAGNET

N

S

CURRENT IN

WIRE LOOP

ROTATION

SHAFT

CURRENT OUT

TRANSFORMER

(STEP-DOWN)

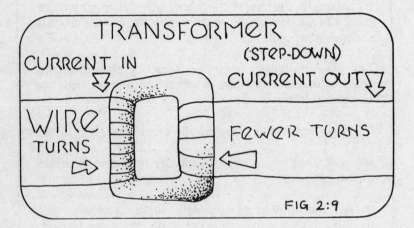

CURRENT IN

CURRENT OUT

WIRE TURNS

FEWER TURNS

FIG 2:9

SHORT CIRCUITS & FUSES

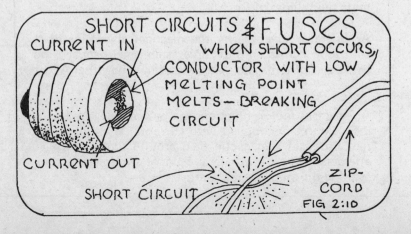

CURRENT IN

WHEN SHORT OCCURS, CONDUCTOR WITH LOW MELTING POINT MELTS—BREAKING CIRCUIT

CURRENT OUT

SHORT CIRCUIT

ZIP-CORD

FIG 2:10

Fuses are rated in amperes. If a current exceeds a fuse in amperes, the fuse will blow. All household electrical systems have fuse boxes (or circuit breakers, which serve the same function). Almost all pieces of electronic equipment have fuses.

GROUND

Since electricity is everywhere, the earth (the largest hunk of matter-energy hereabouts) serves as a fixed reference for all electrical activity. The earth is our only drainage field for unconsumed electrical buildups.

Since electrical energy is everywhere, static charges collect and can do harm to electrical circuits. By connecting a wire from a circuit to the ground, we can avoid electrical excesses and also safeguard ourselves from short circuits and their high currents. Such currents, seeking the earth's reference, tend to flow through the human body if it presents itself as the only convenient path.

In some pieces of electronic equipment, the electrical ground differs from the earth ground. In these cases, the electrical ground is the reference for all electrical measurement inside the equipment. All household electrical systems, electrical devices, and power transmission systems are grounded. In a three-prong plug, the third prong supplies the ground connection. These plugs are required by safety codes in many areas.

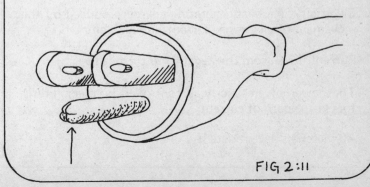

FIG 2:11

REPLAY

Electricity is a heat-generating energy produced by the movement of electrons (current) in conductors.

Current flows from the negative to the positive.

The power of electricity is controlled by placing resistors in the path of current.

All materials have resistivity.

The relationships among a current's pushing force (voltage), the rate of current flow (amperage), the impedance in the path of current (resistance in ohms), and the current's heat-generating energy (wattage) make up the laws that govern the use of electrical energy in conductors to produce heat, light, or motion.

Ohm's Law states that E (volts) equals I (amperes) times R (ohms).

Wattage is equal to voltage times amperage.

In a circuit, the fewer the ohms (resistance) the more the amperes (flow rate), and thereby the more the watts (heat generation).

The given voltage in a circuit does not change except across individual resistances when those resistances are connected in series.

DC is current which flows only in one direction.

AC is current which changes rapidly from one direction to the opposite.

In AC the number of complete direction changes per second equals a current's number of cycles per second.

Current can be generated by moving a wire across a magnetic field's lines of force.

A generator operates by the mechanical turning of a wire loop across lines of force established between the two poles of a magnet. Generators may be either AC or DC.

An electric motor functions via a shaft attached to a loop externally supplied with current. The loop's current produces a magnetic field around the wire which interacts with the magnetic field of the magnet, thus rotating the loop and the shaft.

A transformer works on the principle of induction: AC in a wire coil produces a magnetic field around that coil. Another wire coil close to it picks up this magnetism and thus AC current is induced in the second coil.

Short circuits result when two wire strands conducting the flow of current in and out of a circuit make contact.

Fuses are weak links in conductive paths. They blow when the heat is too great, thus protecting the various electronic components through which the current is flowing.

Ground, which in some cases is a third wire, serves to drain off excess electrical buildups and protect users from the shocks of short circuits. This third wire carries the current into the earth, which is a fixed reference for all electrical activity hereabouts.

ELECTRONICS
INTELLIGENCE ENERGY

We have noted that electrons flowing in conductors generate heat, which in turn can provide light. This flow of electrical energy also produces a magnetic field which in electric motors can create motion. Generally, electricity provides the energy to do work like cook foods, warm houses, light streets, rotate turntables, etc.

In electronics, moving electrons are considered mini-transducers. Remember, a transducer converts energy from one form to another in order to conserve information. Electronic devices use energy to receive, carry, and deliver signals—coded energy.

Before discussing some of the specifics of electronics, we need to reorient ourselves from thinking of electrical energy as being simply the movement of particles to thinking of it as being waves and fields produced by the movement of electrons.

In an atom, electrons are most likely to be found in those areas around the nucleus which we call **orbits**. But the orbits of electrons are not nice and neat like those of the planets around the sun; electron orbits may be anywhere around the nucleus. So in this case, an orbit would best be described as a zone of probability.

Electrons farther from the nucleus occupy orbits of higher energy levels. Those closer to the nucleus are less energetic. Each orbit is separated by a distinct energy gap. In order for an electron to jump up to another orbit, it must gain energy from an external source; or, to drop down an orbit, an electron can give up energy.

When an electron is provided with enough energy to get it beyond the bond of the nucleus, it becomes freed from its atom. This process is called **ionization**, and the abandoned atom with its net positive charge is called an **ion**. (An equal number of protons and electrons make up a neutral atom.) The work factor involved in changing energy levels is referred to as the potential difference or voltage difference.

The process of ionization bears out everything said here so far about electrical energy. We have also stated that by placing a positive charge at one end of a conductor and a negative charge at the other end, we can cause a flow of current.

Electric current is actually wave motion produced by the movement of electrons. Electrical energy travels at a much greater speed than that of the moving electrons themselves. For instance, in AC the electrons do not flow, but gyrate back and forth within a general location. The wave-like flow of current is the result of gyrating electrons nudging their neighbors and passing along electrical energy. In electronics, this theory of electrical energy as wave motion supplants the particle theory.

IMPEDANCES

Impedances are the tools of electronics engineers. There are several types of impedances which affect the flow of current in conductors. Resistance, the loss of energy through heat, is one type of impedance. Unlike resistance, some other impedances do not dissipate energy. Impedances might be thought of as conditions which alter the movement of electrons somewhat like the valves and gates which affect the flow of water.

For the most part, when designing electronics, you first figure out what you want to end up with, and then you figure out how to get there. It's like planning the itinerary of a trip from the last stop to the first. For example, suppose you want to reproduce music at home. The first consideration must be the ear of the listener. In order to hear anything at all, a finite amount of energy must reach the ear—about a milliwatt. In order to generate a milliwatt of power in an average room, a speaker must produce 1–10 watts of acoustical power. For a speaker to produce that power it must be driven by 10–100 watts of electrical power. And so we travel from the end to the beginning. Keep this in mind, as it will be helpful in grasping the seemingly ass-backward logic of electronics.

INDUCTANCE

We know that current in a wire produces a magnetic field around that wire. When any current is first introduced in a wire, it takes a certain amount of time for the magnetic field to build up to its peak intensity. During that time, as the lines of force move, a counter-current is induced in the wire. This second current runs in the opposite direction from the source current and acts to impede it. This action is called **inductance** (see fig 2:13).

In the case of a wire coil, the lines of force cut across more of the wire, thereby inducing an even greater counter-current than in a straight wire. When DC is

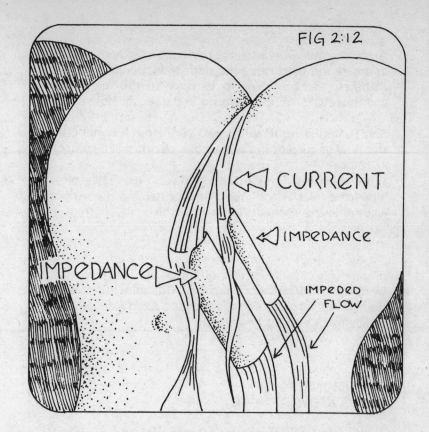

FIG 2:12

CURRENT

IMPEDANCE

IMPEDANCE

IMPEDED FLOW

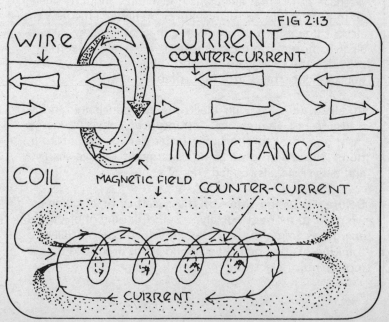

FIG 2:13

WIRE

CURRENT

COUNTER-CURRENT

INDUCTANCE

COIL

MAGNETIC FIELD

COUNTER-CURRENT

CURRENT

supplied, as in a battery, this phenomenon lasts only until the maximum current is built up and flowing through the coil. At that time the lines of force are stabilized and no longer move. The greater the number of turns and the shorter the coil, the greater the amount of inductance. A unit of inductance is called a **henry**. The symbol for inductance is L.

If the current is AC, the lines of force continue to fluctuate with the changes of current direction. The higher the frequency, the higher the voltage in the countercurrent. To determine the amperage of AC in coils we use a modification of Ohm's Law ($I = E \div R$): I (amperage) equals E (voltage) divided by X_L (inductive reactance in ohms).

Inductive reactance is a form of impedance. It might be seen as a storing phenomenon. The action of the countering current impedes the source current without dissipating energy. The electrical energy is actually stored in the magnetic field around the wire. X_L (inductive reactance) equals $2 \pi fL$, which means 2 times 3.14 times the frequency (number of AC cycles) times L (inductance of the coil).

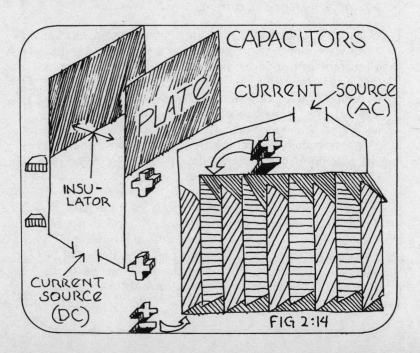

CAPACITORS

PLATE

CURRENT SOURCE (AC)

INSU-LATOR

CURRENT SOURCE (DC)

FIG 2:14

CAPACITANCE

While inductance is the storage of electrical energy in a magnetic field, **capacitance** is the storage of electrical energy in an electric field. Devices which provide capacitance are called **condensers** or **capacitors**.

A capacitor usually has two metal plates separated by some kind of insulator, a material through which current barely flows (sometimes even air is used). A good insulator is called a **dielectric** and is practically nonconducting. In a manner of speaking, the potential difference of the source current is suspended between the plates.

Here's an example of what a capacitor does in a DC situation: Remember that in a simple circuit, current flows from the negative terminal of a battery through a resistor and back into the positive terminal. By replacing the resistor with a capacitor, we in effect break the circuit; the plates are separated by the insulator, so current flows from the negative terminal to the first plate and is held there (see fig. 2:14). Once the current source—in this case, the battery—is emptied of its store of current, it then draws the electrons of the atoms from the second plate to it like a pump. Current, in turn, flows up to the first plate. In this way, the positive-negative polarity is established across the plates, and electrical energy can then be stored at points in a circuit beyond the current source.

The amount of stored charge in a capacitor depends on the voltage of the source current applied to the plates. To express this, we use the formula Q (stored charge) equals C (capacitance) times E (voltage). Capacitance is measured in **farads**, but more commonly, in **microfarads** (millionths of farads), **picofarads** (billionths of farads), and **micromicrofarads** (millionths of microfarads).

The capacitance of a capacitor is in proportion to the area of the plates divided by the distance between them and is a function of the type of insulator used. **Variable capacitors** are those which can store different amounts of charge due to the fact that the space between the plates or the area of the plates can be altered.

As you may have guessed, the storage of AC in capacitors is another story. The positive-negative polarity is constantly changing back and forth from plate to plate. As the polarity reverses there is a process of emptying and filling of electrons from plate to plate. As in the case of inductance, this process effectively acts as an impedance and is called **capacitative reactance**, and it is measured in ohms. The formula is X_C (capacitative reactance) equals $1/2 \pi fC$, (f equals the frequency of AC and C represents capacitance).

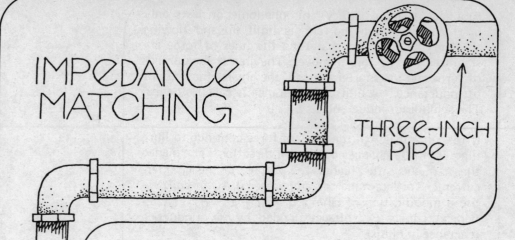

IMPEDANCE MATCHING

THREE-INCH PIPE

IMPEDANCE MATCHING

Inductance and capacitance are effects which occur around and at the surface of conductors. Both cause some amount of electrical energy to be stored beyond the limits of the conducting medium. We must be able to calculate the effect such impedances have on the voltage and amperage of a current.

When we speak of matching impedances, we mean that when we connect two components or circuits, the flow of current from one to the other should occur without unwanted changes to the voltage and amperage of the incoming signal. Connecting, say, a low-impedance device to a high-impedance device is somewhat like connecting a three-inch-diameter pipe to a quarter-inch pipe. Impedance-matching transformers act somewhat like pipe connectors which allow those three-inch pipes to be tied into quarter-inch pipes

It's fairly easy to understand why, in some circumstances, connecting a high impedance into a low impedance is okay. Though not ideal, like the quarter-inch pipe connected to the three-inch pipe, the flow will be minimally affected. But don't make a practice of it, since such connections can cause blowouts in transistorized equipment.

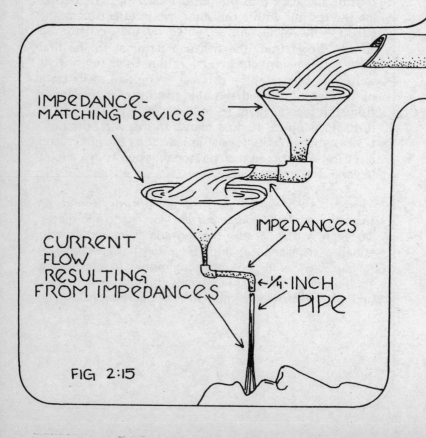

IMPEDANCE-MATCHING DEVICES

IMPEDANCES

CURRENT FLOW RESULTING FROM IMPEDANCES

¼-INCH PIPE

FIG 2:15

RESONANT FREQUENCY

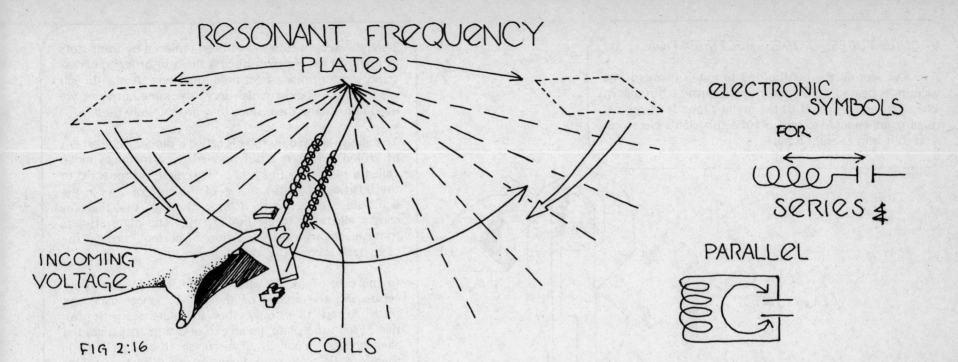

PLATES

INCOMING VOLTAGE

COILS

FIG 2:16

ELECTRONIC SYMBOLS FOR

SERIES &

PARALLEL

RESONANT FREQUENCIES

Inherent in combining inductance and capacitance in the same AC circuit is a **resonant frequency**. Let's say you are an electron being pushed in a swing. Those points at which the swing reaches highest are analogous to the plates of a capacitor; the electrons fill one plate, empty, then fill the other, and so on. The ropes suspending the swing act similarly to the coil, or inductor, providing a limit to the possible flight; the electrons pass through the coil, building up inductance to impede the flow. The push of the swing can be likened to the incoming voltage. Incoming voltage in a radio tuner, for instance, is the frequency of a received broadcast signal. We can say that the swing is tuned for a specific kind of push only. If you are pushed with too much force, you will be lifted beyond the range of the ropes and as you fall back you will snap against them. If you are pushed while in return flight your momentum will be broken

and you will twist and bounce to a halt. The resonant frequency the swing is tuned for is that push which is regular and, with minimum force, smoothly maintains steady flight and return.

Inductive and capacitative reactances can be aligned to establish a particular resonant frequency. A resonant frequency is inherent to the circuit which has in combination an equal amount of inductive and capacitative reactance.

Resonant frequency is figured by the following formula: $f = 1/2 \pi \sqrt{LC}$. If we make a parallel connection of the capacitor and coil we minimize the total impedance of the circuit. If we connect in series we maximize impedance. A parallel circuit that has a particular resonant frequency will not allow current to flow at other frequencies much different than its own. The range of frequencies allowed to pass is called **bandpass** and is determined by the resistance of the circuit.

VACUUM TUBES: DIODES—RECTIFICATION

As we've seen in the lightbulb, a tungsten filament in a vacuum is heated up by the flow of current through it. The high melting point of the metal allows for temperatures great enough to boil off the tungsten's electrons. And so it is in vacuum tubes.

Though vacuum tubes have been replaced by transistors in many cases, we shall discuss them in order to understand some primary electronic functions. And although gas-filled tubes exist which serve the same purposes, we need not discuss them since they are so rarely used.

The simplest vacuum tube is called a **diode**. Its filament of coiled tungsten is surrounded by a metal cylinder called a **plate** (see fig. 2:17). This plate is connected to the positive (paucity) charge of the current. As in the lightbulb, the current flowing through the filament causes electrons to be boiled off. The plate attracts those electrons, creating a flow of current through the plate back toward the source of current.

In the case of AC, in which the polarity constantly reverses and the charge of the plate changes back and forth, current flows only when the plate charge is positive. When the plate has an excess charge (negative) the electrons are repelled. The current that does flow is therefore DC; it only flows in one direction. This changing of AC to DC is called **rectification** and so this type of diode is called a **rectifier**.

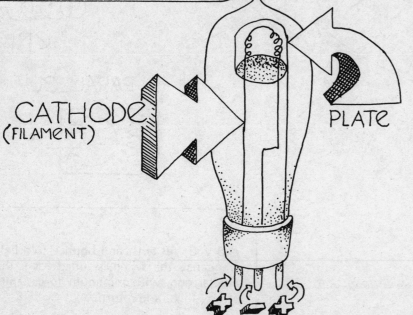

CATHODE (FILAMENT)

PLATE

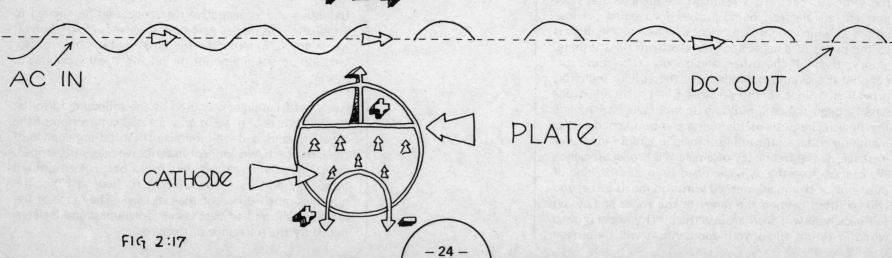

AC IN

DC OUT

PLATE

CATHODE

FIG 2:17

VACUUM TUBES: TRIODES—AMPLIFICATION

There are also **triodes** (see fig. 2:18), which add to diodes a wire mesh between the filament and the plate. This mesh, called a **grid**, sits closer to the filament and serves as a valve. (*Valve*, by the way, is the word the British use for vacuum tube; and in schematics, tubes are noted V-1, V-2, etc.) By placing a charge on the grid, the flow from the filament to the plate can be controlled. If the charge placed on the grid is, say, an audio signal from a microphone, those signal variations which represent voice variations will function to let more or less current cross from the filament to the plate.

With just slight variances in the signal we can effectively allow large amounts of current to pass. This function is called **amplification** and the triodes that perform it are called **amplifiers**. Other devices which function to amplify principally the same way as do triodes are **tetrodes**, which have two grids, and **pentodes**, which have three grids.

Let's restate the meaning of potential difference: In an electronic circuit we can measure a potential difference at a number of points in that circuit. Remember, a potential difference is like a waterfall. The excess (negative) is the top of the fall which drops to the paucity (positive), the bottom.

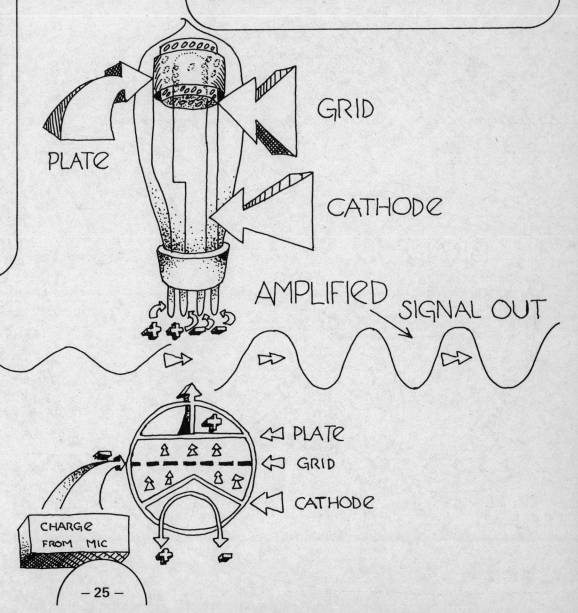

PLATE

GRID

CATHODE

AMPLIFIED SIGNAL OUT

SIGNAL IN

PLATE

GRID

CATHODE

CHARGE FROM MIC

FIG 2:18

FEEDBACK /
DRIVING AS AN EXAMPLE

It's possible for the voltage on the grid of a triode to be higher (more negative) than the voltage on the filament. In this way, the flow from the filament to the plate is nil, because the grid is at the top (negative) of the fall in relationship to the filament. The grid then functions like a closed gate. If the grid voltage is lower than that of the filament, its paucity (positive) charge attracts the excess of the filament, so current can flow onto the plate.

Whether the grid is positive or negative is determined by its relationship to the filament. Under certain circumstances, the grid might be positive to the filament and negative to the plate. The point is that the excess-paucity relationship, at any point in the circuit, is critical in determining the characteristics of the current flow.

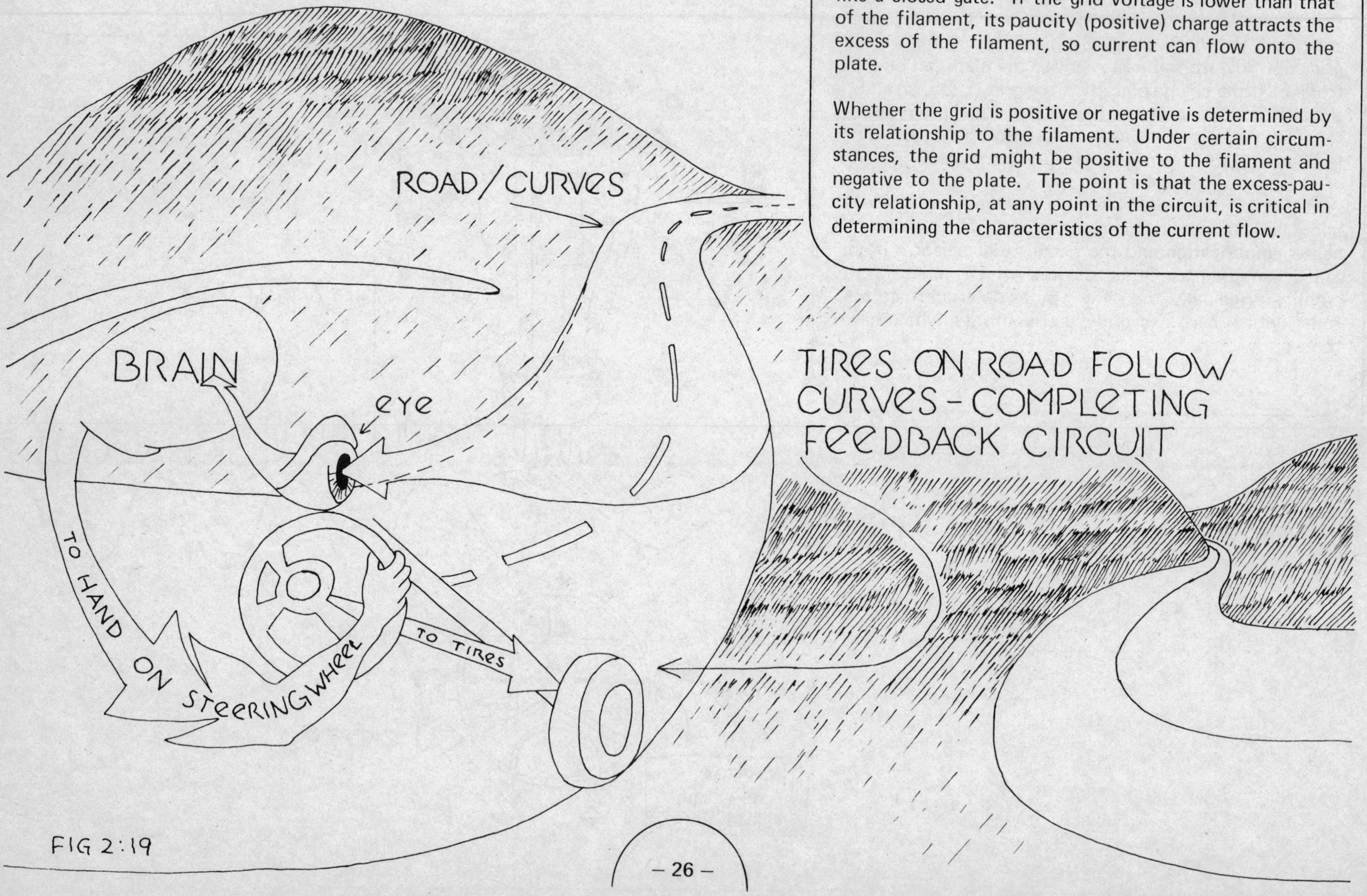

ROAD / CURVES

BRAIN

eye

TIRES ON ROAD FOLLOW CURVES - COMPLETING FEEDBACK CIRCUIT

TO HAND ON STEERING WHEEL

TO TIRES

FIG 2:19

OSCILLATORS

Triodes are also important when used as **oscillators**, which generate specific AC frequencies. Specific AC frequencies act as carriers for transmitting radio and TV signals. They are also used for timing signals to control picture scanning in TV tubes. The primary form for an oscillation circuit contains a capacitor and coil, which in combination provide a resonant frequency which passes frequencies only within close range to itself. Such circuits are called **tuned circuits** (see fig. 2:16).

The generation of a continuous specific frequency is achieved by feeding the plate current (output) back to the grid (input). The same frequency is thus produced over and over again. This process is called **feedback** (see fig. 2:19).

Rectification, amplification, and oscillation are the three primary uses of electronic circuits. To rectify means to change AC to DC. To amplify means to increase the level of a given signal. To oscillate means to generate continuous AC frequencies.

PHASE

When two or more alternating currents of the same frequency are connected but are not in step, they are said to be out of **phase**. Phase differences can be anything from direct opposition to nearly exact agreement. They are measured in degrees, direct opposition being 180° out of phase.

There can also be phase differences between the amperage and the voltage within a single AC source. In circuits within which capacitance, inductance, or both exist, amperage and voltage will be out of phase.

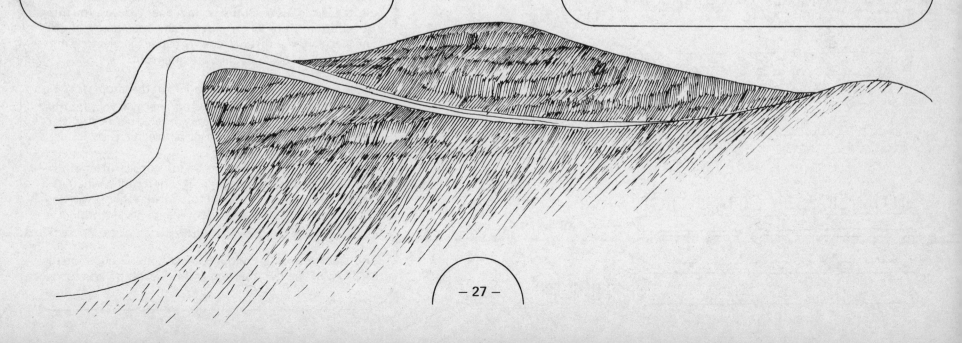

ATOM-ENERGY LEVELS

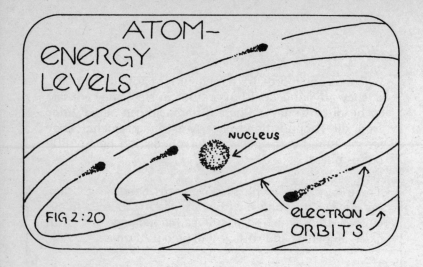

NUCLEUS

ELECTRON ORBITS

FIG 2:20

CONDUCTOR

MAXIMUM ENERGY LEVEL

MINIMUM

WHEN CHARGE IS APPLIED ELECTRONS MOVE TO A HIGHER LEVEL, CAUSING CURRENT TO FLOW

FIG 2:21

INSULATOR

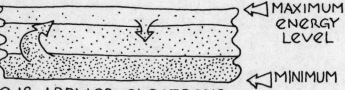

MAXIMUM LEVEL

ENERGY GAP

MINIMUM

FIG 2:22

INTRINSIC SEMICONDUCTOR

FIG 2:23

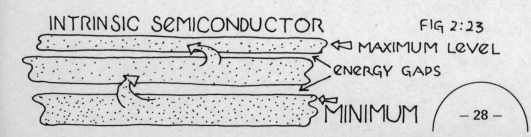

MAXIMUM LEVEL

ENERGY GAPS

MINIMUM

TRANSISTORS AND SEMICONDUCTORS

A heated filament in a vacuum tube acts as an electron source. Tube-type electronic devices take some time to warm up in order to achieve sufficiently high temperatures to cause the necessary copious emission of electrons. Twenty-five to thirty percent of the electronic system's power is used to maintain these high temperatures. It requires only about one hour after tubes warm up for them to reach their stable operating level. Tubes always degenerate from use, and are also relatively bulky and fragile.

On the other hand, **transistors**, since they function by using electrons from the material of which they are made, waste no power generating electrons. Transistors require about four or five hours to stabilize. Transistors are extremely small and virtually indestructible.

Transistors are semiconductors made of elements such as silicon, germanium, indium, and phosphorus. To understand how the electrons of an element are used in semiconductors, let's take a look at energy levels. A specific energy level, or **quantum**, can be ascribed to specific electrons spinning on their axes orbiting around the atom's nucleus. According to present theory, such electrons can assume only certain energy levels (**quanta**). In addition, in order to move from one energy level to another across a distinct energy gap, each electron must either gain or give up a discrete quantum.

Looking at the scientific model of the atom (see fig. 2:20), every possible orbit is an energy level. In other words, there are specific energy levels for specific electrons, and there are energy gaps between energy levels.

In crystalline solids, energy bands consist of many energy levels grouped together. To determine whether a crystalline solid is a conductor, insulator, or semiconductor we look to see which energy level within the band the electrons normally inhabit.

The electrons of a **conductor** normally occupy energy levels well below the maximum level of the band.

Therefore, an applied voltage which increases the energy level of the electrons will easily act to cause the flow of current.

The electrons of an **insulator** normally occupy the maximum level of a band. If an extreme voltage is applied, the energy gap to another band can be jumped, but moderate voltages have no effect upon the electrons, so no current flows.

A **semiconductor** is a material which can build up sufficient heat energy to move some of its electrons from their place in the maximum level of one band to any level in the next band. The energy gaps in semiconductors are narrow. Though few in number, the electrons in the new band move freely and easily up the ladder of energy levels in response to small voltages. Normal environmental temperatures contribute to the optimum functioning of semiconductors. Extreme cold retards their function. Too much heat and they blow.

Transistors are manufactured by adding impurities to intrinsically semiconductive crystalline solids. Remember, the combining of atoms is achieved by the mixing of electrons in their outer orbits. In making transistors, two types of atoms are used: those of the pure semiconductive element, and those of elements with either one more or one less electron in their outer orbits than the number of electrons in the outer orbits of the pure semiconductive element.

For instance, a germanium atom has four electrons in its outer orbit, and an arsenic atom has five. Therefore, if germanium atoms are deliberately replaced by arsenic atoms some extra electrons (called free electrons) are gained. Current can be made to flow through such a transistor which is called an **n-type** (negative) **semiconductor** (see fig. 2:24).

If germanium atoms, which have four electrons in their outer orbits, are replaced with boron atoms, which have three; holes—positive charges—will be left where electrons ought to be. Placing a potential difference across

this combination of elements will cause electrons to move in to fill these holes, while vacating other holes. Thus the holes—which can be considered positively charged particles—move toward the negative charge. Transistors of this type are called **p-type** (positive) **semiconductors.**

The movement of electrons and holes through semiconductive materials can be controlled in order to achieve the same ends accomplished by vacuum tubes. The term **solid-state** describes the electronics of transistor circuitry.

TRANSISTORS

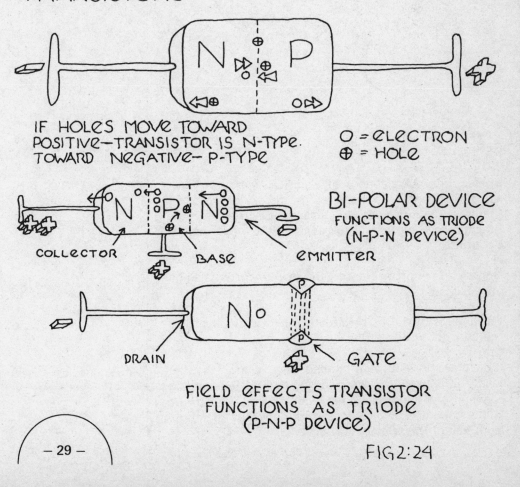

IF HOLES MOVE TOWARD POSITIVE—TRANSISTOR IS N-TYPE. TOWARD NEGATIVE— P-TYPE

O = ELECTRON
⊕ = HOLE

BI-POLAR DEVICE
FUNCTIONS AS TRIODE
(N-P-N DEVICE)

COLLECTOR   BASE   EMMITTER

DRAIN   GATE

FIELD EFFECTS TRANSISTOR
FUNCTIONS AS TRIODE
(P-N-P DEVICE)

FIG 2:24

REPLAY

In electronics, the theory of electrical energy as wave and field phenomena displaces the theory of electrical energy as the movement of particles. Electric current is actually wave motion propagated by the movement of electrons.

Under certain circumstances, the flow of current can be impeded.

Impedances other than resistance act to store electrical energy without dissipating it.

Inductance is a form of impedance produced by the magnetic field that is generated by current flowing in a conductor. The magnetic field induces a second current in the conductor which runs in the opposite direction from that of the primary current.

Inductance is greater in coils than in straight wires. If the current is DC, the counter-current exists only while the initial surge of current is building up to its peak rate of flow. Inductance is measured in henries.

In AC, inductance continues to generate a magnetic field as the changes of current direction repeatedly occur. This phenomenon is called inductive reactance and is measured in ohms.

Capacitance is the storage of electrical energy in an electric field and is also considered an impedance. Devices which provide capacitance are called capacitors. They function to store a potential difference across two metal plates separated by an insulator. Capacitance is measured in farads.

In an AC situation, the positive-negative polarity on a capacitor is constantly reversing. The effect to the flow of current is called capacitative reactance and is measured in ohms.

Variable capacitors allow for the storage of different amounts of charge because the space between the plates or the areas of the plates can be altered.

Impedance matching is important when combining circuits in order to avoid unwanted changes to the voltage and amperage of an incoming signal.

A resonant frequency is inherent to a circuit that has an equal amount of capacitative and inductive reactance in combination. Reactances can be aligned in order to establish a particular resonant frequency.

A parallel connection of capacitor and coil will minimize the total impedance of the circuit. A series connection of capacitor and coil will maximize the total impedance.

A parallel circuit which has a particular resonant frequency will not allow current to flow at frequencies much different than itself. The range of frequency that is allowed to pass is called bandpass and is determined by the resistance of the circuit.

Vacuum tubes are being replaced by transistors, but are still important to know about. A diode, the simplest vacuum tube, works somewhat like the lightbulb. It has a filament of tungsten from which, as current flows through it, electrons are boiled off. The diode also has a plate or metal cylinder which, when charged positive in relation to the filament, attracts the free electrons from the filament.

In the case of AC, in which the charge of the plate is constantly reversing, current will not flow when the plate is negative. In this way, we can change AC to DC, a process called rectification. Such a diode is called a rectifier.

Triodes have an added element called a grid, located between the filament and the plate. A signal put to the grid will act to control the flow of electrons from the filament to the plate.

Amplification is the process by which the strength of the signal put to the grid is increased. Triodes and other devices which effect this process are called amplifiers.

Triodes can also serve as oscillators to generate high frequency AC. The circuit which produces a resonant frequency combines with the triode, and feeds that frequency to the grid which in turn generates it to the plate; from the plate it is again directed to the grid, and so on. This process is called feedback.

Phase is considered in two cases of current flow: 1) when two or more AC sources with the same frequency are connected, and 2) when a single AC flows in a circuit in which either or both capacitance and inductance exist—in which case, amperage and voltage are said to be out of phase.

Transistors, unlike vacuum tubes, are almost indestructible, extremely small, and waste no power generating electrons, since they get their electrons from the material of which they are made.

The molecular structure of an n-type (negative) semiconductor contains some free electrons which can be made to flow with small voltages.

The molecular structure of a p-type (positive) semiconductor contains some free holes which, in response to a voltage, move toward the semiconductor's negative charge.

In solid-state electronics, the combination of p-type and n-type components allows us to achieve the same results obtained using bulkier vacuum tubes.

RADIATING POINT SOURCE

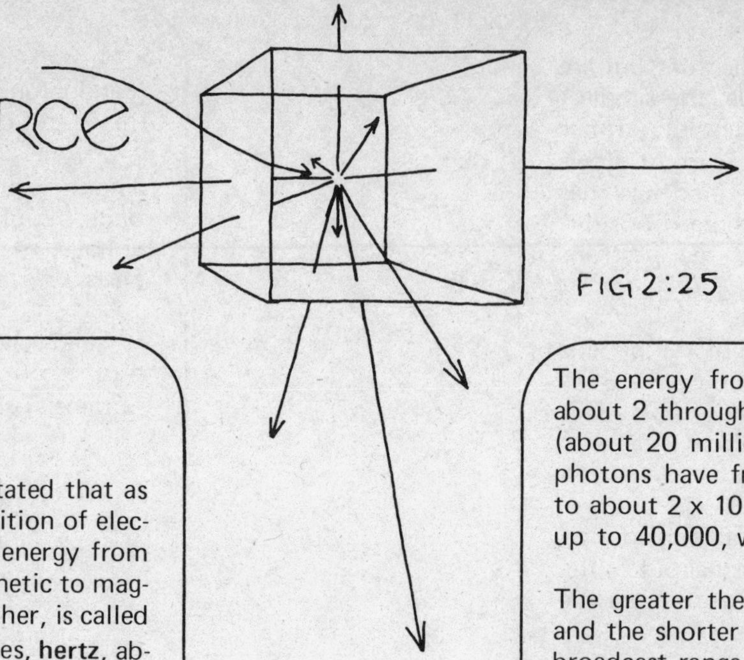

FIG 2:25

AM FM
CODING LIGHTSPEED

In **THE BIG WORKS** (page 3), we stated that as energy travels through space there is a transition of electric and magnetic fields. A transition of energy from electric field to electric field, or from magnetic to magnetic field, or sometimes from one to the other, is called a cycle. (When referring to radio frequencies, **hertz**, abbreviated as Hz, is another name for cycle. The German physicist, Heinrich Hertz, played a significant role in the development of radio frequency transmission. He discovered radio waves, and was subsequently honored by the coining of the terms "hertz," "kilohertz," "megahertz," etc.)

The distance traveled during a cycle is called a wavelength. A wavelength can be expressed in fractions of centimeters (from shortwave to gamma rays), or in meters (from radio wave to long wave). The number of hertz is a wave's frequency. Frequency multiplied by wavelength always equals the velocity of light. Electromagnetic waves travel at 3×10^{10} centimeters per second (about 186,000 miles per second).

Remember too, the photon, which is the most discrete bundle of energy in an electromagnetic wave. Photons come in all sizes. Consider them as particles having certain energy levels which can be expressed as **ev** (electron volt potential differences).

The energy from photons of visible light ranges from about 2 through 4 ev, which is shorter than 10^{-6} meters (about 20 millionths of an inch) in wavelength. These photons have frequencies ranging from about 10^{15} Hz to about 2×10^{15} Hz. X-ray photons have ev potentials up to 40,000, while gamma rays are well beyond that.

The greater the ev potential, the higher the frequency and the shorter the wavelength. In the communications broadcast range, the wavelengths are from about 3 centimeters to around 300 meters, with frequencies ranging from 10,000 Hz to 1 Hz (one million cycles per second).

Also note: From a radiating point source, waves travel out into space in all directions. Any single wave travels in a straight line (see fig. 2:25). A wave has frequency, wavelength, and amplitude. What we call a sinusoidal or sine wave is a wave that is regular, smooth, and persistent. The sine waveform is the mathematical plotting of amplitude and time (see fig. 2:26). Any irregular waves can be analyzed as a combination of sine waves of various amplitude and frequency.

MODULATION

In electronics, communication depends upon the ability to effect change—to **modulate**. All modulating systems feature two basic components: 1) a carrier or vehicle, and 2) a method of change. For instance, the carrier for writing is the pen, and the method of change is a set of predetermined marks (the alphabet) which in groupings can convey information.

AMPLITUDE MODULATION (AM) AND TRANSMISSION

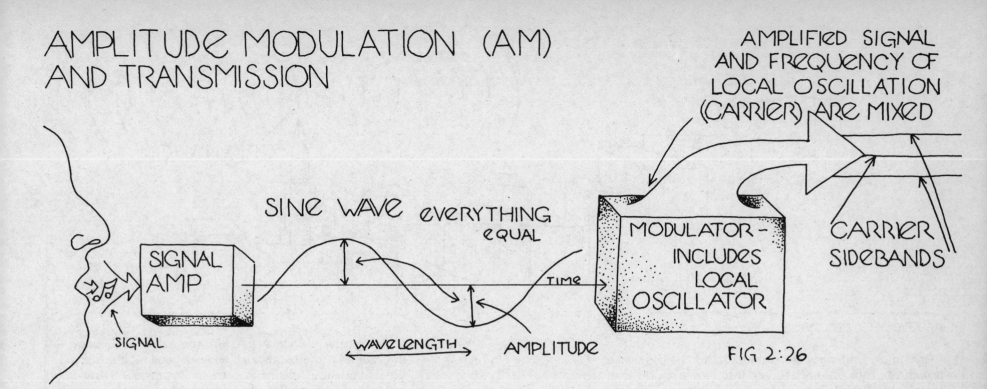

SINE WAVE everything equal

AMPLIFIED SIGNAL AND FREQUENCY OF LOCAL OSCILLATION (CARRIER) ARE MIXED

SIGNAL AMP

SIGNAL

TIME

WAVELENGTH

AMPLITUDE

MODULATOR - INCLUDES LOCAL OSCILLATOR

CARRIER SIDEBANDS

FIG 2:26

Radio Frequency (RF) modulation refers to radio wave frequencies used to transmit audio and TV signals either through the air or along conductive paths in circuits and in coaxial cable. A modulating system contains three devices to transport information (signals): a transmitter, antennas or cable, and a receiver. This hardware functions to generate AC signals at RF frequencies for demodulation—reception—at some other point.

TRANSMITTERS

The transmitter is designed to generate a carrier frequency in the RF range by utilizing an oscillator which, remember, generates a specific frequency AC. Let's say we have a carrier frequency of 100,000 Hz AC. Our signal (the information we want sent) is at 1,000 Hz AC. The two signals are mixed and transmitted side by side. Actually, three RF frequencies leave the transmit-

ter: 1) the carrier frequency at 100,000 Hz; 2) the signal frequency added to the carrier frequency, 101,000 Hz; and 3) the signal frequency subtracted from the carrier frequency, 99,000 Hz.

In RF modulation the frequency range extending from the carrier is called the bandwidth. The regions above and below the carrier, extending to the limits of the bandwidth, are called sidebands. All information is carried in the sidebands.

Since the two sidebands are, in a sense, mirror images of each other and therefore carry duplicate information, one of them can be blocked or suppressed by using a filter in the transmitter. This creates a single sideband transmission. A TV channel, for instance, has a bandwidth of 6 MHz (megahertz) and is a vestigial sideband, meaning that most of the lower sideband has been blocked.

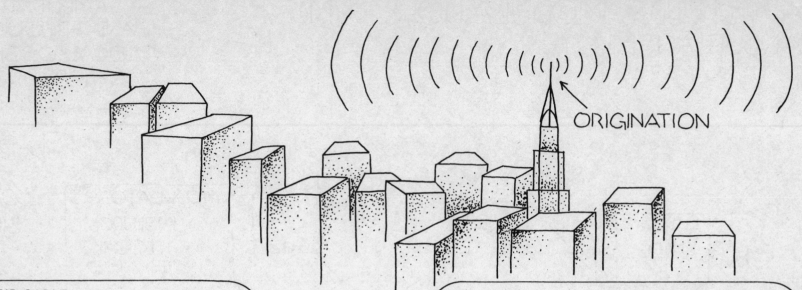

ORIGINATION

ANTENNAS AND CABLE

Very simply, **antennas** are conductors of the RF signals broadcast from transmitters and into receivers. Made of metal and shaped in a variety of ways to project and catch wave patterns, antennas are electromagnetic sensors tuned to the RFs they are to transmit or receive.

Since most independent video is closed circuit, cablecasting is more important to us than is broadcasting. **Cable** is a conductor specifically designed to handle a number of signals simultaneously. If the proper amplification is placed along the path of the conductor, some cable can carry as many as thirty 6-MHz bandwidths—thirty TV channels.

RECEIVERS

A receiver is a device which receives RF signals and then makes them perceptible to the senses. A receiver must be tuned to the carrier frequency in order to pick up an RF signal. A TV set, for instance, has a number of predetermined carrier frequencies—channels—to which it can be set. An incoming RF signal, made up of a carrier frequency and sideband frequencies, must be separated, and the signal passed on into the circuits.

Often receivers change or shift the carrier frequency, but maintain the bandwidth and sideband relationships. This frequency shifting is used in TV receivers and is called the **Intermediate Frequency** (IF) stage. After a signal is taken from the air or cable, the IF is used to transport the signal within the set at a standardized frequency which is generally the same in all TV receivers (about 41–47 MHz).

Note that the carrier frequency must always be great enough to accommodate the accompanying bandwidth. For instance, a 1,000-Hz signal and a 500-Hz carrier wouldn't work. The lower sideband would not be able to contain the 1,000-Hz signal. Usually bandwidth ranges are determined by two major factors: 1) the Federal Communications Commission, as manager of broadcast airspace, and 2) certain frequencies and thus their wavelengths, which are suitable for certain types of transmissions and not others. This second factor usually is dependent on the desired range of transmission.

There are three major methods of RF modulation: **amplitude modulation—AM**, **frequency modulation—FM**, and **phase modulation—PM**. All these methods employ the system that has been described, but differ as to how the information is "packaged."

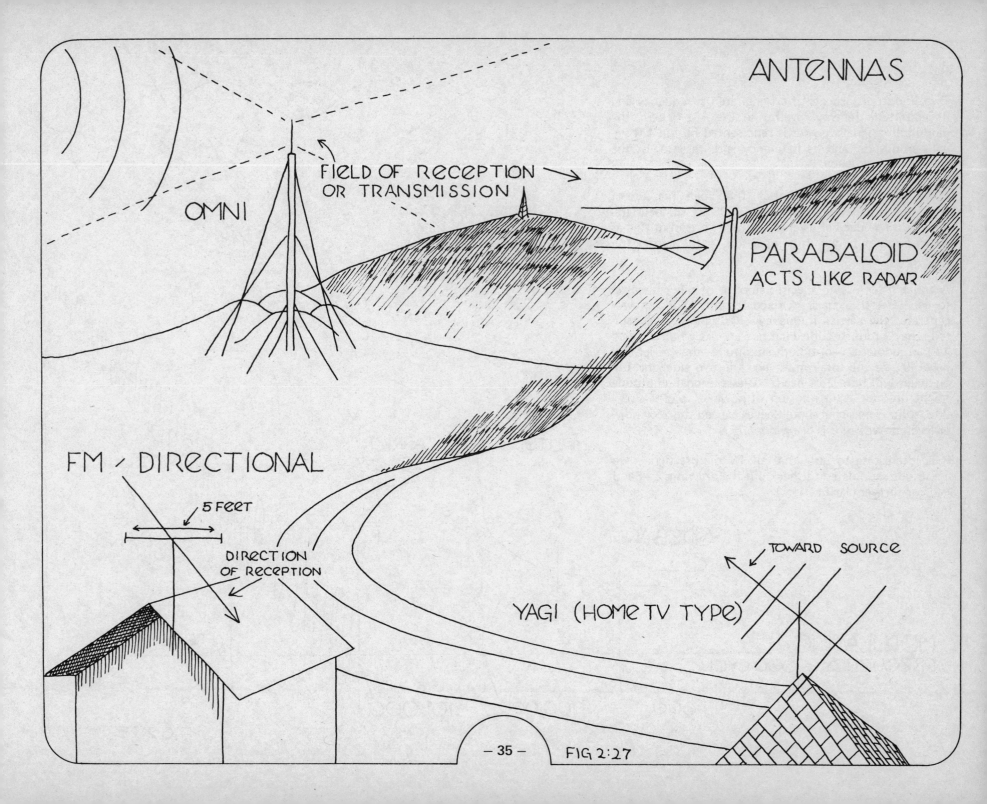

ANTENNAS

OMNI

FIELD OF RECEPTION
OR TRANSMISSION

PARABALOID
ACTS LIKE RADAR

FM - DIRECTIONAL

5 FEET

DIRECTION
OF RECEPTION

TOWARD SOURCE

YAGI (HOME TV TYPE)

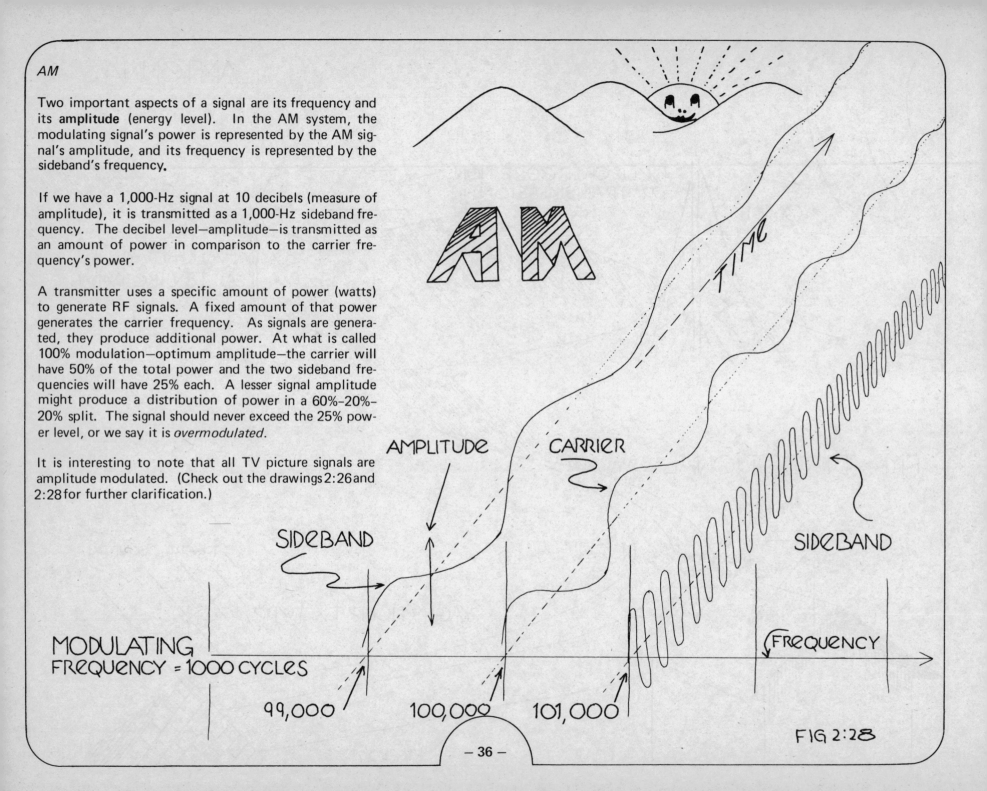

AM

Two important aspects of a signal are its frequency and its **amplitude** (energy level). In the AM system, the modulating signal's power is represented by the AM signal's amplitude, and its frequency is represented by the sideband's frequency.

If we have a 1,000-Hz signal at 10 decibels (measure of amplitude), it is transmitted as a 1,000-Hz sideband frequency. The decibel level—amplitude—is transmitted as an amount of power in comparison to the carrier frequency's power.

A transmitter uses a specific amount of power (watts) to generate RF signals. A fixed amount of that power generates the carrier frequency. As signals are generated, they produce additional power. At what is called 100% modulation—optimum amplitude—the carrier will have 50% of the total power and the two sideband frequencies will have 25% each. A lesser signal amplitude might produce a distribution of power in a 60%–20%–20% split. The signal should never exceed the 25% power level, or we say it is *overmodulated*.

It is interesting to note that all TV picture signals are amplitude modulated. (Check out the drawings 2:26 and 2:28 for further clarification.)

AM

TIME

AMPLITUDE

CARRIER

SIDEBAND

SIDEBAND

FREQUENCY

MODULATING FREQUENCY = 1000 CYCLES

99,000   100,000   101,000

FIG 2:28

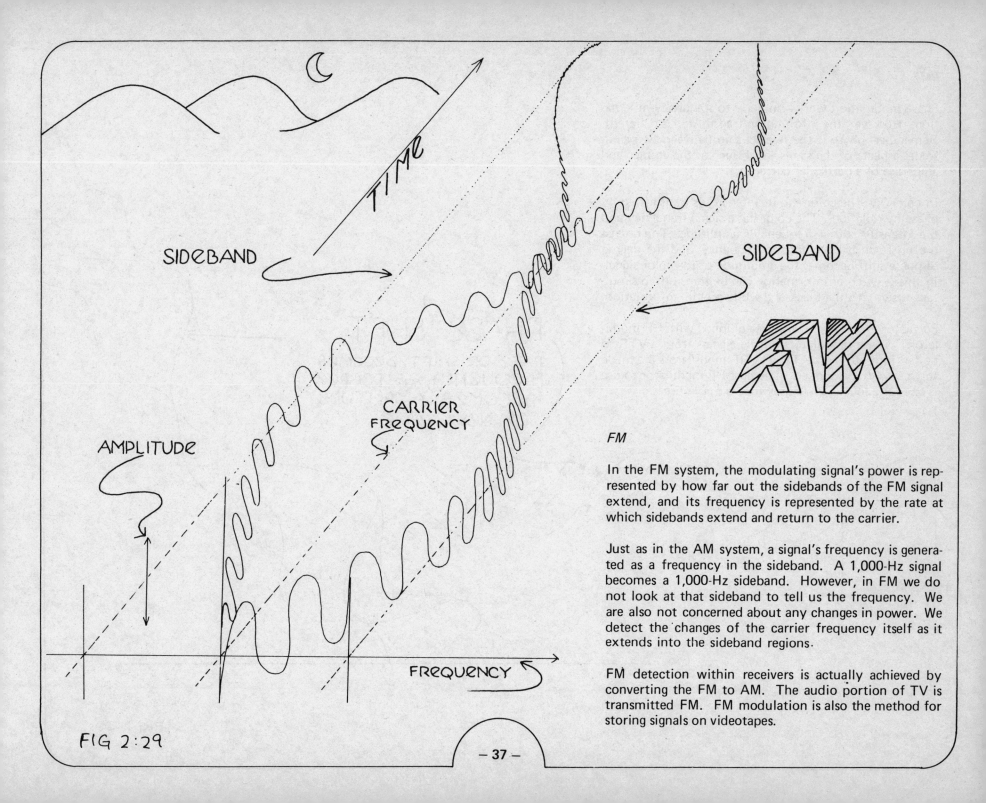

SIDEBAND

TIME

SIDEBAND

AMPLITUDE

CARRIER FREQUENCY

FREQUENCY

FM

FM

In the FM system, the modulating signal's power is represented by how far out the sidebands of the FM signal extend, and its frequency is represented by the rate at which sidebands extend and return to the carrier.

Just as in the AM system, a signal's frequency is generated as a frequency in the sideband. A 1,000-Hz signal becomes a 1,000-Hz sideband. However, in FM we do not look at that sideband to tell us the frequency. We are also not concerned about any changes in power. We detect the changes of the carrier frequency itself as it extends into the sideband regions.

FM detection within receivers is actually achieved by converting the FM to AM. The audio portion of TV is transmitted FM. FM modulation is also the method for storing signals on videotapes.

FIG 2:29

Phase modulation works similarly to frequency modulation. However, the information transmitted is different. Remember, phase is the relationship between two sinusoidal aspects of the same signal, such as the voltage and amperage of a particular current.

In color TV, the color and its intensity is transmitted by phase modulation. The color has a signal frequency and the intensity is that frequency's amplitude. The rate of the phase shift becomes the frequency, and the degree of phase shift becomes the amplitude of the color signal. In this way, color information can be transmitted simultaneously with the black-and-white picture information.

Portable video systems can be equipped with RF modulators. These modulators enable signals from a VTR to be fed into any home TV set. RF modulators are made for many VHF channels. The best RF modulator to use is one for a local TV channel that is not in use.

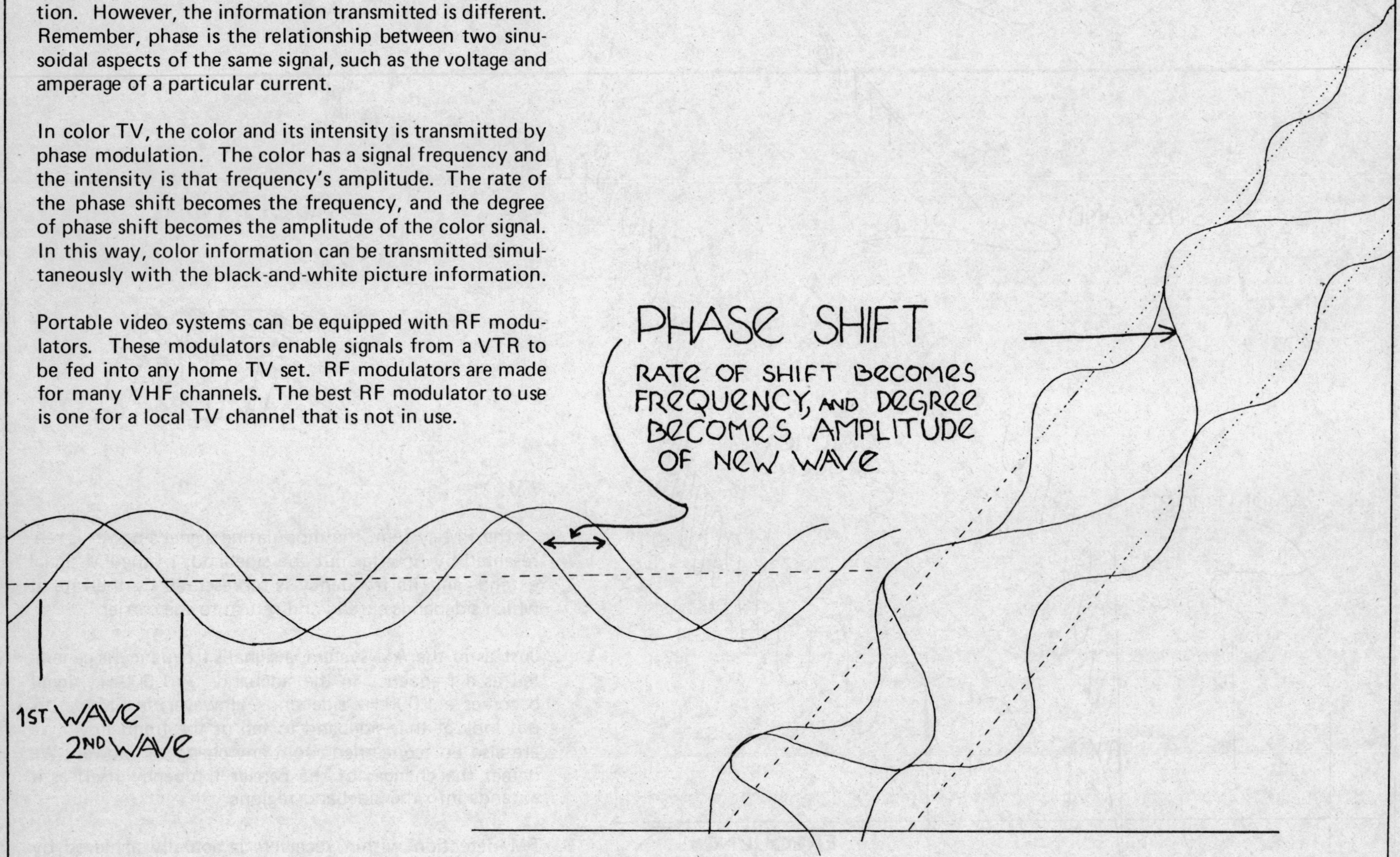

PHASE SHIFT
RATE OF SHIFT BECOMES FREQUENCY, AND DEGREE BECOMES AMPLITUDE OF NEW WAVE

1ST WAVE
2ND WAVE

FIG 2:30

THE PHOTOELECTRIC EFFECT
ELECTRICITY FROM LIGHT

Simply stated, the **photoelectric effect** is the process of light generating electricity from metals. Remember the discussion in the introduction of *Electronics* in this section, dealing with quanta. Electrons occupy orbits at varying distances from an atom's nucleus. Each orbit can be equated with an energy level or quantum. Orbits farther from the nucleus have higher energy levels; closer orbits have lower levels. For an electron to become free of the nucleus' hold, it must gain energy from an external source.

Remember, too, that light (electromagnetic waves) consists of photons which can be considered particles of energy. Photons carry specific amounts of energy (see *AM FM* in this section). It follows that photons of certain energy levels—frequencies—hitting certain materials will raise the energy levels of those materials' electrons, and act to free them from their atoms. And if a voltage is placed near those free electrons, they will be made to flow and current will be produced.

The materials that most readily free electrons when irradiated by light are the alkali metals. The first TV camera, called an iconoscope, employed cesium, which releases its electrons more easily than any other metal.

Another thing to note is that the magnitude of the current produced as described above is proportional to the intensity of the light. A light's intensity—viewing light as a stream of photons—is actually the number of photons bombarding a point. Therefore, photons that have an energy level sufficient to liberate electrons free them in proportion to the number of photons which hit a given point on a photoconductive surface. (See **VIDEO-WORKS**, page 59 , for a discussion of the function of photoconductance in the video camera's light-sensing circuit.)

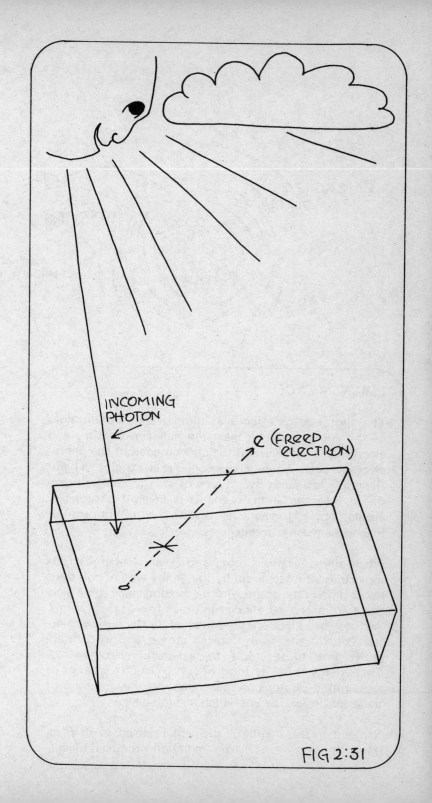

INCOMING PHOTON

e (FREED ELECTRON)

FIG 2:31

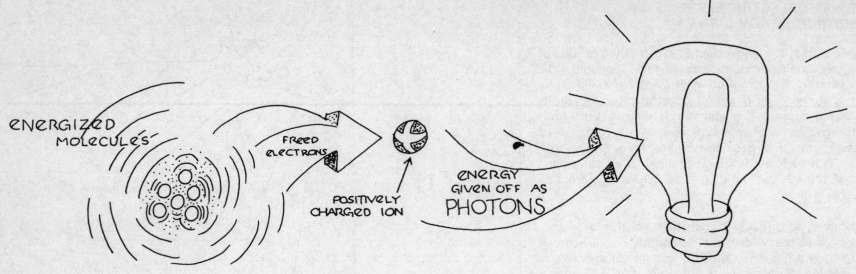

ENERGIZED MOLECULES

FREED ELECTRONS

POSITIVELY CHARGED ION

ENERGY GIVEN OFF AS PHOTONS

FIG 2:32

LUMINESCENCE

The photoelectric effect and **luminescence** are two sides of the energy-matter conversion between photons and electrons. The reverse of the phenomenon of the photoelectric effect, luminescence converts electricity to light. Generally speaking, two types of energy can be introduced into the atom to enable it to emit photons of visible light: 1) mechanical agitation and 2) photons of higher-than-visible frequencies.

When any substance becomes sufficiently energized, its molecules vibrate so rapidly that many violent collisions occur among the atoms. In this circumstance some electrons are energized enough to break free of their atoms. As these free electrons are attracted by the positive electric field of the newly ionized atoms, and in turn are drawn into those atoms, the electrons release energy. That energy is in the form of light. The frequencies of the emitted photons are dependent on the velocities of the electrons and atoms which recombine.

Remember the lightbulb filament referred to in *Electricity* (page 13). Thermal radiation produced by cur-

rent causes the release of electrons and the subsequent emission of light. Lights which require heat to operate are called incandescent lamps and are characterized by their need for high temperatures in order to produce light.

Luminescence describes the process whereby light can be produced at room temperature. The screen of a TV consists of many tiny crystals of phosphors which, when bombarded by electrons, become luminescent. In other words, as fast-moving electrons strike a phosphor crystal, they are absorbed by the molecules, and the electrons of that crystal are raised to higher-than-normal energy levels. As the electrons drop back to their unexcited states, they give off visible light.

There are two kinds of luminescence: **fluorescence** and **phosphorescence**. Fluorescence refers to the short light-life or afterglow of certain phosphors. Phosphorescence denotes the relatively long light-life of other phosphors. For the purposes of TV, fluorescent phosphors are employed. These shorter light-life phosphors serve the high-speed functioning of the cathode ray tube (see **VIDEOWORKS**, page 92).

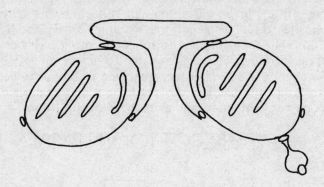

OPTICS
SIGHT SEEING

In the previous section we established the interaction between photons of light and a substance's electrons. Keep in mind that optics can be described as the behavior of light in transparent media other than air. Since our ultimate concern is lenses, the transparent medium of greatest importance is glass.

First, understand that the velocity of light differs as it travels through various media, and as light's velocity changes, so does its wavelength. Also, as light passes from one medium to another, there are impedance problems. So, besides being slowed down, a light wave can be reflected, refracted, dispersed, and diffracted. These are the phenomena which determine how lenses will focus and filter light.

Remember, as is discussed in *Transduction* (page 7): focusing is the process of placing an incoming photon on the point of a selected surface (vidicon face, inner eye, etc.) that corresponds to the point from which the photon was reflected in the field of vision.

ABSORPTION

When we say plants get energy from the sun, we are saying that photons of solar frequencies are being absorbed by the atoms of the plant—photosynthesis or photon absorption. Like the photoelectric effect, **absorption** occurs when an electron is bombarded by a photon with enough energy to raise it up an energy level or even to free it.

During the period in which the electron contains excess energy, the electric field of the excited atom is changed, in turn effecting the states of neighboring atoms. This chain of effects works to distribute the new energy throughout the group of atoms. As the originally energized electron is attracted back into the fold by an excited atom, it may or may not have enough remaining excess energy to emit a low-frequency photon. Those photons which are emitted, even at lower frequencies than when received, are said to be re-emitted.

Black, for instance, absorbs all the frequencies of light and re-emits photons in the lower frequencies of the infrared spectrum. Gray absorbs some photons and reflects others. White reflects all light's frequencies.

REFLECTION

A mirror **reflects** the vast majority of light that falls on it—the photons hitting any given point are bounced off unchanged. The coarse surface of a piece of white paper disperses photons in all directions, but mirror reflections retain the details of light—its location, frequency, and intensity.

Glass is **transparent**, meaning that photons do not interact with the electrons of glass. Light travels through glass more slowly than it travels through air; this in turn shortens the wavelength but doesn't change the frequency.

Light reflects off the surface of transparent glass, as it does off a mirror. The angle of reflection is exactly opposite to the angle of the incoming wave (see fig. 2:33). The light loss due to reflection of glass is about 4% per surface. Lenses are coated to reduce reflection. The coating is an impedance-matching technique which acts as an intermediary to smooth out the changes of velocity as light enters and exits the glass and the air.

REFLECTION (MIRROR)

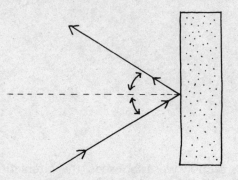

REFLECTION (GLASS)

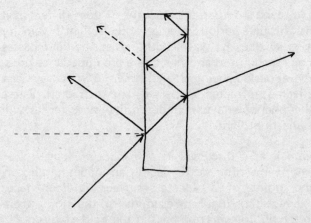

FIG 2:33

REFRACTION

As a light wave exits one medium and enters another in which it travels at a different velocity, its direction is bent, unless the wave enters at right angles to the medium's surface (see fig. 2:34). The change of velocity causes a change in direction, or bending of the light. The velocity change is accompanied by a change in the light's wavelength but not in its frequency. The ratio of the two light velocities traveling through the two media is the measure of the extent of **refraction** and is called the **index of refraction**.

FIG 2:34

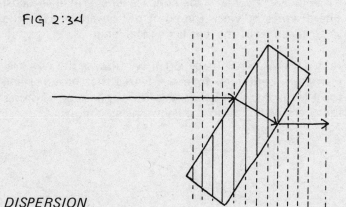

DISPERSION

Dispersion occurs when different frequencies of light travel at different velocities through the same material. As they pass through the material, each different frequency wave goes in its own direction. What entered the medium as one wave, exits the medium as a number of separate waves (see fig. 2:35).

FIG 2:35

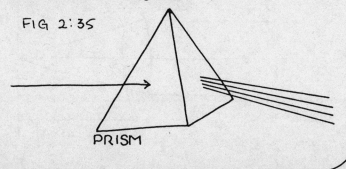

PRISM

DIFFRACTION

Shadows contain some light. Although an obstacle casts a shadow by blocking light, some photon energy is **diffracted** into the shadow region. The light can be considered to be bent around the edges of an obstacle (see fig. 2:36).

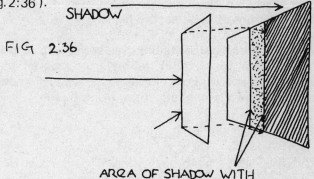

FIG 2:36

SHADOW

AREA OF SHADOW WITH DIFFRACTED LIGHT

A BASIC LENS IS SIMPLY MADE OF TWO PRISMS ONE PLACED ON TOP OF THE OTHER

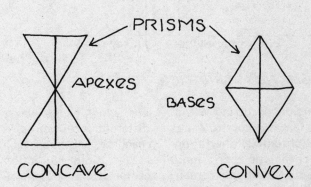

PRISMS

APEXES

BASES

CONCAVE   CONVEX

FIG 2:37

POLARIZATION

Remember that the electromagnetic wave consists of electric and magnetic fields. When the electric fields of a wave are pointed up and down, that wave is said to be vertically **polarized**. Waves can be vertically, horizontally, circularly, or randomly polarized, depending upon the orientations of their electric fields.

Polaroid material transmits only the waves of a particular orientation, filtering out the rest from a wave that is randomly polarized. Polaroid sunglasses are well known for cutting down strong reflections from the sun.

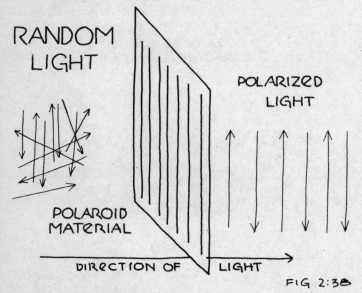

FIG 2:38

CHROMATIC ABERRATION

Dispersion occurring within a lens, which causes waves of different colors to focus at different focal points, is called **chromatic aberration**. In each single element of a lens, chromatic aberration takes place. **Color correction** is the method used to realign the focal point by grouping a number of different elements together. In **VIDEOWORKS** (page 51), we see how multi-element lenses are color corrected.

LENSES

Every lens has what is called a **principal focus**. Most optical lenses are spherically concave or convex. A convex lens bends light to a point of mutual convergence. From that point of convergence (principal focus) to the lens' vertical center is the **focal length** of the lens. For lenses of the same diameter, the greater the degree of curvature, the shorter the focal length.

A concave lens refracts light out from the center. It too has a principal focus which is determined by continuing the lines of divergence back in front of the lens. Where these lines converge is the concave lens' principal focus. The distance between the point of convergence and the vertical center of the lens is its focal length.

In VIDEOWORKS (page 50), we discuss the way elements are combined to make lenses that have varying focal lengths (zoom lenses) and the application of optics for directing light into the light-sensing circuits.

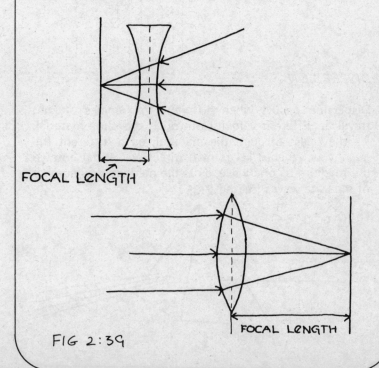

FOCAL LENGTH

FOCAL LENGTH

FIG 2:39

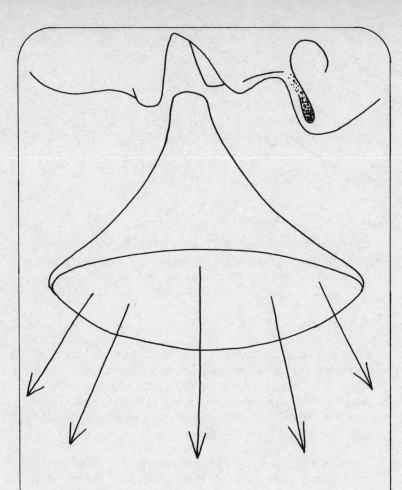

ACOUSTICS
SOUND WAVES, TOO

Referring back to **THE BIG WORKS** (page 6), remember that things that go bump in the universe are generally mechanically energized. Sound waves have wavelength and frequency. Sound puts pressure on a substance and causes its particles to be momentarily moved. That pressure-movement effect is passed on down the line through the substance. The density of the substance determines a sound's speed of travel. A sound's frequency is the number of times the pressure causes the maximum particle density from the norm. The sound's wavelength is the distance between the two maximum points.

Sound waves are considered as compressional or longitudinal waves. At sea level, sound travels in air at a rate of 1,100 feet per second. The speed of sound is affected by temperature—it is increased by heat, decreased by cold. Most of the sounds of speech are in the range of 100–10,000 Hz. The overall audible range for humans is about 20–20,000 Hz.

A frequency of 17,600 Hz has a wavelength of ¾ inch. A low audible tone of, say, 22 Hz has a 50-foot wavelength. The formula, frequency times wavelength equals velocity, applies for sound as well as light. There are three categories of sound waves: infrasonic, or below audible range; sonic, within the range of human hearing; and ultrasonic, above audible range.

Sound waves radiate in all directions. As they move farther from their source, their energy is dissipated. Cupping one's mouth to direct a yell is an example of a "handmade" acoustical—sound-controlling—device. The horn shape used in loudspeakers, megaphones, and musical instruments, functions to concentrate sound waves in the direction in which the horn is aimed. In this way, the horn also serves as an impedance-matching device, smoothing the transition of a sound from a confined space or source into an open space or air of the real world.

Let us focus on the relationship between sound and the electronic devices which handle it. In **VIDEOWORKS** (page 110), you'll find a rundown of audio equipment. To prepare for that we'll deal now with decibels, signal-to-noise ratio, and dynamic range.

We sense changes of sound intensities by comparing the present sound level with the previous one. We do not judge relative loudness in terms of differences of power, but in ratios of power. We say a sound is a bit louder, twice as loud, or a hell of a lot louder than another sound, whether those sounds are faint or very loud. Thus, a difference in power which might be barely detectable in comparing two loud sounds would be tremendous when comparing two faint sounds. It is the ratios of power to sound that we compare.

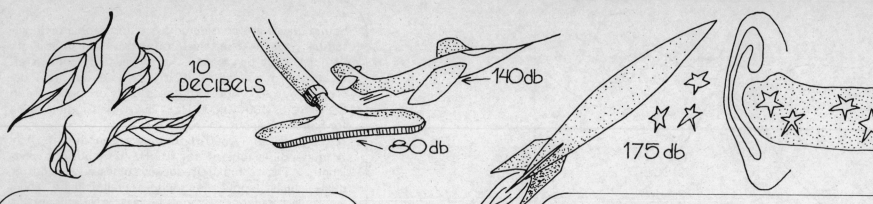

DECIBELS

If one sound is 10 times as powerful as another, it is said to be **10 decibels (db)** stronger than the first. A sound 100 times more powerful is 20 db stronger than the first; 1,000 times more powerful, 30 db stronger; 10,000 times more powerful, 40 db stronger; 100,000 times more powerful, 50 db stronger; and 1,000,000 times more powerful, 60 db stronger. The scale also goes into the minus region: If a sound is 1/10 the strength of another, it is -10 db; if it is 1/100 as strong, it is -20 db, etc. Technically, the number of decibels is 10 times the logarithm to the base 10 of the ratio of the sound powers.

For convenience, an absolute value for 0 db has been established and is expressed in acoustical watts. At 0-db intensity, we can barely hear. Leaves rustling in the wind are near 10 db. From about thirty feet away, the engine noise of a car produces a level of about 50 db; a pneumatic drill, 90 db. Sounds at levels near 140 db are intense enough to cause pain. A 115-db sound is ten billion times as powerful as a sound of 10 db.

Consider an electronic component that is generating sound: If its power in watts is doubled, the change in volume is 3 db. The ear detects increases and decreases in increments of about 3 db, which means a doubling or halving of volume.

The output of an amplifying stage in a string of electronic components can be expressed in decibels. In this case, the decibels equal 20 times the logarithm of the ratio of the two voltages or amperages. Zero decibel-milliwatts (dbm) equals 1 milliwatt in 600 ohms.

NOISE AND DYNAMIC RANGE

Electronic devices produce what is called **noise**—random energy—from the voltages generated within them. The higher the frequency, temperature, and resistance of the system, the more the noise. A high **signal-to-noise ratio** means a strong and clear signal; a low signal-to-noise ratio, a weak and masked signal.

The signal-to-noise ratio of any component of a system is expressed in decibels. A system that has a 40-db ratio of signal-to-noise has a range of 10,000 signal strengths. In other words, the maximum signal strength is 10,000 times greater than the noise.

In black-and-white TV, the contrast scale is about 20 to 1: Twenty gradations of tone, from black through gray to white, make up the visible TV image. The ratio of the black signal to the white signal is called the **dynamic range** of the contrast. In ½-inch video systems, the signal-to-noise ratio is about 40 db. The dynamic range of both audio and video information must fit well within the span defined by the system's signal-to-noise ratio. The dynamic range of contrast signals has more than enough room within the 10,000 signal ratio of the system. The contrast scale may be viewed as a bandwidth within the larger bandwidth of the signal-to-noise ratio.

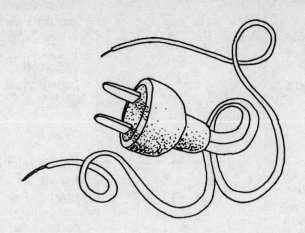

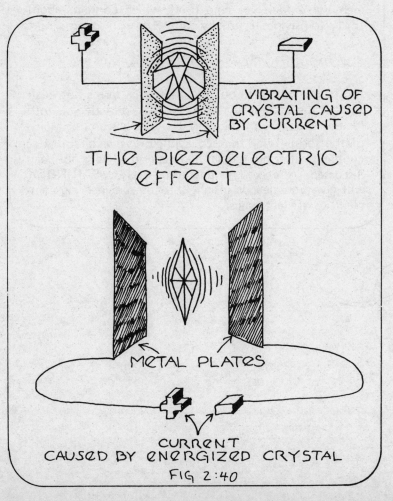

VIBRATING OF
CRYSTAL CAUSED
BY CURRENT

THE PIEZOELECTRIC EFFECT

METAL PLATES

CURRENT
CAUSED BY ENERGIZED CRYSTAL

FIG 2:40

LOOSE WIRES
IMPORTANT MISCELLANY

Thus far we have dealt with what I call the origins of video systems. For my own head, and I hope for yours too, the material provides a stimulus to look still further into electronic media. But before we go on, there are a few other things it will be helpful to understand.

THE PIEZOELECTRIC EFFECT

Some crystals, acting as electromechanical transducers, can be utilized to change AC into mechanical energy, or sound. Properly cut, a small crystal sliver can be mechanically energized if placed between two metal plates connected to a voltage source. And conversely, a mechanically energized piece of crystal will produce a voltage.

This property of some crystalline materials is called the **piezoelectric effect** and is used in microphones which transform mechanical vibrations of sound into electrical signals. These crystals are also used in making tuned circuits (crystal resonators) for generating high-frequency oscillations at a constant rate within especially narrow bandwidths.

ELECTROSTATIC

The term "static" applied to both electric and magnetic fields describes fields that neither move nor change intensity. A stationary charge produces a **static** field; a stationary magnet, a **magnetostatic** field; a stationary electric charge, an **electrostatic** field.

ELECTROLYSIS

Electrolysis is the production of chemical changes by passing current through an **electrolyte**. An electrolyte is an ionized (positively charged) material that allows electrical energy to flow through it. Usually, it is a liquid or chemical paste used either as a conducting medium between the terminals of a battery, or as a dielectric in a capacitor.

When we discuss battery power for video systems, we will see the importance of this process.

SERVOMECHANISMS

More commonly called **servos**, servomechanisms are systems of control which read their own output (feedback) to determine the degree of further output as compared to the input. Automatic temperature control devices are servomechanisms. A furnace is controlled by a thermostat in accordance with a room's temperature, which is the output of the system. The input is the setting made on the thermostat. We see in **VIDEOWORKS** (page 79), how servomechanisms function to coordinate a video recorder's mechanical and electrical components.

INTEGRATED CIRCUITS (CHIPS)

For specific common circuits requiring a number of transistors, **ICs** (integrated circuits) have been developed. Also called **chips**, they are manufactured like individual transistors but grouped together on a single rectangular piece of material which measures about 1 inch by ¼ inch. A chip itself, which contains about thirty transistors, is usually about 1/8-inch square.

A WORD ABOUT THE GLOSSARINDEX

At the rear of this book are additional terms not dealt with in the text. They are included to provide you with further exposure to the workings of electronics. Many of the terms refer to such applications of circuitry as coupling, filtering, regulating, etc., which have not been discussed. A relaxed reading over the **GLOSSARINDEX** will give you deeper insight into the engineering complexities of electronics.

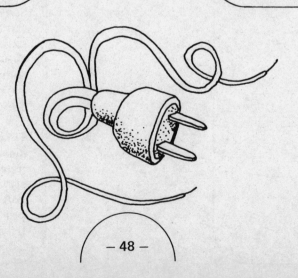

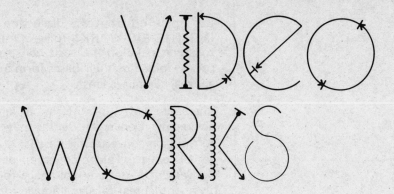

VIDEO WORKS

INTRODUCTION

This section focuses on the actual tools of video and how they work. The solutions of electronic design problems are many, and what makes each video equipment manufacturer different from the next is the way its engineers have chosen to deal with the electronic problems they face.

All video systems are principally the same. Each has a light-sensing circuit with focusing optics of some kind to direct the incoming light. Each must transduce light energy into electrical signals. Each incorporates circuitry to encode the information and carry it to a monitor for decoding and display or into recording circuitry for storage.

In this book, ½-inch video systems of recent vintage are given the most emphasis, since they are the systems most often employed by the independent video user. Though there are differences in design from brand to brand, your understanding of one system will lead to a basic understanding of them all, including 1-inch and 2-inch systems. We will be talking here primarily about black-and-white systems. Color systems will be mentioned separately.

CAMERA
SEEING CIRCUITS

The video camera will be dealt with in four parts: 1) the zoom lens, 2) the vidicon, 3) video amplifiers, and 4) the signal drive circuits. Though these four parts usually are packaged as a unit—which with a viewfinder make up the camera—they sometimes are packaged separately. Signal drive circuits and video amplifiers can be housed in the recording deck. Detachable viewfinders are common in small studio cameras.

LENSES IN GENERAL

Let's pick up from the discussion of lenses in **WORK-ING THE BIG WORKS** (page 44). Two prisms joined together make up the basic construction of a lens. The prisms joined at their bases form a **convex lens**; at their apexes, a **concave lens**.

There are two types of simple lenses—**convergent** and **divergent**. Convergent lenses may be bi-convex, plano-convex, or convergent-miniscus. Divergent lenses may be bi-concave, plano-concave, or divergent-miniscus. Convergent lenses are real-image forming (positive), and divergent lenses are virtual-image forming (negative).

Inherent in simple lenses are the following defects: 1) chromatic aberration, 2) spherical aberration, 3) curvature of the field, 4) distortion, 5) flare, 6) coma (a form of spherical aberration), and 7) astigmatism.

BASIC LENSES

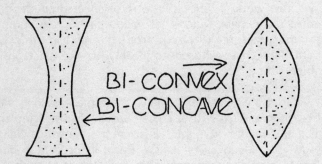

BI-CONVEX
BI-CONCAVE

PLANO-CONVEX
PLANO-CONCAVE

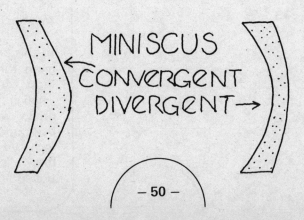

MINISCUS
CONVERGENT
DIVERGENT

FIG 3:1

Chromatic aberration, as mentioned in **WORKING THE BIG WORKS** (page 44), is the focusing, at different focal points, of the different colors of a wave of light. In lens-making, many types of materials are added to silicon dioxide—the basic substance of which lenses are made—in order to achieve different indexes of refraction in a piece of glass. Chromatic aberration can be corrected by the careful combination of pieces of glass which have different dispersive and refractive qualities.

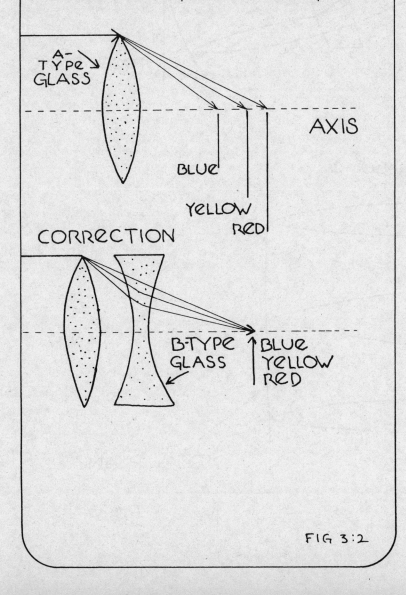

FIG 3:2

Spherical aberration results from the curved surfaces of lenses. Light waves passing through the edges of the lenses have focal lengths different from those passing through the centers. To correct spherical aberration, lenses are positioned so that the refractive deviation is shared among the surfaces of the lenses.

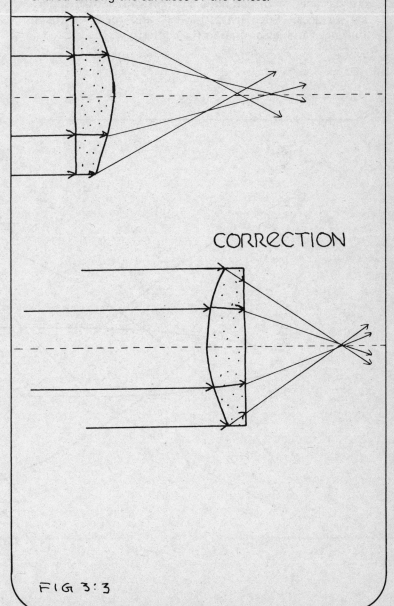

FIG 3:3

Curvature of the field is a problem which also has to do with the curved surfaces of a lens. Light waves passing through the edges of the lens have focal lengths which fall short of the picture plane (in our case, the vidicon face). The best lenses to correct curvature of the field are designed with parabolic surfaces rather than spherical surfaces. Such lenses have greater focal lengths at the edges and lesser ones in the center.

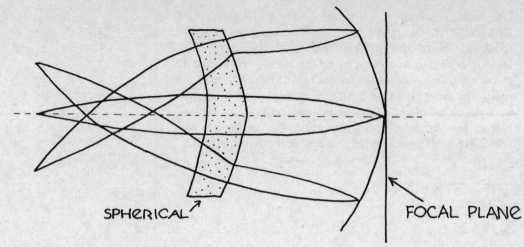

SPHERICAL

FOCAL PLANE

CORRECTION

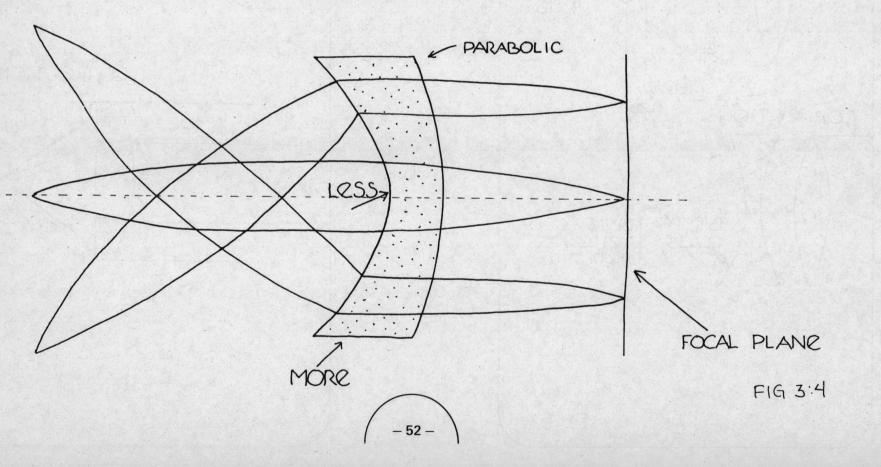

PARABOLIC

LESS

MORE

FOCAL PLANE

FIG 3:4

PINCUSHION

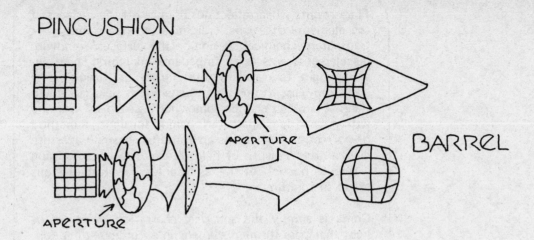

APERTURE

BARREL

APERTURE

Distortion results from the placement of the diaphragm (iris) of a lens. Pincushion distortion occurs when the lens is in front of the diaphragm. Barrel distortion occurs when the lens is behind the diaphragm. Correction is achieved by placing opposite lens elements in front of and behind the diaphragm. This combination of simple lenses makes up a rapid rectilinear lens.

CORRECTION

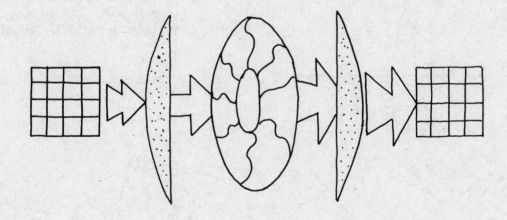

FIG 3:5

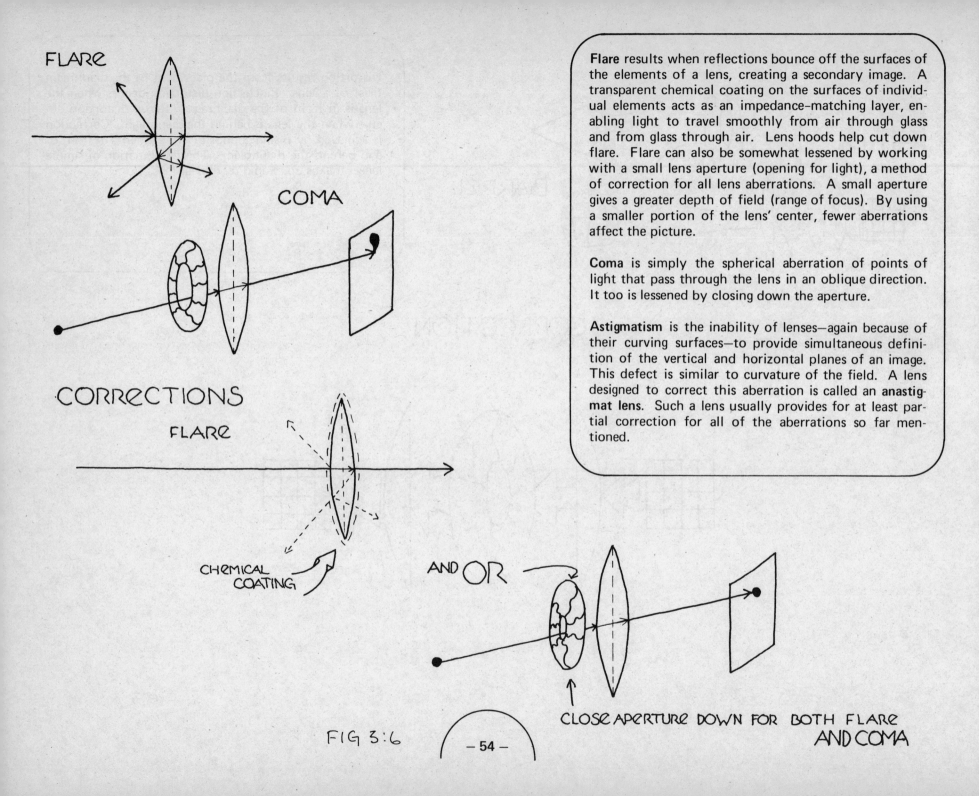

FLARE

COMA

CORRECTIONS

FLARE

CHEMICAL COATING

AND OR

CLOSE APERTURE DOWN FOR BOTH FLARE AND COMA

Flare results when reflections bounce off the surfaces of the elements of a lens, creating a secondary image. A transparent chemical coating on the surfaces of individual elements acts as an impedance-matching layer, enabling light to travel smoothly from air through glass and from glass through air. Lens hoods help cut down flare. Flare can also be somewhat lessened by working with a small lens aperture (opening for light), a method of correction for all lens aberrations. A small aperture gives a greater depth of field (range of focus). By using a smaller portion of the lens' center, fewer aberrations affect the picture.

Coma is simply the spherical aberration of points of light that pass through the lens in an oblique direction. It too is lessened by closing down the aperture.

Astigmatism is the inability of lenses—again because of their curving surfaces—to provide simultaneous definition of the vertical and horizontal planes of an image. This defect is similar to curvature of the field. A lens designed to correct this aberration is called an **anastigmat lens**. Such a lens usually provides for at least partial correction for all of the aberrations so far mentioned.

FIG 3:6

The quality of a lens depends on the degree to which it has been corrected for defects. Since the video image is less refined than the photographic image, video lenses need not be of superior quality (in fact, defects in the video lens occasionally provide some desirable optical effects).

Some important lens terms:

C-mount denotes the size of the lens receptor ring of the camera body—standard for most video cameras and 16mm film. Adaptors for using other lens mounts with a C-mount are available.

Depth of field indicates the range of acceptable sharpness in front of and behind the plane of focus. Smaller apertures and shorter focal lengths provide for greater depths of field.

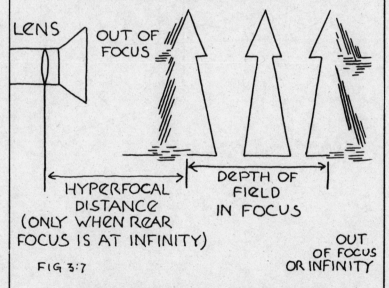

LENS
OUT OF FOCUS
OUT OF FOCUS OR INFINITY
HYPERFOCAL DISTANCE (ONLY WHEN REAR FOCUS IS AT INFINITY)
DEPTH OF FIELD IN FOCUS

FIG 3:7

Hyperfocal distance is the distance from the nearest plane of the depth of field to the lens, when the farthest plane of the depth of field is at infinity, i.e., everything from the focused point nearest the lens on out to infinity is in focus.

Focal length is the distance between the center of the lens and its points of convergence.

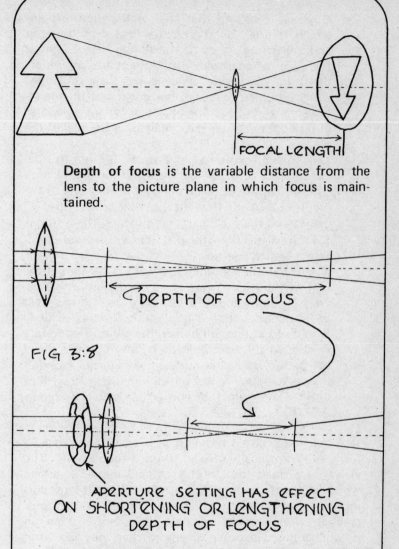

FOCAL LENGTH

Depth of focus is the variable distance from the lens to the picture plane in which focus is maintained.

DEPTH OF FOCUS

FIG 3:8

APERTURE SETTING HAS EFFECT ON SHORTENING OR LENGTHENING DEPTH OF FOCUS

Lens angle describes in degrees the vertical and horizontal angles that the lens takes into view. It is determined by the focal length of a lens.

Aspect ratio is an image's width divided by its height. The aspect ratio for the video image (TV screen) is 4:3. However, this ratio is more commonly expressed as 3 by 4.

Coverage refers to that area of the picture plane which is filled by the circular image of the lens, and **vignetting** refers to the falling off of light at the edges of an image. Both effects are easily identified in very wide angle lenses (fisheye lenses) which produce coverage that might not fill the total area of the picture plane, or an image whose outer edges may be less bright than the rest of the picture.

Lens speed, expressed in **f-stops**, is the ratio between the size of the aperture and the focal length of the lens, the distance the light must travel to the picture plane. If the lens diameter or aperture is 2 inches and the focal length is 8 inches, the f-stop is f 4. At a focal length of 8 inches, f 8 would indicate a 1-inch aperture.

T-stops are measurements based on the light at the rear of the lens. There is no fixed relationship between f-stops and T-stops, since small differences in lens construction can affect the T-stop, while f-stop calculations will remain the same. T-stops are calculated by electronically measuring the light at the picture plane—in our case, the vidicon face and the automatic light control circuit. (For film buffs: The vidicon in normal use is comparable to ASA 100.)

It should be pointed out that in most video systems a scene is electronically viewed through the camera. The viewer is a small (usually 1-inch or 3-inch) TV screen which shows the picture just as you will see it later during the tape playback. Unlike the filmmaker and photographer, who need to calculate the effect of light on photochemicals in order to ensure that they get what they want, videomakers have a direct relationship to their product. A lighting problem can be noticed in the viewer and a correction immediately can be made, whether it involves getting more light, changing position, shielding the lens, or opening or closing the aperture.

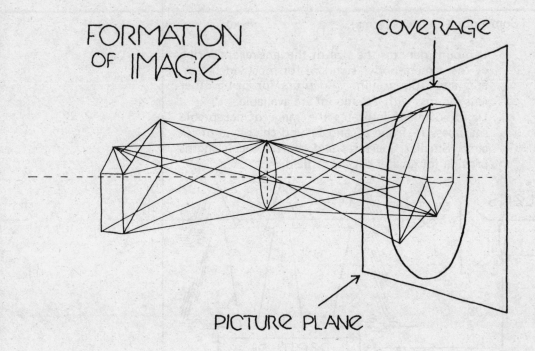

FORMATION OF IMAGE

COVERAGE

PICTURE PLANE

FIG 3:9

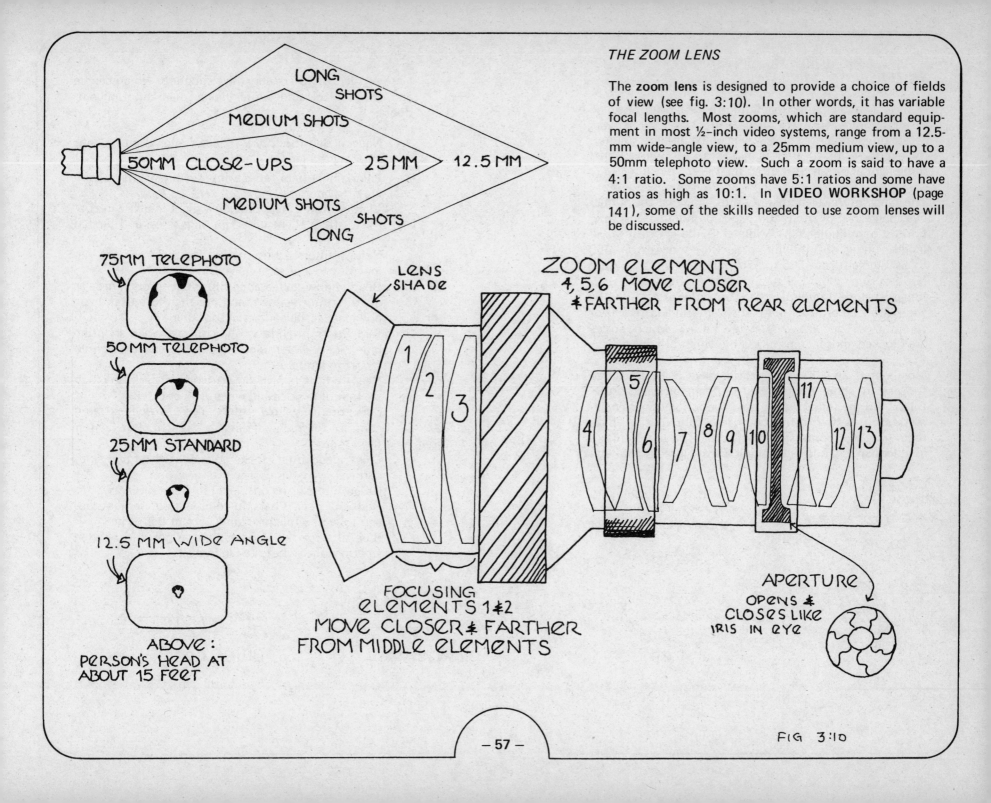

LONG SHOTS

MEDIUM SHOTS

50MM CLOSE-UPS   25MM   12.5 MM

MEDIUM SHOTS

LONG SHOTS

The **zoom lens** is designed to provide a choice of fields of view (see fig. 3:10). In other words, it has variable focal lengths. Most zooms, which are standard equipment in most ½-inch video systems, range from a 12.5-mm wide-angle view, to a 25mm medium view, up to a 50mm telephoto view. Such a zoom is said to have a 4:1 ratio. Some zooms have 5:1 ratios and some have ratios as high as 10:1. In **VIDEO WORKSHOP** (page 141), some of the skills needed to use zoom lenses will be discussed.

75MM TELEPHOTO

50MM TELEPHOTO

25MM STANDARD

12.5 MM WIDE ANGLE

ABOVE:
PERSON'S HEAD AT
ABOUT 15 FEET

LENS SHADE

ZOOM ELEMENTS
4, 5, 6 MOVE CLOSER
& FARTHER FROM REAR ELEMENTS

1 2 3
4 5 6 7 8 9 10 11 12 13

FOCUSING
ELEMENTS 1 & 2
MOVE CLOSER & FARTHER
FROM MIDDLE ELEMENTS

APERTURE
OPENS &
CLOSES LIKE
IRIS IN EYE

FIG 3:10

FILTERS

A **filter** is a device for regulating the intensity or color of light coming through a lens. Filters are used to exaggerate or eliminate specific wavelengths of light, to modify exposure, or to alter light tones. A filter absorbs some light and transmits other light.

The range of wavelengths in white light that the human eye perceives is from 400 to 700 millimicrons (millionths of millimeters). Violet has the shortest wavelength—under 450 millimicrons. Blue ranges from 450 to 500, green from 500 to 570, and yellow from 570 to 590. From about 590 to 610 is orange, and red is longer than 610 millimicrons. The color saturation of a filter itself determines the color(s) it will absorb and/or transmit. The drawings below show which colors are blocked and/or transmitted by which filters.

Most optics and their accessories have been developed for use in conjunction with photochemical exposure. Filters aid the filmmaker in the production of special effects such as fog, diffusion, partial obscuration, haze reduction, sky contrast control, etc. The use of filters in videomaking, however, should be explored separately.

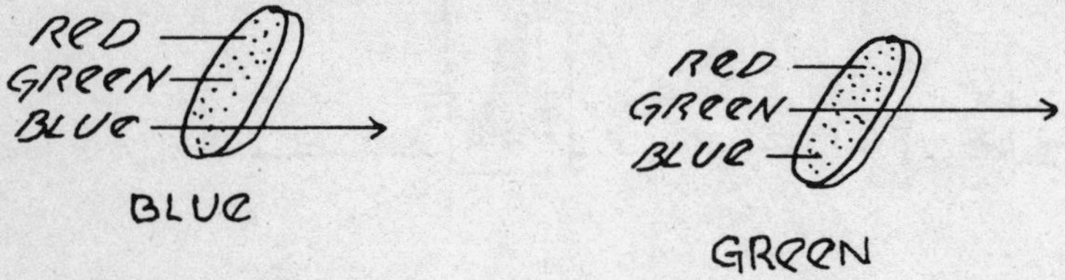

Here is a list of filters and their functions which can be applied to black–and–white video when shooting outdoors:

Neutral density filters reduce the amount of light entering the lens.

Polarizing filters reduce intense highlights reflecting off water and snow.

Light yellow filters provide a slight increase in contrast; they slightly darken blue skies, and lighten faces a bit.

Yellow filters do essentially the same as light yellow, but to a lesser extent.

Deep yellow and **orange** filters cut through haze as do the other yellows, and are therefore useful for open landscape and aerial shooting.

Red filters provide strong contrast when shooting blue skies, water, and clouds; they also lighten faces moderately.

Deep red filters provide extreme contrast—so much so, that blue skies and water appear black.

Dark orange-yellow filters also provide extreme contrast for night effects in daylight, but lighten flesh tones.

Light green filters make greenery lighter and skies darker.

Green filters bring out detail in green subjects.

Red and green filters, in combination, darken skies and foliage, while providing correct flesh tones.

Blue filters make blues as light as possible, lending an atmospheric haze to landscapes.

BLUE

GREEN

YELLOW

RED

MAGENTA

BLUE - GREEN

FIG 3:11

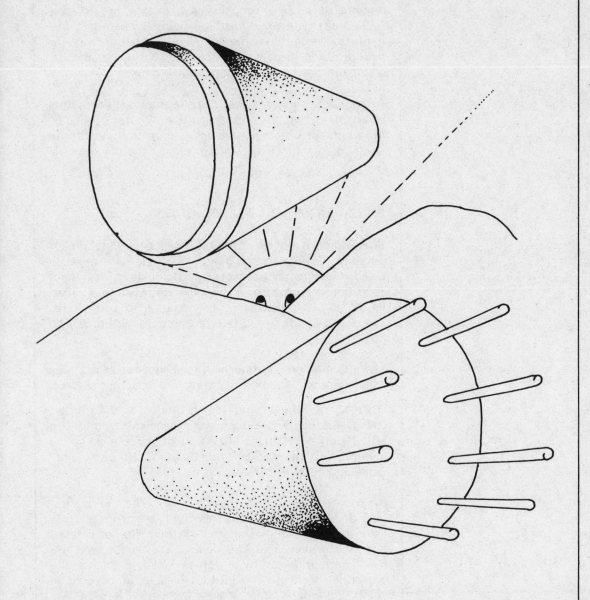

THE VIDICON

The **vidicon** is a vacuum tube which consists of a face, or target, an electron gun, and deflection coils (see fig. 3:12). The **face** is comprised of three layers and a target ring. The outside of the face is glass, which preserves the vacuum and provides transparency so that incoming photons can pass through it. Inside the glass is a layer of conductive material applied so thinly that it too is transparent so that photons can pass through. Next is the **photoconductive layer**, which when struck by photons, undergoes a reduction in resistivity. This lower resistance permits the electrons generated by the electron gun to pass onto the **conductive layer**. The number of electrons permitted to pass is proportional to the number of photons striking a given point on the photoconductive surface within a finite period of time. The immediate response time of the photoconductive layer to incoming photons is in millionths of a second. The effects of the photons upon the photoconductive layer decay in 1/60–1/30 of a second.

The **target ring** encircles the conductive layer and acts to drain off the electrons from that layer. These electrons produce the electrical energy that represents the picture or video signal—it's an AC voltage which is amplified by the video amplifier farther down the line in the system.

The **electron gun**, at the back end of the vidicon, is the heated filament which gives off a steady flow of electrons. The direction of the flow and the size of the stream is determined by electrodes within the tube: the *beam*, the *accelerator*, the *focus*, and *mesh*. Together, these electrodes create the electric fields that control the stream of electrons called the **electron beam**.

The **deflection coils** locate the electron beam in the picture plane. The picture plane is two-dimensional—vertical and horizontal. The electron beam moves from right to left and from the bottom to the top. Remember that the image is inverted by the lens. The action of the electron beam is controlled by two sets of deflection coils which are placed around the outside of the vidicon.

The above process is called **scanning**. The deflection coils generate magnetic fields which steer the electron beam. A sweep along one horizontal line from right to left takes 56.5 microseconds. The return from left to right takes 7 microseconds and is called **retrace** (see fig. 3:15). During retrace, the electron beam is **blanked** (cut off).

Simultaneous to this horizontal scanning, the electron beam sweeps from bottom to top, but at a much slower rate. For every 262.5 horizontal lines scanned there is only one vertical scan, and that occurs every 1/60 of a second. Thus, every 1/60 of a second and 262.5 lines compose what is called a **field**.

Two fields constitute a **frame**, or 525 lines every 1/30 of a second. A frame is a total picture. Fields are **interlaced**, meaning the first field skips every other line, which is subsequently filled in by the second field.

There are two types of interlacing: **random interlace**, which means that the horizontal and vertical are not interlocked and thus interlace sloppily; and **2:1 interlace**, which means the horizontal and vertical are generated from the same oscillator and interlocked, thereby interlacing equidistantly (see fig. 3:20).

The 525-line, 30-frames-per-second scanning system is standard for color and black-and-white in the U.S., South America, and Japan. In Europe, France and Belgium and the U.S.S.R. use a standard of 819 lines and 25 frames per second for black-and-white. All the rest of Europe and Britain uses 625 lines and 25 frames per second for color. In Britain, it's 405 lines and 25 frames per second for black-and-white. Note that the number of fields per second corresponds to the AC hertz standard of that area.

You will notice in camera specifications that horizontal resolution is expressed in *lines* of resolution. For in-

stance, a camera may have a horizontal resolution of 300 lines. This figure refers to the frequency response of the system in detecting black and white changes on one horizontal line—roughly meaning that one horizontal line can be broken into 300 points. The horizontal resolution determines the contrast and sharpness of the picture. The greater the resolution, the higher the frequency response and the better the picture.

A complete video signal thus contains information about photon intensity and location. Photons reflected off an object onto the vidicon face are transduced into electrical signals to be transmitted to the video amplifiers.

OTHER LIGHT-SENSING CIRCUITS

The vidicon is not the only tube of its type used in TV cameras. Similar to it is the silicon diode—the so-called **tivicon**—which has been developed for use in low-light conditions. Instead of a chemical coating on the target, its coating is composed of thousands of silicon diodes. These semiconductor diodes are extremely sensitive to light.

The **plumbicon** is another low-light-sensitive tube which has a lead oxide coating on its target surface.

Whereas the vidicon and silicon diode tubes are interchangeable in most ½-inch system cameras, plumbicon installation necessitates alteration of the camera. The plumbicon is the standard tube used in both black-and-white and color Big TV cameras.

On the near horizon for popular use is the charge-coupled device which uses no free-flying electrons. It is a light-sensing circuit composed of discrete diodes placed in a two-dimensional grid comparable to the eye of a fly. These units can be extremely small, as small as the proverbial deck of cards. Also available, but expensive as yet, are what are called light intensifiers or light amplifiers. These types of elements fit on the lens, and amplify the light before it hits the vidicon target.

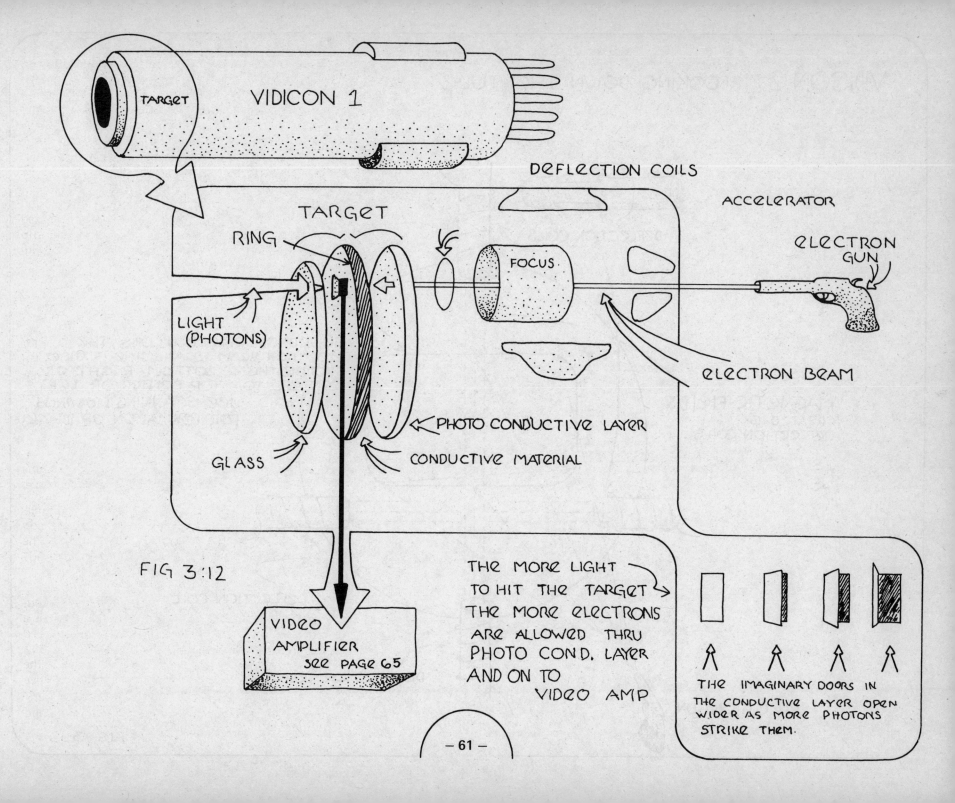

TARGET

VIDICON 1

DEFLECTION COILS

ACCELERATOR

ELECTRON GUN

TARGET

RING

FOCUS

LIGHT (PHOTONS)

ELECTRON BEAM

PHOTO CONDUCTIVE LAYER

GLASS

CONDUCTIVE MATERIAL

FIG 3:12

VIDEO AMPLIFIER SEE PAGE 65

THE MORE LIGHT TO HIT THE TARGET THE MORE ELECTRONS ARE ALLOWED THRU PHOTO COND. LAYER AND ON TO VIDEO AMP

THE IMAGINARY DOORS IN THE CONDUCTIVE LAYER OPEN WIDER AS MORE PHOTONS STRIKE THEM.

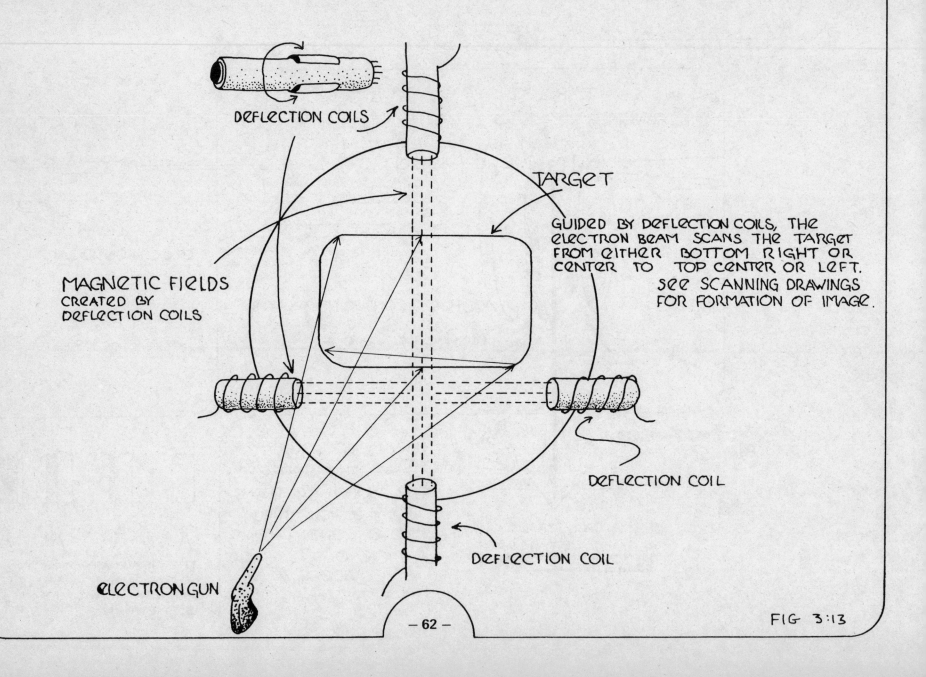

VIDICON 2   LOOKING DOWN THE TUBE

DEFLECTION COILS

TARGET

GUIDED BY DEFLECTION COILS, THE
ELECTRON BEAM SCANS THE TARGET
FROM EITHER BOTTOM RIGHT OR
CENTER TO TOP CENTER OR LEFT.
SEE SCANNING DRAWINGS
FOR FORMATION OF IMAGE.

MAGNETIC FIELDS
CREATED BY
DEFLECTION COILS

DEFLECTION COIL

DEFLECTION COIL

ELECTRON GUN

FIG 3:13

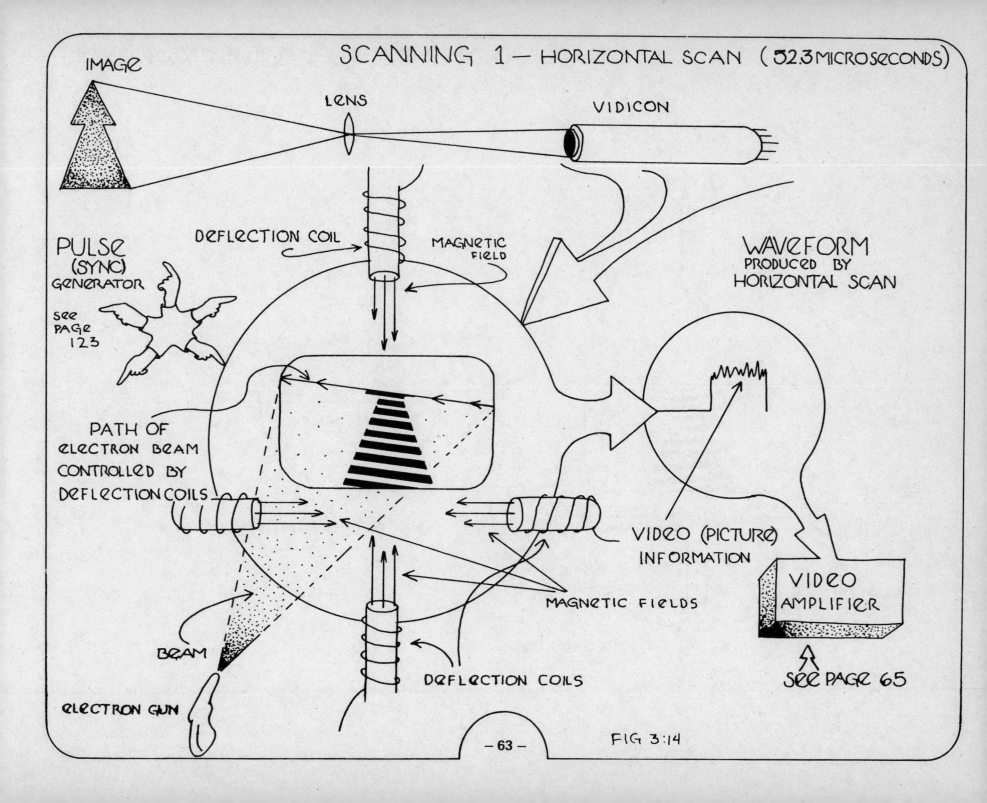

SCANNING 1 — HORIZONTAL SCAN (52.3 MICROSECONDS)

IMAGE

LENS

VIDICON

DEFLECTION COIL

MAGNETIC FIELD

PULSE (SYNC) GENERATOR

see PAGE 123

WAVEFORM PRODUCED BY HORIZONTAL SCAN

PATH OF ELECTRON BEAM CONTROLLED BY DEFLECTION COILS

MAGNETIC FIELDS

VIDEO (PICTURE) INFORMATION

DEFLECTION COILS

VIDEO AMPLIFIER

BEAM

ELECTRON GUN

SEE PAGE 65

-63-

FIG 3:14

SCANNING 2-HORIZONTAL RETRACE (11.21 MICROSECONDS)

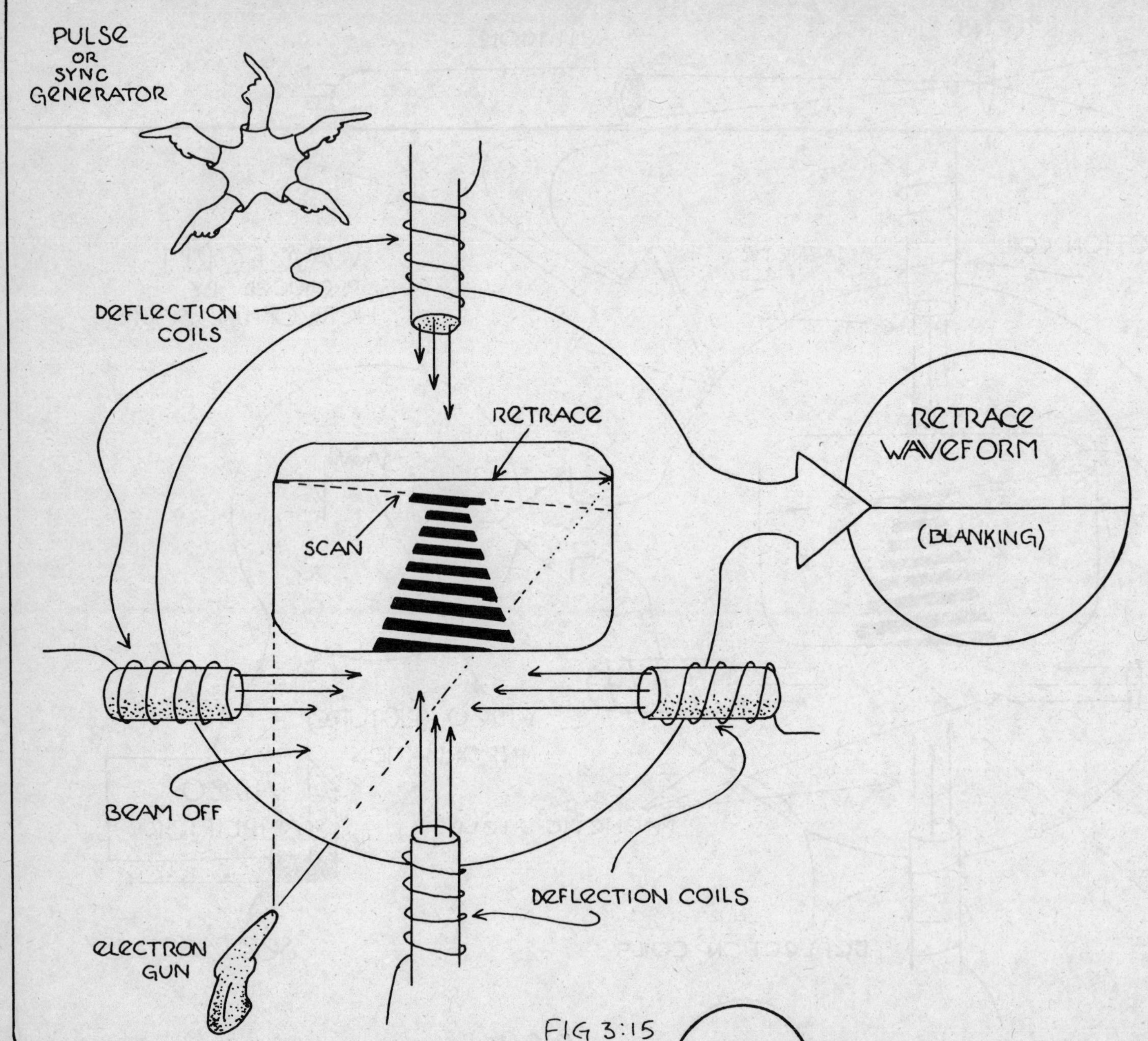

PULSE OR SYNC GENERATOR

DEFLECTION COILS

RETRACE

SCAN

RETRACE WAVEFORM

(BLANKING)

BEAM OFF

DEFLECTION COILS

ELECTRON GUN

FIG 3:15

VIDEO AMPLIFIERS

Coming off the vidicon from the target ring is the picture signal which has small AC voltages. The target itself has a fixed voltage to attract the beam electrons. Those electrons represent each horizontal line of about 56.5 microseconds of signal. They are conducted through a number of video amplifiers in order to increase the signal strength.

To examine one section of video amplification, let's follow the picture signal from the vidicon through a few amplification stages. A resistor, which is coupled to the first transistor (an NPN device, see fig. 2:24) carries out the first stage of amplification.

The target, from which the signal is coming, is high impedance. It generates variable voltages with very small current changes. Transistors are low-impedance devices which are sensitive to large currents and small voltage changes. The primary objective of this stage of amplification is to match impedances and increase signal strength.

Pi-networks are circuits that match impedances, and are similar to resonant circuits containing inductance and capacitance. A pi-network connects the target and first transistor. This circuit extends high-frequency response of the system and filters out set frequencies in order to eliminate noise.

The first three transistors in the circuit form a negative feedback amplifier loop. The signal is passed directly from one transistor to the other. Negative feedback means that some of the signal—180° out of phase—is taken from the third transistor collector and is conducted to the base of the first transistor. In this way, the input impedance of the low-impedance transistor is increased, helping to match the high impedance of the signal from the target. Large amounts of negative feedback serve to fix the overall gain of the feedback loop.

By the time the video signal passes through the camera's various stages of amplification (not all using the feedback technique), it is increased many times.

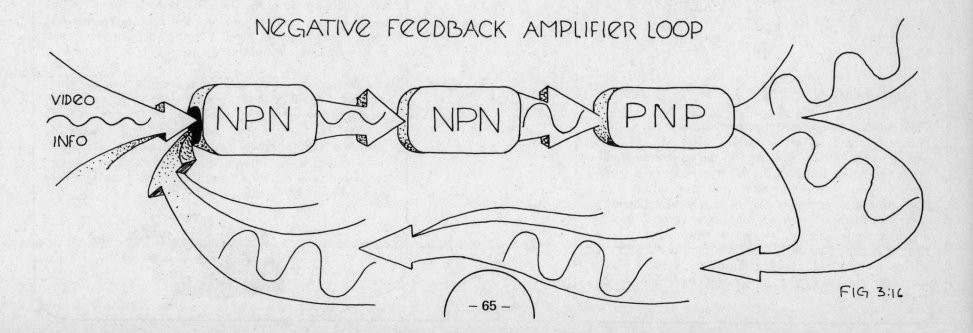

NEGATIVE FEEDBACK AMPLIFIER LOOP

FIG 3:16

An **Automatic Gain Control** (AGC) system (sometimes called an Automatic Light Control system) controls the fixed target voltage in inverse proportion to the average amount of light on the face of the vidicon. This system raises and lowers the sensitivity of the vidicon and holds the picture signal constant over a wide range of light values. At very low light levels the AGC action is disabled.

SIGNAL DRIVE CIRCUITS

Five pulses are generated to drive the camera: 1) the **horizontal ·sync** (synchronization) pulse, which starts and stops the horizontal trace; 2) the **horizontal blanking** pulse, which turns off the electron beam during horizontal retrace; 3) the **vertical sync** pulse, which starts and stops the vertical trace; 4) the **vertical blanking** pulse, which turns off the beam during vertical retrace; and 5) the **equalizing** pulses, which ensure that the vertical scan begins every 1/60 of a second and keeps the horizontal oscillator running during the vertical blanking. This last set of pulses does not take place in ½-inch equipment.

It is important to note that the *timebase stability* of a system is its ability to ensure that the horizontal lines occur during an exact time duration. Imprecision in this timing can cause problems which will show up on video-tape if the tape is stretched. Transferring, editing, and transmitting will therefore be troublesome. We will explain these problems when discussing the recorder and timebase correctors.

The horizontal sync pulse drives the horizontal deflection coils of the vidicon, and the vertical sync pulse drives the vertical deflection coils. Blanking simply means cutting off the electron beam in the vidicon. All horizontal, vertical, and equalizing pulses are generated from one complex circuit source, the **pulse generator**.

In our 525–line black–and–white system, the vertical frequency is 60 Hz and the horizontal frequency is 15.75 kHz. (In color TV, the frequencies of these signals are slightly different. See *Color Video*, page 102.) These frequencies are generated by oscillators and sent to driver circuits which control the deflection coils. These frequency signals are simultaneously directed to the electronic viewfinder deflection coils, to the **blanking amplifier** (which controls the electron beam of the vidicon), and to the **sync mixer** (which combines the picture signal with the horizontal, the vertical, the blanking, and the equalization pulses).

Out of the sync mixer comes the composite video signal which is amplified and passed to the video recording deck and the electronic viewfinder of the camera (see fig. 3:19). Due to the high-voltage requirements of both the viewfinder's TV tube and of the vidicon, a high-voltage converting circuit is needed. This convertor is basically a power amplifier-transformer-rectifier which develops the requisite high voltages.

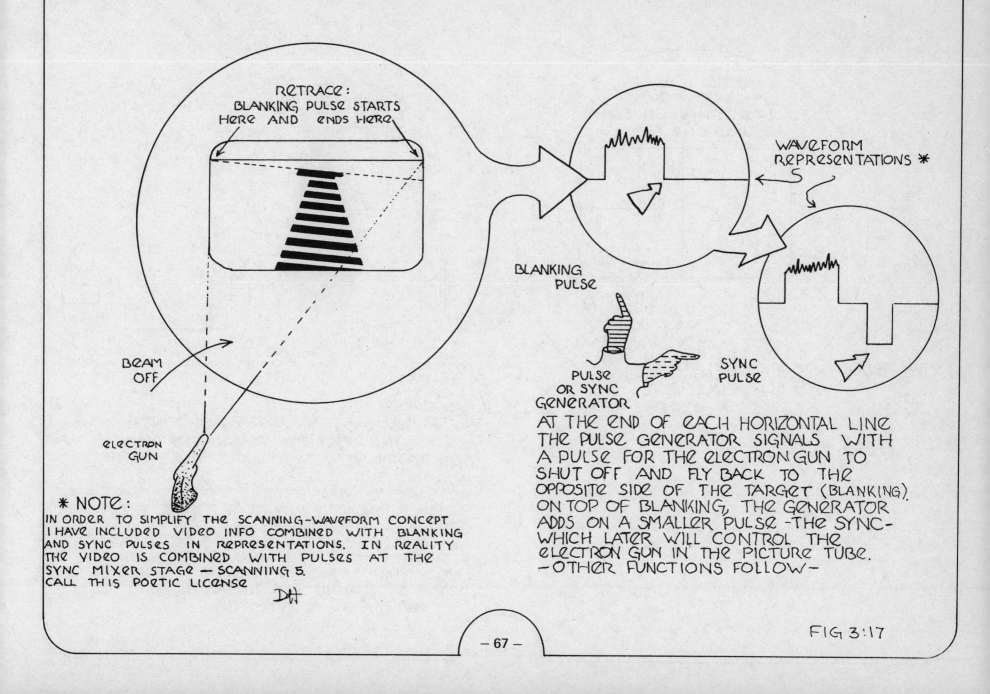

SCANNING 3 — HORIZONTAL BLANKING & SYNC PULSES

RETRACE:
BLANKING PULSE STARTS
HERE AND ENDS HERE

WAVEFORM
REPRESENTATIONS ✳

BEAM
OFF

BLANKING
PULSE

ELECTRON
GUN

PULSE
OR SYNC
GENERATOR

SYNC
PULSE

✳ NOTE:
IN ORDER TO SIMPLIFY THE SCANNING-WAVEFORM CONCEPT
I HAVE INCLUDED VIDEO INFO COMBINED WITH BLANKING
AND SYNC PULSES IN REPRESENTATIONS. IN REALITY
THE VIDEO IS COMBINED WITH PULSES AT THE
SYNC MIXER STAGE — SCANNING 5.
CALL THIS POETIC LICENSE
DH

AT THE END OF EACH HORIZONTAL LINE
THE PULSE GENERATOR SIGNALS WITH
A PULSE FOR THE ELECTRON GUN TO
SHUT OFF AND FLY BACK TO THE
OPPOSITE SIDE OF THE TARGET (BLANKING).
ON TOP OF BLANKING, THE GENERATOR
ADDS ON A SMALLER PULSE -THE SYNC-
WHICH LATER WILL CONTROL THE
ELECTRON GUN IN THE PICTURE TUBE.
—OTHER FUNCTIONS FOLLOW—

FIG 3:17

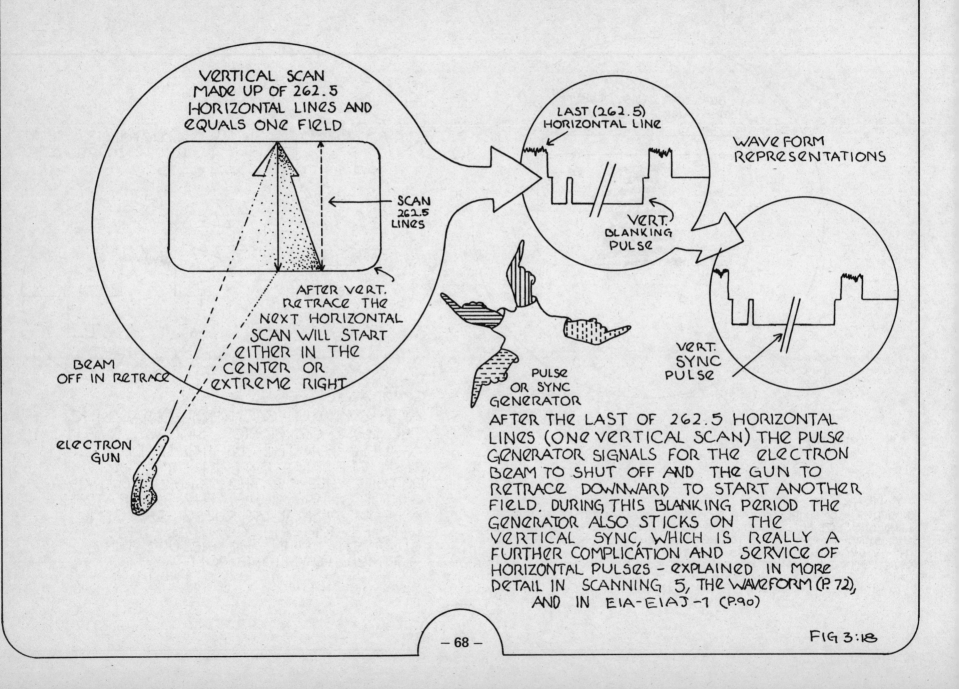

SCANNING 4 — VERTICAL SCAN (1/60 SECOND)
RETRACE AND BLANKING AND SYNC PULSES

VERTICAL SCAN MADE UP OF 262.5 HORIZONTAL LINES AND EQUALS ONE FIELD

SCAN 262.5 LINES

AFTER VERT. RETRACE THE NEXT HORIZONTAL SCAN WILL START EITHER IN THE CENTER OR EXTREME RIGHT

BEAM OFF IN RETRACE

ELECTRON GUN

LAST (262.5) HORIZONTAL LINE

WAVEFORM REPRESENTATIONS

VERT. BLANKING PULSE

PULSE OR SYNC GENERATOR

VERT. SYNC PULSE

AFTER THE LAST OF 262.5 HORIZONTAL LINES (ONE VERTICAL SCAN) THE PULSE GENERATOR SIGNALS FOR THE ELECTRON BEAM TO SHUT OFF AND THE GUN TO RETRACE DOWNWARD TO START ANOTHER FIELD. DURING THIS BLANKING PERIOD THE GENERATOR ALSO STICKS ON THE VERTICAL SYNC, WHICH IS REALLY A FURTHER COMPLICATION AND SERVICE OF HORIZONTAL PULSES — EXPLAINED IN MORE DETAIL IN SCANNING 5, THE WAVEFORM (P. 72), AND IN EIA-EIAJ-1 (P.90)

FIG 3:18

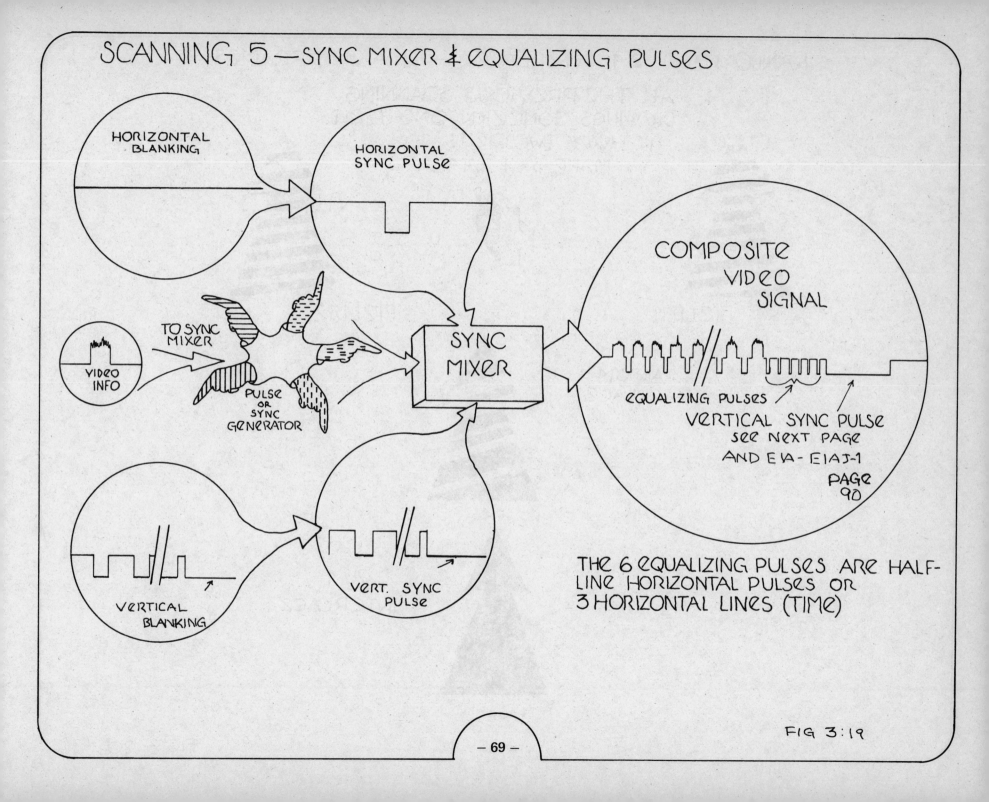

SCANNING 5—SYNC MIXER & EQUALIZING PULSES

HORIZONTAL BLANKING

HORIZONTAL SYNC PULSE

COMPOSITE VIDEO SIGNAL

VIDEO INFO

TO SYNC MIXER

PULSE OR SYNC GENERATOR

SYNC MIXER

EQUALIZING PULSES

VERTICAL SYNC PULSE
SEE NEXT PAGE
AND EIA- EIAJ-1
PAGE 90

VERTICAL BLANKING

VERT. SYNC PULSE

THE 6 EQUALIZING PULSES ARE HALF-LINE HORIZONTAL PULSES OR 3 HORIZONTAL LINES (TIME)

FIG 3:19

RANDOM AND 2:1 INTERLACE — MAKING FRAMES

ALL THE PREVIOUS SCANNING
DRAWINGS CONCERN ONE FIELD.
IT TAKES TWO FIELDS TO
MAKE A FRAME

FIELD 1

FIELD 2

RANDOM
INTERLACE

2:1
INTERLACE

FIG 3:20

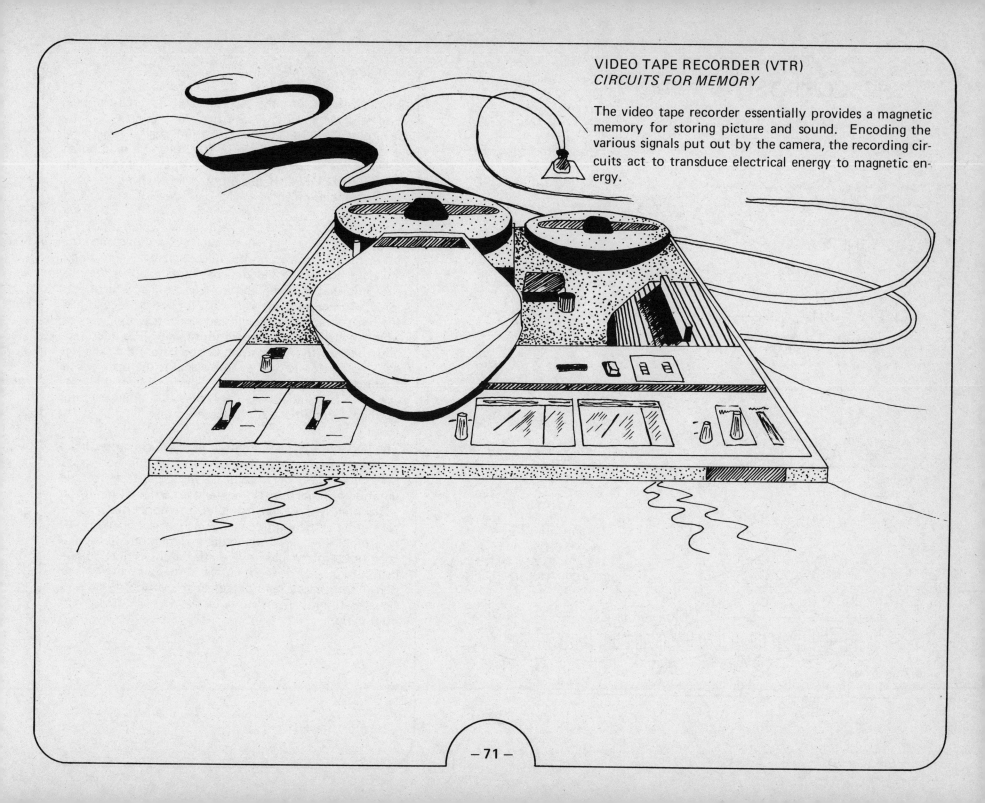

VIDEO TAPE RECORDER (VTR)
CIRCUITS FOR MEMORY

The video tape recorder essentially provides a magnetic memory for storing picture and sound. Encoding the various signals put out by the camera, the recording circuits act to transduce electrical energy to magnetic energy.

THE COMPOSITE VIDEO WAVEFORM

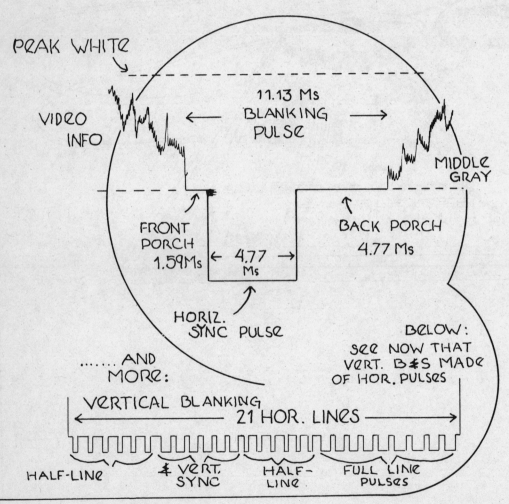

PEAK WHITE

VIDEO INFO

11.13 Ms BLANKING PULSE

MIDDLE GRAY

FRONT PORCH 1.59Ms

4.77 Ms

BACK PORCH 4.77 Ms

HORIZ. SYNC PULSE

BELOW: SEE NOW THAT VERT. B&S MADE OF HOR. PULSES

.......AND MORE:

VERTICAL BLANKING
21 HOR. LINES

HALF-LINE

& VERT. SYNC

HALF-LINE

FULL LINE PULSES

FIG 3:21.

THE WAVEFORM

Before getting into the recorder and its circuitry, let's discuss some specific areas of concern about videotape recording. As the drawings have indicated, every signal is represented as a waveform which can be read on an oscilloscope. We discuss oscilloscopes in **MAINTENANCE AND REPAIR** (page 179), along with other electronic test equipment.

Using a color standard broadcast signal, which is now replacing the black-and-white standard, let's examine the make-up of the composite video signal: A broadcast standard composite video signal is made up of the picture information from the horizontal line, which lasts for 52.3 microseconds with an 11.13-microsecond gap for horizontal blanking. In sequence, it is followed by what is called the **front porch** (optimally, 1.59 microseconds), a very short transition period before the sync signal. Just prior to the picture signal is the **back porch** (optimally, 4.77 microseconds), during which the voltage level is **clamped**—set for black. Clamping circuits set the DC conditions of the waveform.

The horizontal sync pulse itself lasts 4.77 microseconds. The vertical blanking pulse lasts for the duration of 21 horizontal lines. The vertical sync pulse lasts for the duration of 6 horizontal lines, and it carries within it the horizontal sync which maintains the horizontal oscillator during vertical retrace. During vertical blanking, 16 horizontal lines have no picture information. Six equalizing pulses occur before and after each vertical pulse—in itself composed of six pulses. Video circuits are designed to generate and/or detect the voltage levels and signal durations in order to form and read the picture information.

THE FM SIGNAL

Remember, the bandwidth required for the video signal frequency range is 4.2 MHz (although in some VTRs it's as low as 2.2 MHz); for a TV channel (video and audio information) it's 6 MHz. The bandwidth covered by doubling a frequency is called an **octave**. Tape is usable over a range of about 10 octaves. The bandwidth of a video signal covers about 18 octaves: let's say from 25 Hz to 4.2 MHz. Therefore, some kind of translation must be made from the signal range to the tape range.

The signal is FM–modulated at a high frequency in order to reduce its octave range. A 6-MHz carrier modulated by a 4-MHz signal will generate sidebands of 6 minus 4 MHz and 6 plus 4 MHz (2 MHz to 10 MHz). This will result in a frequency range of about 3 octaves, which is well within the capacity of the tape response.

Two types of modulating systems are commonly used: the multivibrator (square wave oscillator) and heterodyne (sine wave oscillators).

A **multivibrator modulating system** has a free–running frequency which represents the video blanking level. The changing of video levels causes changes of frequency. In other words, voltage levels of signals are translated into frequencies of square pulses.

In the **heterodyne modulating system**, the video signal modulates a high–frequency oscillator. Another oscillator with a fixed frequency is mixed with the first. Heterodyning is a form of the modulation process described in **WORKING THE BIG WORKS** (page 32).

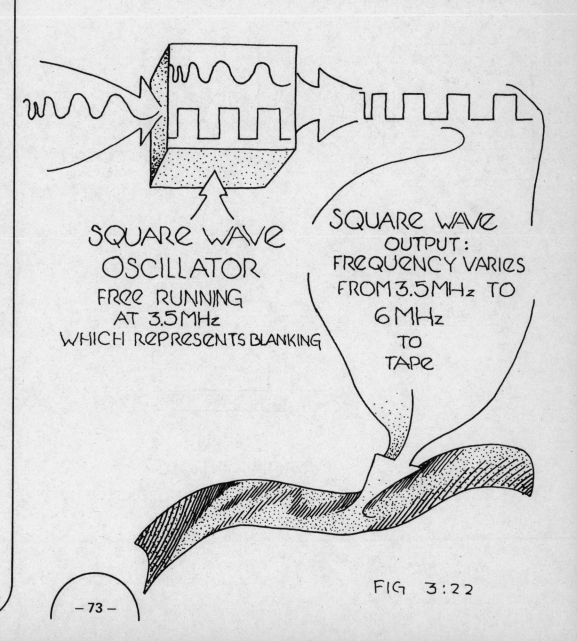

MULTIVIBRATOR

SQUARE WAVE OSCILLATOR
FREE RUNNING AT 3.5MHz
WHICH REPRESENTS BLANKING

SQUARE WAVE OUTPUT:
FREQUENCY VARIES FROM 3.5MHz TO 6MHz
TO TAPE

FIG 3:22

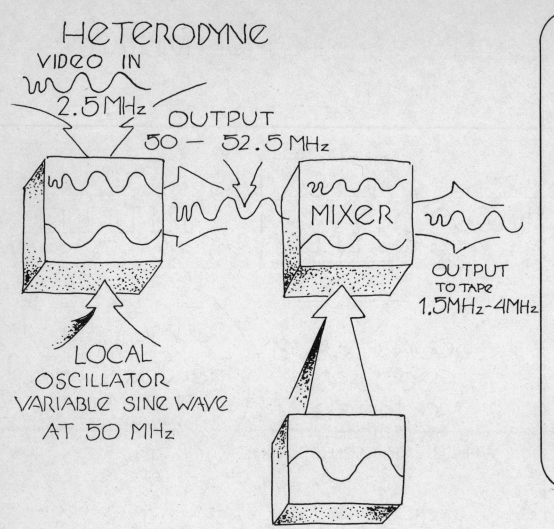

HETERODYNE

VIDEO IN 2.5 MHz

OUTPUT 50 – 52.5 MHz

MIXER

LOCAL OSCILLATOR VARIABLE SINE WAVE AT 50 MHz

OUTPUT TO TAPE 1.5 MHz – 4 MHz

LOCAL OSCILLATOR FIXED AT 54 MHz

FIG 3:23

Demodulation systems are of several types, two of which we will discuss: pulse counter demodulation, and heterodyne demodulation.

Pulse counter demodulation is mostly used in the VTRs with which we are concerned. Put simply, it is the reversal process of multivibrator modulation. Square pulse frequencies are translated into voltage levels.

Heterodyne demodulation mixes the incoming signal—a carrier with sidebands—with the output of a high-frequency oscillator, which in turn produces new sidebands. These new sidebands are the sum and difference of the two mixed high-frequency signals. One of the sidebands is filtered out and the carrier is removed by a bandpass filter. Thus the signal is demodulated—translated into voltage levels.

Pre-emphasis is a method used to minimize the signal-to-noise ratio of a signal of wide frequency range. Generally, the higher the frequency, the more the noise. Pre-emphasis increases the voltage of a high-frequency signal, thereby increasing the signal-to-noise ratio before recording. (The more power, the less noise at any given frequency.) **De-emphasis** is the reverse process, necessary for returning the voltage to its proper signal level for replay.

FREQUENCY RESPONSE AND SPEED OF WRITING

Frequency response refers to a system's ability to reproduce picture detail. In **VIDEOWORKS** (page 60), lines of resolution are described as the measure of a system's frequency response. Remember that the number of lines of resolution is roughly equal to the number of points into which a horizontal line can be broken. The degree of response is dependent on the entire system—its speed of writing, head characteristics, signal system electronics, and the extent of its bandwidth—for frequency modulation. Frequency response is primarily a function of the recorder. The horizontal resolution of the camera is usually greater than that of the VTR.

There is a relationship between tape speed and frequency response: The wavelength of a signal equals the velocity of the tape divided by the frequency of the signal. In order to recover a signal from the tape, the head on replay must intercept less than one wavelength of the signal. If very high frequencies are to be recorded, the head gap must be of a specific minimum size. By accelerating the tape's velocity—**speed of writing**—the frequency response can be increased. In VTRs both the tape and the heads move in order to achieve the necessary speeds.

METHODS OF SCANNING

Two methods are used for high head-to-tape speed or scanning: quadruplex (transverse) and helical. Quadruplex is the broadcast standard, while helical scan is the system used in the VTRs with which we are concerned.

Quadruplex systems use 2-inch videotape traveling at 15 inches per second. A servo-controlled drum with four heads revolves at a rate of 14,400 revolutions per minute, resulting in a writing speed of 1,561 inches per second. The penetration of the tape by the head is controlled by a vacuum guide at the drum. Tape-to-head penetration (about 2.5 mils) is important to ensure that tape-to-head contact is constantly maintained.

In **helical scan** recording, the tape is wrapped in one of several ways around the head drum assemblies. These assemblies house rotating heads which lay down (print) the information at an angle dependent on the size of the drums and the speed of the tape. Each printed line equals a field. Several widths of tape are used: ¼-inch, ½-inch, ¾-inch, 1-inch, and 2-inch.

In order to obtain a high-frequency response, high writing speed can be achieved by using a large drum. (However, practical limits are set by timebase stability, which we will get to shortly.) The tape speed in most systems of our concern runs 7½ inches per second. The rotational speed of the heads is locked to the 60-Hz frequency of the vertical signal. Tape tension is critical because the tape must be stretched exactly the same amount in replay as in record.

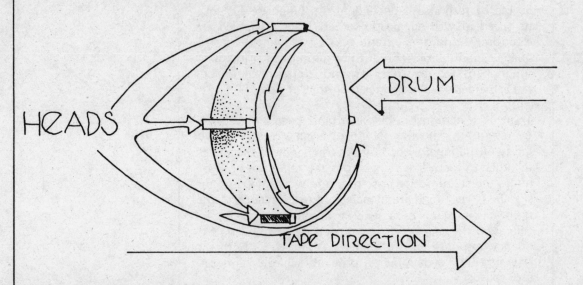

QUADRUPLEX (TRANSVERSE)
2" SCANNING FORMAT

HEADS

DRUM

TAPE DIRECTION

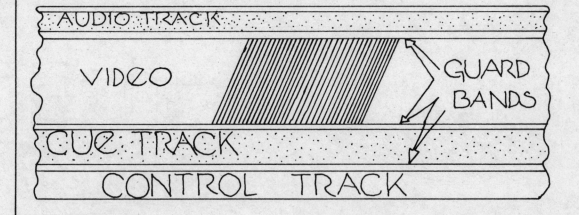

AUDIO TRACK

VIDEO

GUARD BANDS

CUE TRACK

CONTROL TRACK

FIG 3:24

HELICAL SCAN FORMAT ½" or 1"

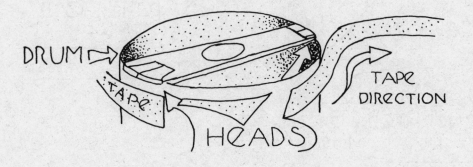

DRUM →

TAPE

HEADS

TAPE DIRECTION

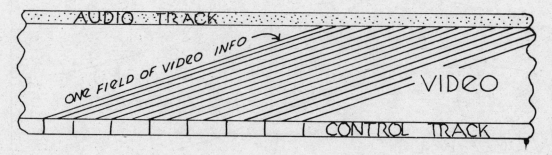

AUDIO TRACK

ONE FIELD OF VIDEO INFO →

VIDEO

CONTROL TRACK

FIG 3:25

TIMEBASE STABILITY

Problems in **timebase stability** result from mechanical errors which take place during recording. These problems are the main reason helical scan VTRs do not record standard broadcast signals. As stated earlier, the timebase stability of a system determines its exactness in timing the horizontal trace. A significant part of the VTR is devoted to the servomechanisms that control the speed and phase of the heads and the tape. However, timing errors do occur, and especially in a broadcast situation—in which interswitching of multiple video sources is routine—timing errors must be held within very narrow limits or TVs will function poorly.

In helical scan systems, timebase instability results because the head is driven by a signal derived from the vertical sync. This signal occurs once every 1/30 of a second, producing a reference once every 525 horizontal lines. In quad systems, the heads are driven by a signal which occurs once every 1/2,000 of a second, producing a reference once every 8 horizontal lines. Since a head is a servo-controlled mechanism which checks its own output by comparing it to a reference signal, it is easy to see that a reference signal occuring 2,000 times a second is preferable to one which occurs only 30 times a second. A lot of instability can go down in 1/30 of a second.

E-E (ELECTRONICS-TO-ELECTRONICS)

The **E-E mode** functions to monitor the picture being recorded by a VTR. Once a signal is modulated within the VTR, it is passed directly to both the recording circuitry and the demodulator. From the demodulator, the signal is processed by all the replay electronics, and can be monitored while it is being recorded. Note that the monitored image does not come from the tape and therefore will not show you exactly what the tape is recording. Any failings in the recording circuitry will not show up on the monitor.

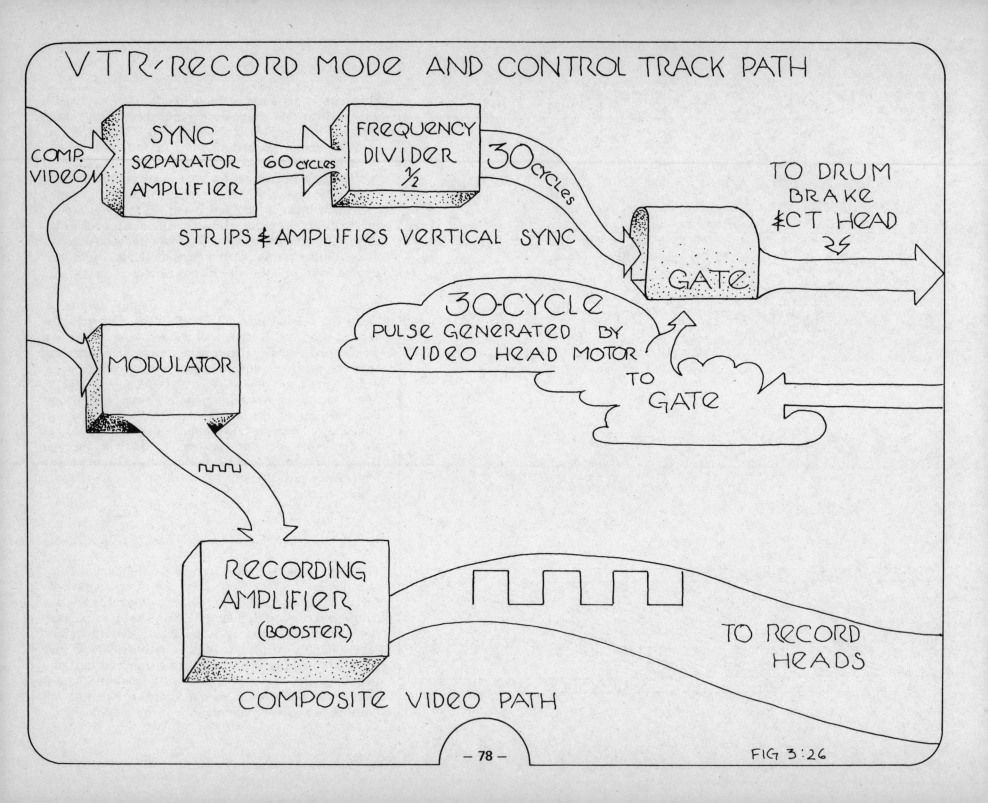

VTR-RECORD MODE AND CONTROL TRACK PATH

COMP. VIDEO

SYNC SEPARATOR AMPLIFIER

60 cycles

FREQUENCY DIVIDER ½

30 cycles

TO DRUM BRAKE & CT HEAD

STRIPS & AMPLIFIES VERTICAL SYNC

GATE

30-CYCLE PULSE GENERATED BY VIDEO HEAD MOTOR

TO GATE

MODULATOR

RECORDING AMPLIFIER (BOOSTER)

TO RECORD HEADS

COMPOSITE VIDEO PATH

FIG 3:26

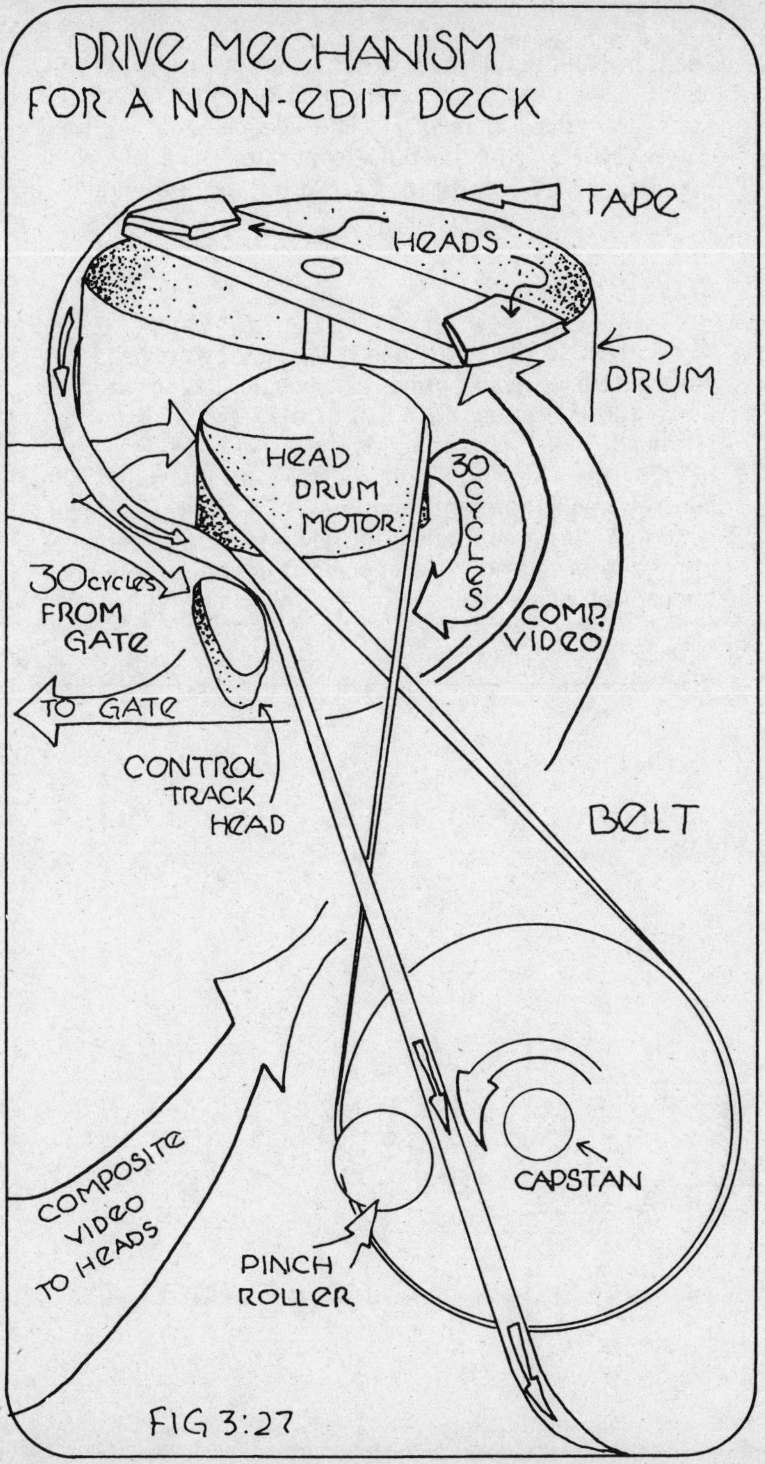

DRIVE MECHANISM FOR A NON-EDIT DECK

TAPE

HEADS

DRUM

HEAD DRUM MOTOR

30 CYCLES

30 CYCLES

COMP. VIDEO

30 cycles FROM GATE

TO GATE

CONTROL TRACK HEAD

BELT

COMPOSITE VIDEO TO HEADS

PINCH ROLLER

CAPSTAN

FIG 3:27

SERVO SYSTEMS

For our purposes, we will discuss only the helical scan recording servo systems. (Enough about quadruplex systems; it would be best to deal with them in a book entitled *Corporate Video!* I think the degree to which quad has been discussed will more than aid the independent video practitioner.)

Remember, the aim of a servo system is to utilize feedback to correct and maintain synchronization of the tape-travel and head rotation (see **WORKING THE BIG WORKS**, page 48). There are two types of servos: **head drum servo** and **capstan servo**.

HEAD DRUM SERVO

The head drum is free-running at slightly more than 30 Hz; it drives the two video heads which are attached to the opposite ends of a flat metal bar. Traveling at 30 revolutions per second, each head is in contact with the tape for a bit more than half a revolution—1/60 of a second. (Only one head records at a time—head switching occurs during the vertical blanking.) Thus, every printed line represents a field. It starts and ends within the vertical sync time, printing 262.5 lines of horizontal information during that time.

The vertical sync of the incoming composite video is also **counted down** (separated and divided by 2) which produces a 30-Hz signal. This signal acts as a reference for all the servo functions of the VTR. In order to drive the head drum servo, the signal is sent to the **gate** which compares it with the head drum speed pulse. This pulse (30 Hz) is generated by a head drum motor coil which is the VTR's pulse generator. To guard against any discrepancy between the two signals, the gate generates the 30-Hz signal to the head drum motor brake which acts to establish and maintain the head drum speed at 30 Hz.

The head drum servo also performs a phase-regulating function. *Phase* here refers to the positioning of the

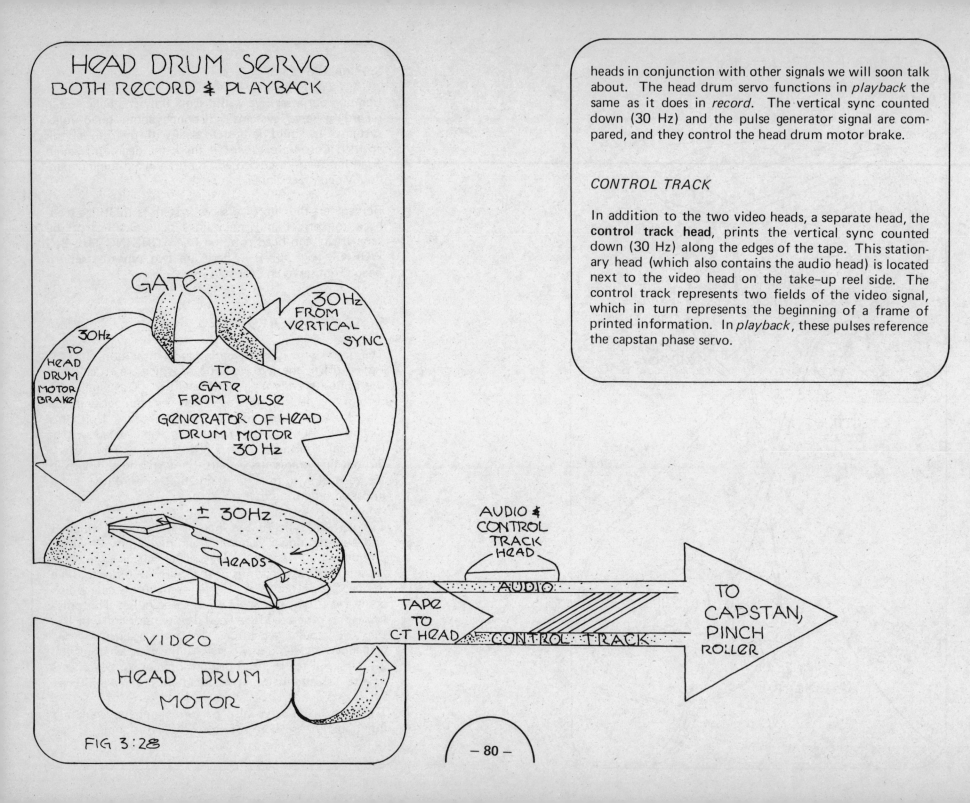

HEAD DRUM SERVO
BOTH RECORD & PLAYBACK

GATE

30Hz
FROM
VERTICAL
SYNC

30Hz
TO
HEAD
DRUM
MOTOR
BRAKE

TO
GATE
FROM PULSE
GENERATOR OF HEAD
DRUM MOTOR
30Hz

± 30Hz

HEADS

VIDEO

HEAD DRUM
MOTOR

AUDIO &
CONTROL
TRACK
HEAD

AUDIO

TAPE
TO
C·T HEAD

CONTROL TRACK

TO
CAPSTAN,
PINCH
ROLLER

FIG 3:28

heads in conjunction with other signals we will soon talk about. The head drum servo functions in *playback* the same as it does in *record*. The vertical sync counted down (30 Hz) and the pulse generator signal are compared, and they control the head drum motor brake.

CONTROL TRACK

In addition to the two video heads, a separate head, the **control track head**, prints the vertical sync counted down (30 Hz) along the edges of the tape. This stationary head (which also contains the audio head) is located next to the video head on the take-up reel side. The control track represents two fields of the video signal, which in turn represents the beginning of a frame of printed information. In *playback*, these pulses reference the capstan phase servo.

CAPSTAN

Another concern, besides head speed and phase, is the speed of the tape. The tape speed is maintained by the **capstan**, a shaft and a pinch-roller which pulls the tape. In the simplest machines, the capstan is driven by a belt connected to the head drum motor. In *playback*, the capstan also uses a motor of its own which acts to modify the phase relationship of the tape travel-to-head position. This motor is servoed by comparing the signal from the control track and the 30-Hz signal from the head drum pulse generator. Any discrepancies between the two signals will retard the capstan motor and momentarily slow the tape speed. This type of signal comparison is a form of capstan servo.

CAPSTAN SERVO

As indicated above, a capstan servo is used in all VTRs during playback. The capstan servo consists of two components: the capstan phase servo and the capstan speed servo. Remember that *phase* refers here to the positioning of the tape and head, and *speed* refers to the maintenance of the correct tape speed (7½ inches per second).

The capstan servo is not belted, but has its own motor. The capstan motor produces a signal from its own frequency generator. The signal is 30 Hz per motor revolution and there are usually about 30 motor revolutions per second. Thus the frequency generator produces a signal of about 900 Hz (30 x 30).

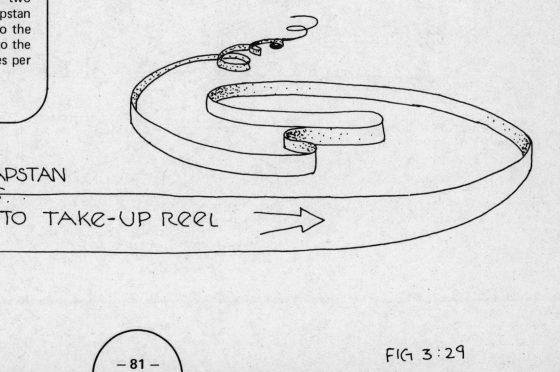

TAPE

CAPSTAN

TO TAKE-UP REEL

PINCH ROLLER

FIG 3:29

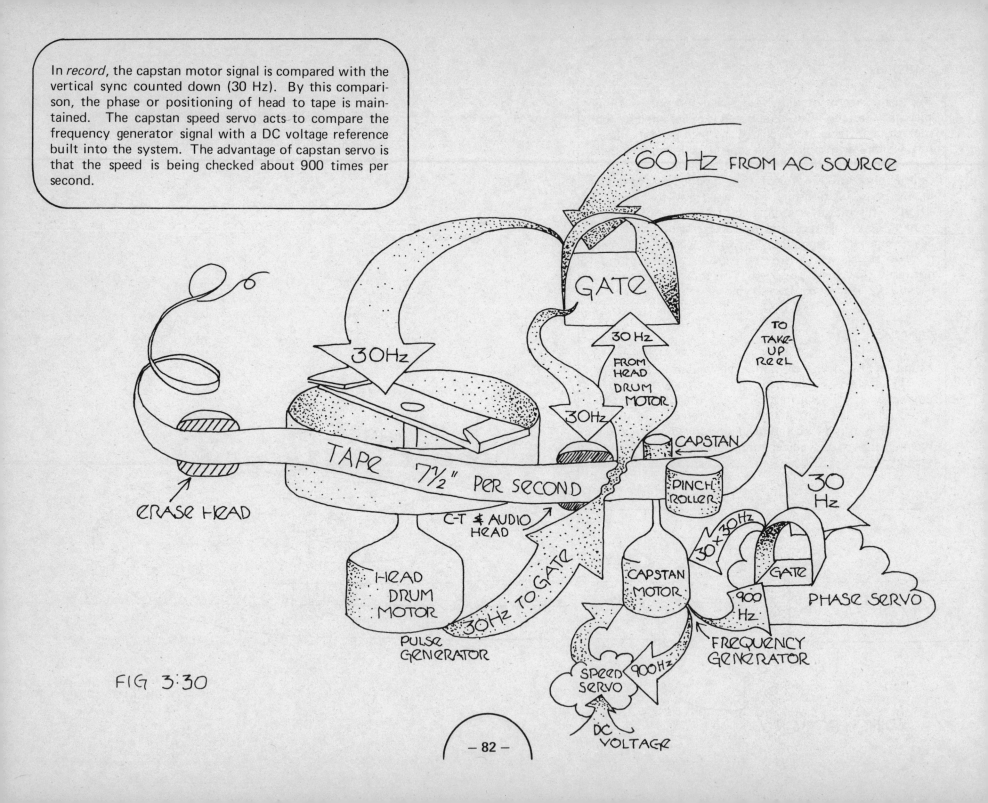

In *record*, the capstan motor signal is compared with the vertical sync counted down (30 Hz). By this comparison, the phase or positioning of head to tape is maintained. The capstan speed servo acts to compare the frequency generator signal with a DC voltage reference built into the system. The advantage of capstan servo is that the speed is being checked about 900 times per second.

60 Hz FROM AC SOURCE

GATE

30 Hz

30 Hz
FROM HEAD DRUM MOTOR

30 Hz

TO TAKE-UP REEL

CAPSTAN

30 Hz

TAPE "7½" PER SECOND

PINCH ROLLER

ERASE HEAD

C-T & AUDIO HEAD

30 x 30 Hz

GATE

PHASE SERVO

HEAD DRUM MOTOR

30 Hz TO GATE

CAPSTAN MOTOR

900 Hz

FREQUENCY GENERATOR

PULSE GENERATOR

SPEED SERVO

900 Hz

FIG 3:30

DC VOLTAGE

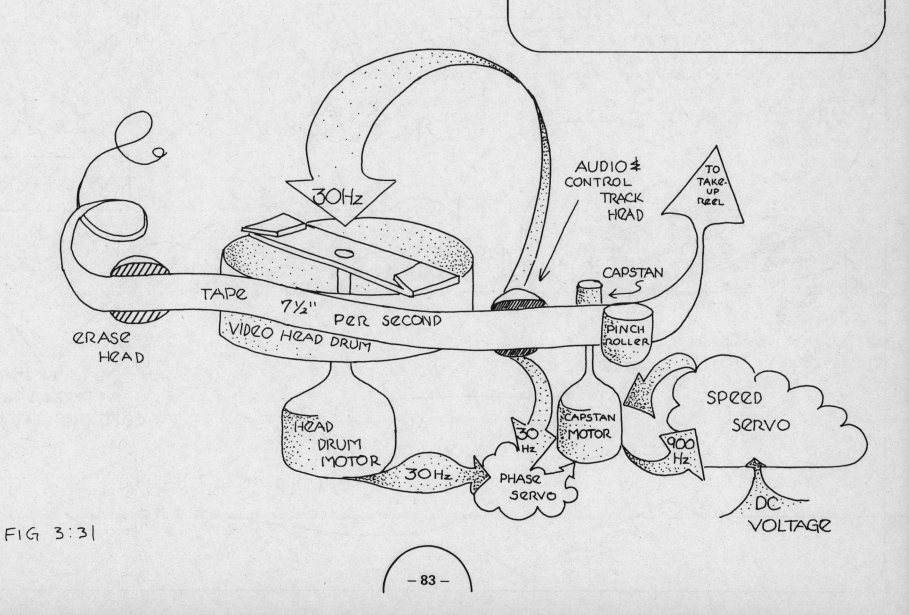

FIG 3:31

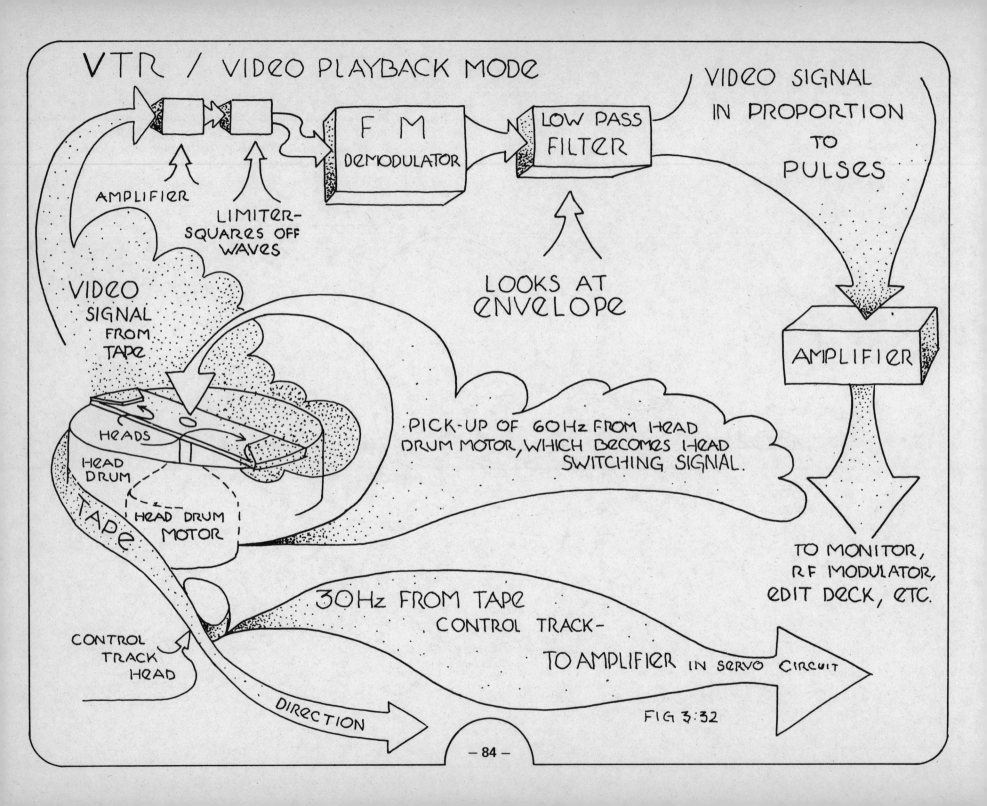

VTR / VIDEO PLAYBACK MODE

VIDEO SIGNAL IN PROPORTION TO PULSES

AMPLIFIER

LIMITER – SQUARES OFF WAVES

FM DEMODULATOR

LOW PASS FILTER

LOOKS AT ENVELOPE

VIDEO SIGNAL FROM TAPE

AMPLIFIER

HEADS

HEAD DRUM

HEAD DRUM MOTOR

TAPE

PICK-UP OF 60 Hz FROM HEAD DRUM MOTOR, WHICH BECOMES HEAD SWITCHING SIGNAL.

TO MONITOR, RF MODULATOR, EDIT DECK, ETC.

30 Hz FROM TAPE CONTROL TRACK –

– TO AMPLIFIER IN SERVO CIRCUIT

CONTROL TRACK HEAD

DIRECTION

FIG 3:32

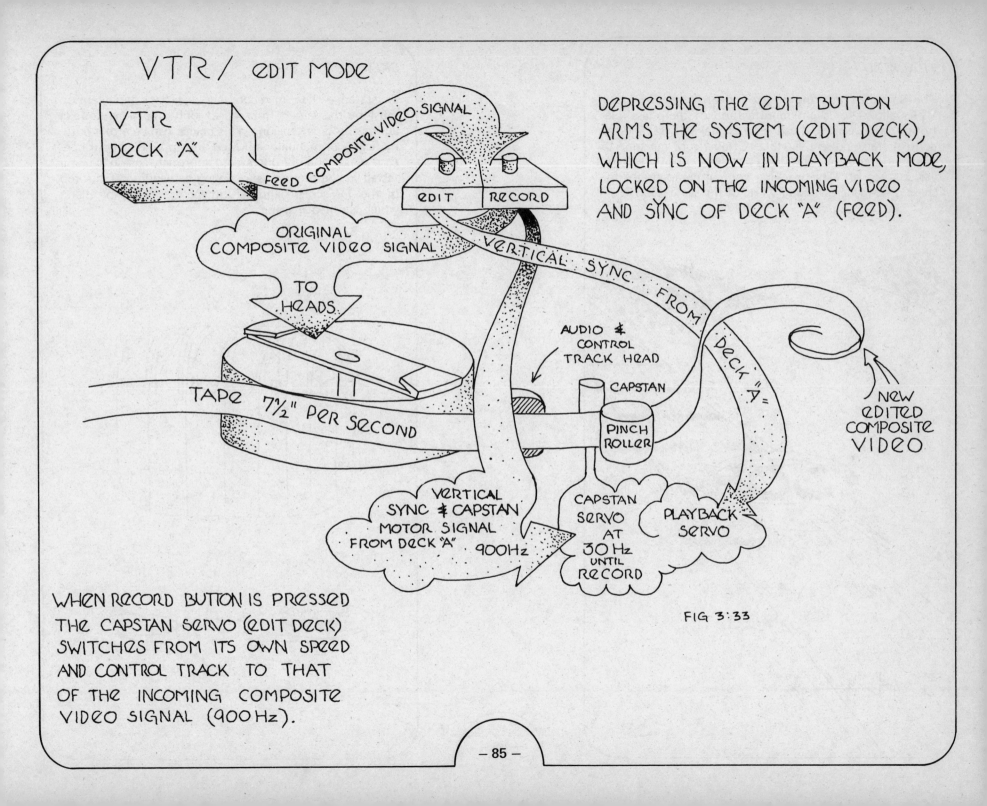

VTR / EDIT MODE

VTR DECK "A"

FEED COMPOSITE VIDEO SIGNAL

DEPRESSING THE EDIT BUTTON ARMS THE SYSTEM (EDIT DECK), WHICH IS NOW IN PLAYBACK MODE, LOCKED ON THE INCOMING VIDEO AND SYNC OF DECK "A" (FEED).

EDIT   RECORD

ORIGINAL COMPOSITE VIDEO SIGNAL

VERTICAL SYNC FROM

TO HEADS

AUDIO & CONTROL TRACK HEAD

CAPSTAN

DECK "A" =

TAPE 7½" PER SECOND

PINCH ROLLER

NEW EDITED COMPOSITE VIDEO

VERTICAL SYNC & CAPSTAN MOTOR SIGNAL FROM DECK "A" 900Hz

CAPSTAN SERVO AT 30 Hz UNTIL RECORD

PLAYBACK SERVO

FIG 3:33

WHEN RECORD BUTTON IS PRESSED THE CAPSTAN SERVO (EDIT DECK) SWITCHES FROM ITS OWN SPEED AND CONTROL TRACK TO THAT OF THE INCOMING COMPOSITE VIDEO SIGNAL (900 Hz).

TRACKING

The so-called **tracking control** incorporated in most VTRs allows for slight modification of the phase relationship between the head drum signal (30 Hz) and the control track pulse (30 Hz). Often, from machine to machine, there are slight discrepancies of position of the various heads. The tracking control compensates for these discrepancies among VTRs of the same standard.

SKEW

As stated earlier, in *record* and *playback* tape tension must be the same. In *playback* only, the **skew control** audits the tape tension. This device can be either automatically or manually adjusted, but in VTRs of our concern it is manually operated. Improper tension is manifested in the picture as a curving or bending at the top of the TV screen—another timebase stability problem, which is called **flagging**.

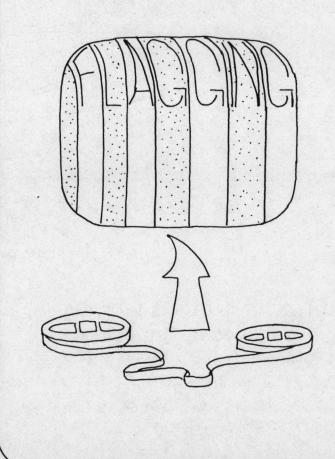

RECORDING HEADS

In all VTRs, the same heads function for both *record* and *playback*. Heads are made from ferromagnetic materials (those made up of atoms which behave like tiny magnets), and are affixed to a **head drum** which serves to position and guide them.

The VTR's *record-playback* head is an electromagnet with a gap between its poles. The current in its coils varies with the signal input. The field formed across the gap of its metal core is affected by changes of current input. As the tape passes the gap it is magnetized. In *playback*, the magnetized tape generates a field between the poles of the head. These varying fields induce voltage in the head's coils in proportion to their rate of change. Therefore, the output is frequency- (number of field changes-) dependent (i.e., doubling the frequency results in doubling the voltage output). Signal losses occur at high frequencies when the wavelength approaches the size of the gap, and at low frequencies when the wavelength is long as compared to the gap. In both, there is little discernable field change. Signal losses are inherent in all phases of the videotape recording system. They result from irregularities in the head gap and poor head-to-tape contact.

In helical scan VTRs, correct head-to-tape contact (penetration) is achieved by proper tension of the tape around the drum and the tip projection of the heads. Excess penetration causes extreme wear upon the head and tape, and can cause heads to clog when tape oxides are scraped off and jam the gap of the head.

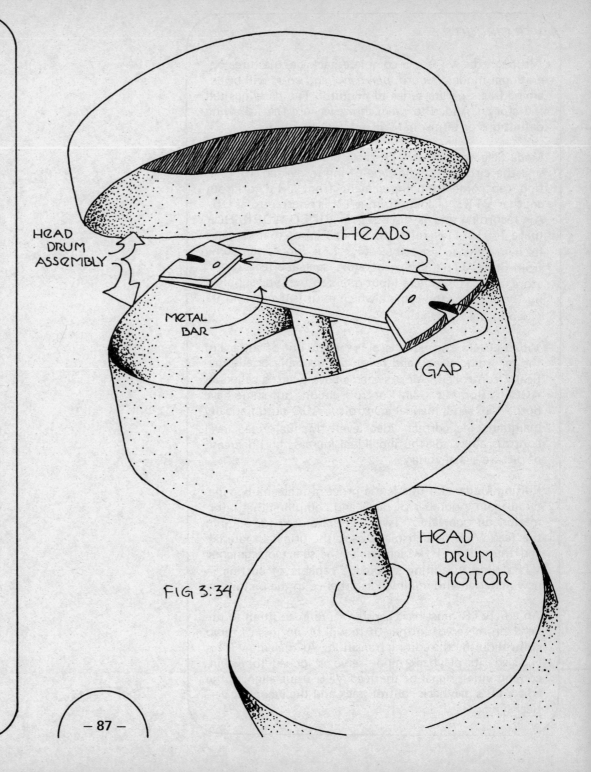

HEAD DRUM ASSEMBLY

HEADS

METAL BAR

GAP

HEAD DRUM MOTOR

FIG 3:34

VTR CIRCUITRY

Although the VTR is a complete package, the three operational modes (*record*, *playback*, and *edit*) will be examined as separate series of circuits. The drawings tell the story. Added to them, however, are the following definitions of terms that will aid understanding:

Mode Selector. Most VTRs have a mode selector which sets the circuits for the type of input. Video information can come from the camera, from a TV, or from another VTR. (Taping from a TV is referred to as Off/Air recording and is discussed in **VIDEO WORKSHOP** (page 170). *Line* refers to a video input that supplies its own sync to drive the VTR. *Line* inputs can come from other VTRs, sync generators, special effects generators, etc. The *camera* input refers to the sync supplied by the VTR to the camera which returns the composite video to the VTR.

Video Level. The video level is the amount of voltage of the recording signal, and it can be manually or automatically controlled. Most systems have what is called an **AGC** (Automatic Gain Control) circuit, but some have both AGC and manual controls. AGC automatically maintains the correct video level. Manual video level controls allow for the individual increase and decrease of picture signal voltages.

Editing Mode. Editing is the process of assembling material from a number of tapes and compiling that information on one tape. Two VTRs are used for editing: the feed VTR, which plays back the original material; and the edit VTR, which copies the selected segments. VTRs used in editing should be capable of cutting in new material with minimal disturbance to the picture.

An edit VTR must have capstan servo in addition to the head drum servo, so that there will be no loss of servo control during the editing transition. As the edit VTR is engaged, its playback mode servo is locked to the incoming video signal of the feed VTR, thus aligning the edit VTR's playback control track and the incoming vertical sync.

As the *record* function goes into effect, the capstan servo of the edit VTR changes from using its own control track and head drum speed (30 Hz) to using the incoming vertical sync and its own capstan motor signals (900 Hz). This change is made in a fraction of a second without loss of servo.

Moire. In most helical scan VTRs, the video erase head is located next to the head drum on the feed reel side of the VTR. Because of this erase head location, a few inches of tape is not erased before being recorded. If there is previous information on the tape, the unerased section of tape produces moire—an effect which shows up as a zigzag pattern over the picture. VTRs with this problem are set up with boosted record currents for the first few seconds of the edit in order to "drown out" the moire.

Newer high-priced VTRs have flying erase heads which revolve in the head drum along with the recording heads, so previously recorded information can be erased instantaneously when recording new information.

Insert. The insert is an editing capability of edit VTRs. Inserting is the process by which a segment of tape is placed between two existing segments. Usually, edited segments are assembled in sequence, one after the other. Little concern is given to the tail of a segment since it will be overlapped by the head of the next. An insert must leave only a minimum trace of picture interruption on an edited tape. In some machines this result is achieved by enabling the edit–arming circuitry to continue for a number of seconds after the *record* function is switched off, allowing for a quick and smooth transition of the capstan servo *record* alignment into the *playback* alignment.

Solenoid Switching. Solenoid switching refers to the action of any kind of electromechanical triggering devices. Most ½-inch VTRs are not solenoid–operated, but some of them have some solenoid switching. A good example of solenoid switching is an edit button which, when hit, sets off a series of electronic events which result in the precision alignment of the edit with the vertical sync. This process, called **vertical interval cutting**, means that the edit only occurs during the vertical blanking, between frames. It's the height of editing: All edits are clean and quick and no moire is seen.

Slow Motion. Slow motion in many VTRs is a playback function which is accomplished simply by bypassing the capstan servo. The capstan speed is then controlled by a variable resistor which allows speeds of 1/15 to 1/5 of the normal speed. This kind of slow motion leaves something to be desired, as it also allows you to see a noise bar which results from having no capstan phase function (tracking). Also, it hops from line to line, sampling only parts of each.

TIME LAPSE

Contrary to slow-motion images, which are produced by retarding the tape speed in playback, **time lapse** images are produced by recording at a slow speed and playing back at normal speed. This form of fast motion can be recorded only by specially designed VTRs, which can operate for a number of hours while actually recording only an hour of tape. When played back at normal speed the result is a one-hour condensation of the number of hours of recording.

VTRs which are capable of time lapse recording can have settings of 6–48 hours of recording and slow playback. The slow playback of some of these VTRs is accomplished by moveable tape guides which correctly position the heads and the tape so that the heads follow a complete line of information without hopping, thus eliminating noise bars. At slower speeds, as the tape guides move, the gaps between the lines of video information are effectively increased in size. The usual set of heads could fall into reading the gaps instead of the information. Therefore, these VTRs often have two set of heads so that uninterrupted scanning is ensured for every line of information.

COMPATIBILITY

The Electronics Industries Association (EIA) is the organization which sets the compatibility standards of electronic products among U.S. manufacturers. However, most of the video equipment we are concerned with is manufactured in Japan and EIA of Japan (EIAJ) has established the EIAJ-1 standards for ½-inch video recording equipment. Most EIAJ-1 equipment is compatible. In some cases dissimilar plugs may be used, but the electronic functions of the equipment will be compatible: the tape speed, the location of the heads, tape size, and the mechanical aspects will all be the same.

The EIA in the U.S. has set the standards for broadcast recording equipment. Compare the signal waveforms for the EIA and EIAJ-1 composite video signal (see figs. 3:35-36). Note the blanking signals and their time durations before and after the sync pulse. The exactness of the EIA standard and the lack of specification of the EIAJ-1 standard causes the timebase problems between the two systems.

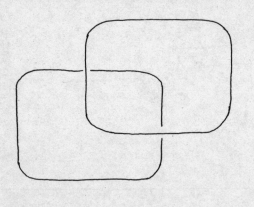

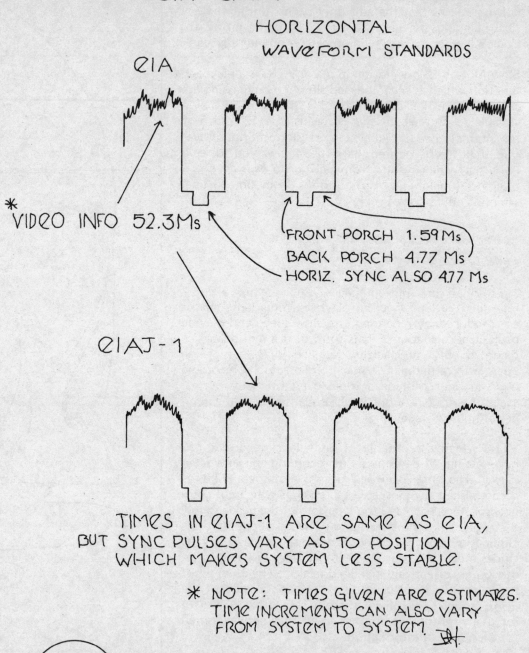

EIA—EIAJ-1

HORIZONTAL WAVEFORM STANDARDS

EIA

* VIDEO INFO 52.3Ms

FRONT PORCH 1.59 Ms
BACK PORCH 4.77 Ms
HORIZ. SYNC ALSO 4.77 Ms

EIAJ-1

TIMES IN EIAJ-1 ARE SAME AS EIA, BUT SYNC PULSES VARY AS TO POSITION WHICH MAKES SYSTEM LESS STABLE.

* NOTE: TIMES GIVEN ARE ESTIMATES. TIME INCREMENTS CAN ALSO VARY FROM SYSTEM TO SYSTEM.

FIG 3:35

EIA–EIAJ-1 CONT. VERTICAL SYNC WAVEFORMS

EIA:

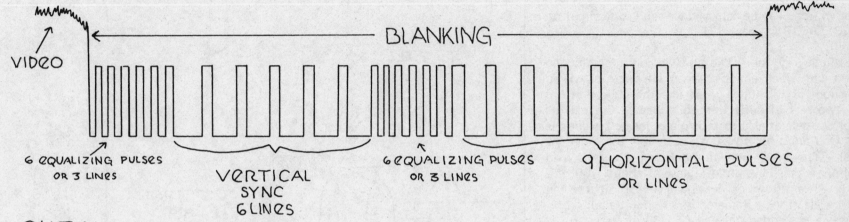

BLANKING

VIDEO

6 EQUALIZING PULSES
OR 3 LINES

VERTICAL
SYNC
6 LINES

6 EQUALIZING PULSES
OR 3 LINES

9 HORIZONTAL PULSES
OR LINES

EIAJ-1:

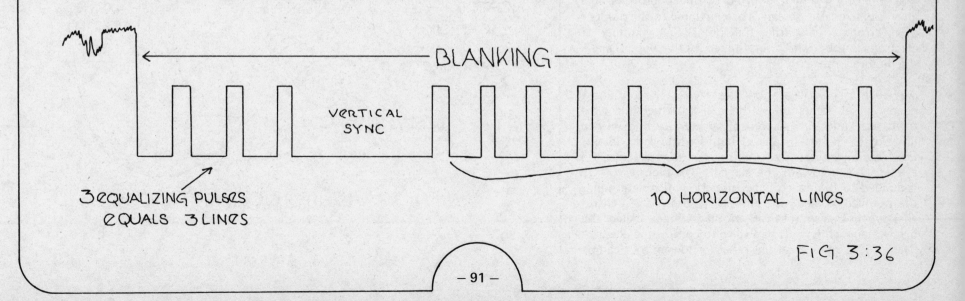

BLANKING

VERTICAL
SYNC

3 EQUALIZING PULSES
EQUALS 3 LINES

10 HORIZONTAL LINES

FIG 3:36

MONITOR AND RECEIVERS
CATHODE RAY TUBE (CRT)

The means for display of a video signal is the reverse of the process which takes place in the camera. Essential to effect display is the **CRT—cathode ray tube** (see fig. 3:37). (At least for the moment this is true—video display will one day be achieved via solid-state circuitry. See **VIDEOWORKS**, page 131.)

The cathode ray tube, like the vidicon tube, has an electron gun which emits a stream of electrons within the vacuum of the tube. Also like the vidicon it has either two sets of deflection coils located outside the tube or two sets of electrostatic plates located inside the tube: One set is for horizontal scanning, the other for vertical. The inner side of the screen is coated with phosphors which have an afterglow of about 1/60 of a second. The phosphor coating gives off light when struck by electrons. Remember, any point along a horizontal line is scanned once every 1/30 of a second. If the afterglow were to persist beyond 1/60 of a second, the scanning beam's electrons hitting a given spot every 1/30 of a second would be smeared by the afterglow of the preceding scan's electrons.

The intensity of light emitted by the phosphors at a given point on the screen is proportional to the number of electrons which strike that point. The number of electrons in the beam is determined by the video signal— the picture voltage.

An electron gun is a triodelike device. It contains a heater which heats the cathode from which the electrons are emitted. A **control aperture**—a grid with a hole in the center—is placed between the cathode and the **focusing anodes**. The focusing anodes accelerate the electron beam toward the screen. The picture voltage is applied to the control aperture grid which determines the number of electrons allowed to pass. The control aperture grid also receives another voltage called the bias voltage which acts as a valve to control the electron beam. This voltage can be raised or lowered. It can be

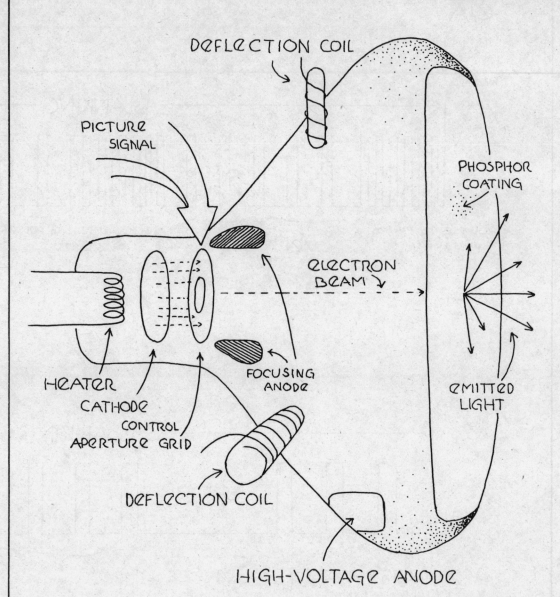

CATHODE RAY TUBE

DEFLECTION COIL

PICTURE SIGNAL

PHOSPHOR COATING

ELECTRON BEAM

EMITTED LIGHT

FOCUSING ANODE

HEATER

CATHODE

CONTROL APERTURE GRID

DEFLECTION COIL

HIGH-VOLTAGE ANODE

FIG 3:37

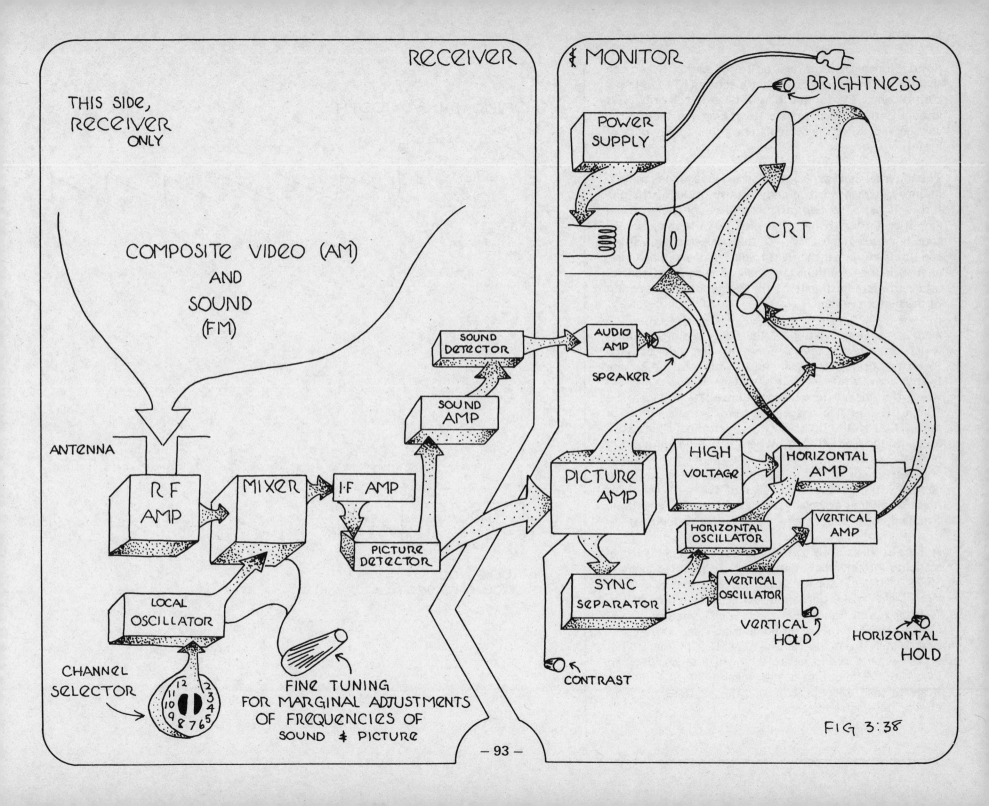

RECEIVER · MONITOR

BRIGHTNESS

THIS SIDE, RECEIVER ONLY

POWER SUPPLY

CRT

COMPOSITE VIDEO (AM) AND SOUND (FM)

SOUND DETECTOR

AUDIO AMP

SPEAKER

ANTENNA

SOUND AMP

RF AMP

MIXER

IF AMP

HIGH VOLTAGE

HORIZONTAL AMP

PICTURE AMP

PICTURE DETECTOR

HORIZONTAL OSCILLATOR

VERTICAL AMP

LOCAL OSCILLATOR

SYNC SEPARATOR

VERTICAL OSCILLATOR

VERTICAL HOLD

HORIZONTAL HOLD

CHANNEL SELECTOR

FINE TUNING FOR MARGINAL ADJUSTMENTS OF FREQUENCIES OF SOUND & PICTURE

CONTRAST

12 1 2 3 4 5 6 7 8 9 10 11

— 93 —

FIG 3:38

positive or negative in relation to the cathode, and can therefore either repel or attract electrons. The external control on a TV for the bias voltage is the *brightness* knob. Extreme *brightness* settings override the picture voltage and cause the screen to be either totally dark or bright.

The external *contrast* control on a TV regulates the difference between positive and negative peaks of the picture voltage. The *contrast* control is connected to an amplifier through which the picture voltage passes before it reaches the CRT. If the peak-to-peak voltage variations are large, the light-to-dark range will be greater than if the variations are small. The *contrast* control also permits adjustment of the degree of amplification of the picture voltage.

Across the inner coating of the CRT is a high voltage which sets up a potential difference from the cathode to attract the electrons in the direction of the screen. In black-and-white sets this voltage is about 12,000 volts; the smaller the screen, the lower the voltage. The 1-inch CRT used for viewers in cameras has a voltage of only 3,000 volts. Color TVs have extremely high voltages—around 25,000 volts. When these high voltages are present, X-rays are generated. Although these X-rays are short-lived in air, they are somewhat harmful to people within a couple of feet of the set. (For this reason, children especially should be kept at least three feet away from a color set when they are watching it.)

A TV also has knobs to regulate horizontal and vertical scanning. Remember that the horizontal frequency is 15.75 MHz; the vertical is 60 Hz; and that two interlaced fields make up a frame which occurs at 30 Hz. The horizontal frequency in TVs is generated by a local oscillator. The incoming composite video carries the sync signals from the camera or VTR. The horizontal sync is separated and fed to the horizontal oscillator to lock it up. The output of the locked-up local oscillator is fed to the deflection coils and thus controls the scanning of the electron beam.

HORIZONTAL SAWTOOTH

VERTICAL SAWTOOTH

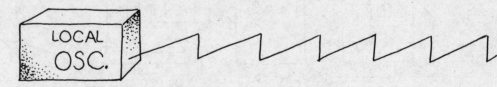

LOCKED ON TO
INCOMING VERTICAL SYNC

FIG 3:39

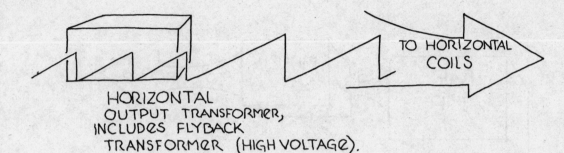

HORIZONTAL
OUTPUT TRANSFORMER,
INCLUDES FLYBACK
TRANSFORMER (HIGH VOLTAGE).

TO HORIZONTAL
COILS

VERTICAL OUTPUT
TRANSFORMER, FEEDS
CURRENT TO COILS.

TO
VERTICAL
COILS

A **sawtooth waveform** is generated by the local oscillator and stepped up by the horizontal output transformer which feeds the deflection coils. As its name suggests, a sawtooth wave has a long, steady ascent reaching a peak, at which point it falls off sharply, hits a low point, and again begins an ascent (see fig. 3:39). This long, steady ascent represents the increasing current fed to the coils, which deflects a horizontal line. At a line's end there is a quick decrease in the current, resulting from a high voltage surge from the transformer. This voltage deflects the electron beam back to the starting point very rapidly—the sharp falling off in the waveform. A part of the horizontal output transformer —the **flyback transformer**—serves as the source for the high voltage needed for the inner coating of the CRT which accelerates the electrons to the screen.

The vertical deflection process is similar to the horizontal one. The sawtooth waveform is generated by a vertical oscillator in the set which is locked to the incoming vertical sync of the video signal. A vertical output transformer feeds current to the vertical deflection coils. The *horizontal hold* controls and the *vertical hold* controls on a TV allow for adjustment of the sawtooth oscillators.

Blanking refers to the shutting off of the electron beam during retrace so no extraneous information is seen. Blanking is signaled by the blanking pulses which are part of the picture signal fed to the control aperture grid. Sensed as negative signals, the blanking pulses stop the flow of the electrons. Remember, within the blanking pulses are the sync signals which are sensed by the **clipping circuitry** which separates the sync signals and feeds them to the horizontal and vertical deflection circuits, signaling them to do their thing.

SOUND

Monitors may or may not have an internal sound system. (See **VIDEOWORKS**, page 113.)

RECEIVERS

As compared to monitors, receivers have additional circuitry for demodulating broadcast signals. A TV receiver is made up of an AM receiver for the picture and an FM receiver for the sound.

Coming from an antenna, the signals are conducted by wire to an RF amplifier. The incoming amplified signals are fed to a mixer which is also fed by a local oscillator. The frequencies of that oscillator are determined by the setting of the channel selector on the TV set.

A heterodyning process takes place in the set which results in transferring the incoming signal frequencies (which match the oscillator's frequencies) to the lower Intermediate Frequencies (IFs) within the receiver. The IFs are standard for all TVs and are 45.75 MHz for picture and 41.25 MHz for sound. This frequency conversion stage is accomplished by the RF amplifier, the mixer, and the oscillator, which together are referred to as the **tuner**.

The IF signals are amplified and fed to picture-sound detection circuitry. Here the picture signals are demodulated and separated from the sound signals. From this point on the demodulated picture signals are dealt with just as they are in the monitor. The sound signal still has a frequency of 4.5 MHz and is fed to an IF amplifier and then to an FM detector which demodulates it. The audio section transforms the sound signals into power for the loudspeaker.

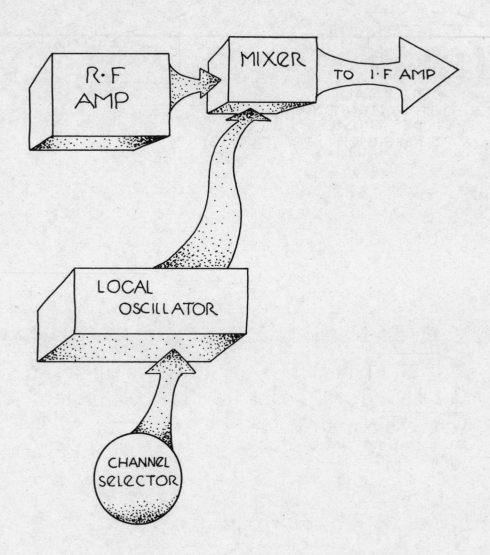

TUNER

FIG 3:40

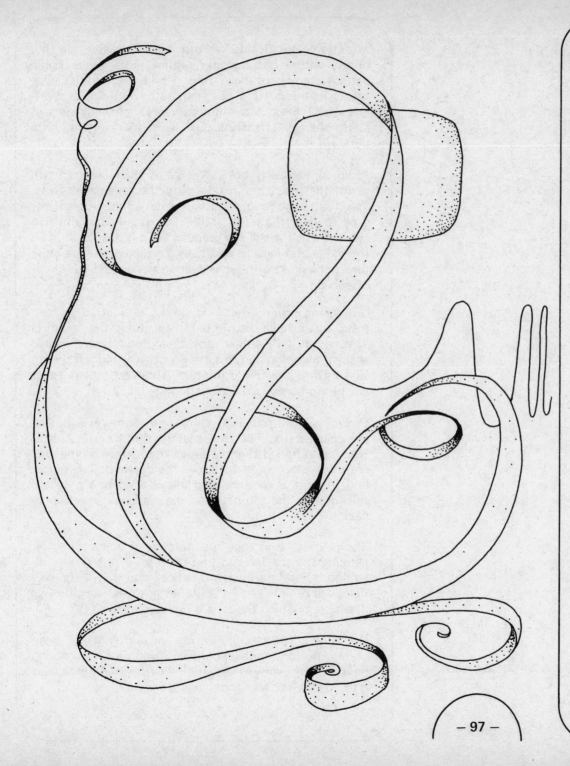

VIDEOTAPE

Videotape is a polyester filmbase coated with minute magnetic particles in a polymeric binder. The characteristics of better tape are good signal-to-noise ratio, low clogging disposition, low dropout rate, low abrasiveness of tape to heads, a minimum of static, and long tape life.

Of greatest importance in the production of high-quality tape is the quality of the magnetic particles used. They affect the sensitivity of the videotape, its signal output, inherent signal-to-noise ratio, etc. Oxides normally used are needle-shaped particles chemically known as gamma ferric oxide. Also used are higher-energy particles which include chromium dioxide, cobalt-doped gamma ferric oxide, and cobalt-alloy metal particles.

Particle energy is measured in **oersteds of coercivity**—the measure of magnetic energy needed to flip the domains of the particles. The higher the oersteds, the more magnetic energy is needed to affect the particles, and the more magnetic energy the particles themselves can contain. Gamma ferric oxide has a coercivity in the range of 250-350 oersteds. The higher-energy particles range higher than 400 oersteds.

Generally, the smaller and more uniform the particle size, the lower the noise at higher frequencies. Particle uniformity also contributes to a more equal distribution of the particles throughout the binder, which helps to uniformly magnetize the tape.

The binder, which suspends the oxide, also affects the final characteristics of the tape. It must have low frictional properties to reduce head and tape wear and to keep down frictional heat, and it must also have low electrical resistance. A binder contains wetting agents (lubricants to minimize head-to-tape friction) and solvents for coating the polyester base with the oxide particles.

The polyester filmbase in better tape is coated with a thin layer of carbon-filled polymeric coating. This carbon backing reduces friction, increases resistance to tape scratches, and minimizes the static charge that can build up on tape and attract dust. (Dust which is wound into the oxide layer of the tape causes **dropouts**—dead areas of recording.)

There are five tape sizes: 2-inch, 1-inch, ¾-inch, ½-inch, and ¼-inch. The video output from a tape drops severely at the edges of the tape. The usable area of 2-inch tape is limited to 83% of the tape; of ½-inch tape, it is only 64%.

A clean tape path on the VTR is essential to avoid dropouts. Some dropouts can be caused by dust which is not permanently lodged in the tape. Foreign particles of this nature are usually ejected from the tape through successive playings. However, after 50-200 passes, any momentary loss of signal associated with permanent dropouts usually becomes so noticeable that the tape is no longer usable.

Tapes should not be left lying around on VTRs, as they easily collect dust. Both the tape and the VTR *must* be kept clean. Cleaners which are safe to use include freon, ethyl alcohol, and isopropyl alcohol. (More on cleaning in **MAINTENANCE AND REPAIR**.)

Cinching of tapes is another problem caused by the VTR's mechanical functions. If, when coming out of either *fast forward* or *rewind*, the *stop* mechanism works too abruptly, the tape may cinch and buckle on the reel, and permanent damage to the tape can result. If the tape cinches, unwind the crinkled portion and rewind it.

Although tape is made under very exacting temperature and humidity controls, it can be used in a wide range of climatic conditions. It functions most efficiently in temperatures of 50ºF-80ºF, and a relative humidity of 50%. There are, of course, problems when working in extreme conditions. Abrasiveness increases with humidity and causes clogging, resulting in a loss of signal and shortening of head life. At low humidities, elements in the coating can evaporate, resulting in shortened tape life. Low humidity also increases electrostatic charges—attracting dust, with its resultant dropouts.

A quick rundown on how tape is manufactured will reveal the problems in reliability the tapemaker faces. The first stage involves mixing the various ingredients used to coat the base. Mixing is usually done in two steps. First, the solid or granular resin is dissolved; then the oxide and various additives are mixed in. The mixture is blended until it is homogeneous and ready for dispersion.

During *dispersion*, the oxide must be wetted by the resin and evenly distributed throughout the mixture. Testing during various stages of the mixture guards against clumping and ensures proper wetting and dispersion. Once the oxide mixture is correctly blended, it can be stored or used for coating the tape base.

Coating of the polyester filmbase is done on wide rollers called webs. The tape is later cut to specific widths. Blades positioned slightly above the surface of the web are most often used to apply the coating. The blades hold back the mixture and allow a coating only the thickness of the gap between the blade and the film to pass.

The next stage in tape manufacture is *orienting*—magnetizing the particles to line them up in the proper direction. For tape used on helical scan VTRs, the particles are oriented at an acute angle to the longitudinal direction in which the tape is pulled on the VTR.

Orienting is followed by *drying* and *curing*, which evaporates the toxic and explosive solvents of the coating mixture. In ovens in which air flows across the tape, it is dried and its heat-setting resins are cured.

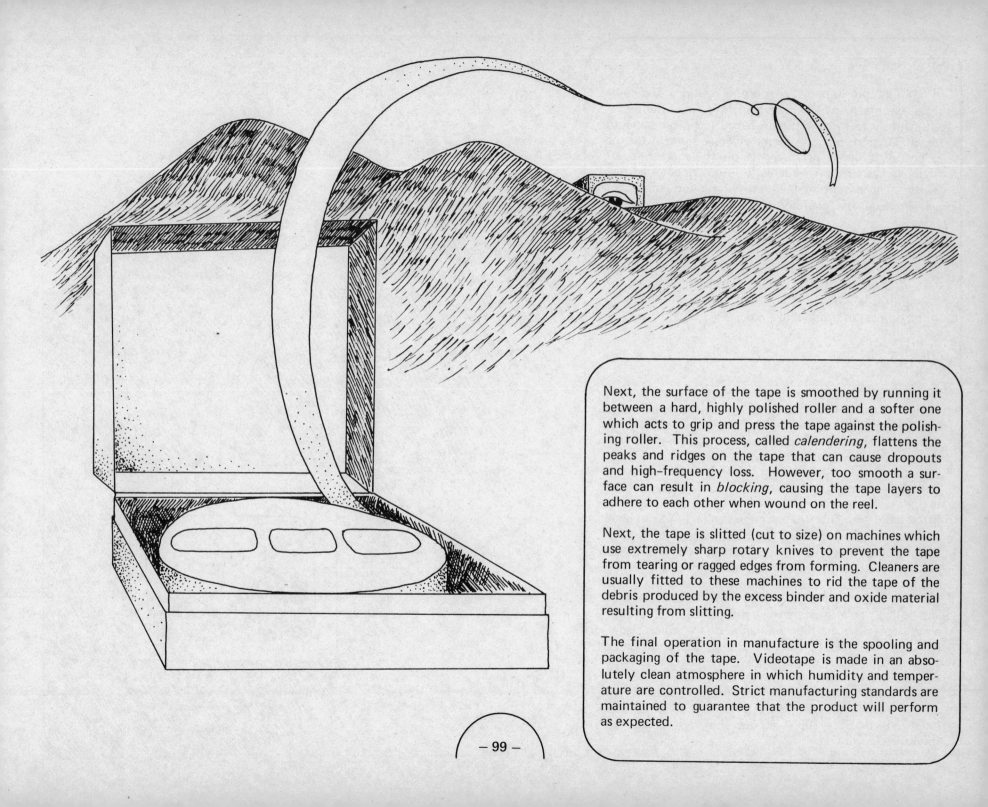

Next, the surface of the tape is smoothed by running it between a hard, highly polished roller and a softer one which acts to grip and press the tape against the polishing roller. This process, called *calendering*, flattens the peaks and ridges on the tape that can cause dropouts and high-frequency loss. However, too smooth a surface can result in *blocking*, causing the tape layers to adhere to each other when wound on the reel.

Next, the tape is slitted (cut to size) on machines which use extremely sharp rotary knives to prevent the tape from tearing or ragged edges from forming. Cleaners are usually fitted to these machines to rid the tape of the debris produced by the excess binder and oxide material resulting from slitting.

The final operation in manufacture is the spooling and packaging of the tape. Videotape is made in an absolutely clean atmosphere in which humidity and temperature are controlled. Strict manufacturing standards are maintained to guarantee that the product will perform as expected.

COLOR VIDEO

In Big TV, color broadcasting is now routine. The color signal waveform which differs slightly from the black-and-white waveform is the preferred technical standard for all TV transmission. Color video equipment for the independent video producer is on the market—color portapak systems are available for use with color editing VTRs. The advent of low-cost color video equipment will increase the usefulness and demand for ½-inch video.

Color and black-and-white equipment operate on the same principle. However, the color camera, VTR, and monitor have additional circuitry to accommodate the color information which is coded, stored, and decoded in the process of producing a color TV image.

COLOR

We distinguish visual detail much more by the intensity of light than by the differences of color. Whereas black-and-white detail on a horizontal line of video is broken down into about 300 picture elements, color need only be broken down to 1–50 picture elements.

The additive and subtractive mixing of light is the basis for the relative simplicity of color video. There are three basic elements that produce color in video: hue (tint), saturation (color), and luminance (intensity). The three primary colors of light are red, green, and blue. Their correspondent complementary colors are cyan, magenta, and yellow. Adding a color and its complement (i.e., red and cyan, green and magenta, or blue and yellow) results in a cancellation of color or level of gray, depending on the luminance of the color signal. Adding the three primary colors in disproportionate quantities of saturation and luminance makes it possible to produce any color in the visible spectrum. For instance, a fully saturated red with no luminance is very dark. Raising the luminance level of that same saturated red to 80%–100% produces a very pastel red (pink).

CAMERA TYPES

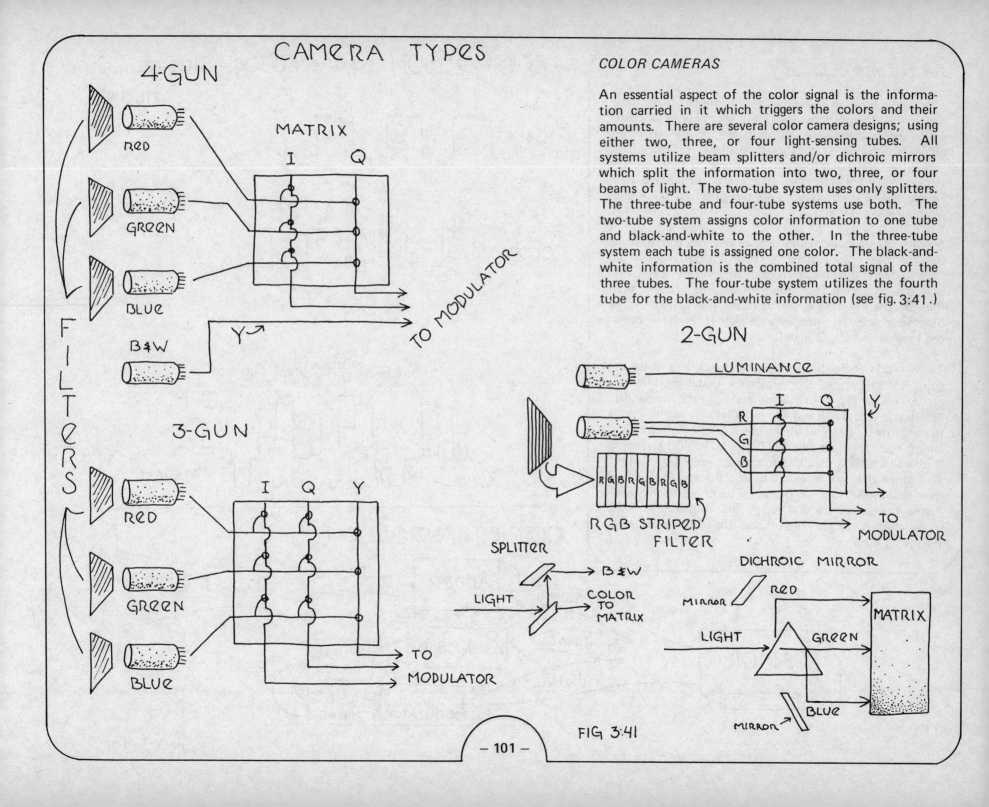

4-GUN

RED

GREEN

BLUE

B&W

FILTERS

MATRIX

I   Q

Y

TO MODULATOR

3-GUN

RED

GREEN

BLUE

I   Q   Y

TO MODULATOR

An essential aspect of the color signal is the information carried in it which triggers the colors and their amounts. There are several color camera designs; using either two, three, or four light-sensing tubes. All systems utilize beam splitters and/or dichroic mirrors which split the information into two, three, or four beams of light. The two-tube system uses only splitters. The three-tube and four-tube systems use both. The two-tube system assigns color information to one tube and black-and-white to the other. In the three-tube system each tube is assigned one color. The black-and-white information is the combined total signal of the three tubes. The four-tube system utilizes the fourth tube for the black-and-white information (see fig. 3:41.)

2-GUN

LUMINANCE

I   Q   Y

R
G
B

TO MODULATOR

RGB STRIPED FILTER

SPLITTER

LIGHT → B&W

COLOR TO MATRIX

DICHROIC MIRROR

MIRROR   RED

LIGHT   GREEN

BLUE

MIRROR

MATRIX

FIG 3:41

THE COLOR SIGNAL

The color signal is made up of **chrominance** and **luminance**. Luminance is the light intensity—black-and-white information—and chrominance is the remaining color information—saturation and hue. In both black-and-white and color systems, scanning is basically the same, except for frequency changes in the color system which makes it compatible for reception on black-and-white or color TV sets.

A matrixing system in the camera encodes the information of the color image. Three distinct signals are formed from the initial voltages of the red, green, and blue (RGB) signals from the light-sensing tubes. One of these is the luminance, and is called the **Y signal**. The other two are the chrominance signals, and are called the **I signal** and the **Q signal**.

To maintain compatibility between black-and-white and color TV broadcast, the luminance signal modulates a carrier frequency of the standard 4.5-MHz bandwidth. The color signals (I and Q) modulate a second and a third carrier. Each of these carriers is a subcarrier at about 3.58 MHz (actually 3.579545 MHz 10 Hz) within the full 6-MHz bandwidth allotted each TV channel. The subcarriers are modulated by the I and Q signals in quadrature—90° out of phase. The phase angle determines the color transmitted. The amplitude of the modulated subcarrier determines the color saturation. (See fig. 3:43.)

COMPARISON: B&W—COLOR SIGNAL

FIG 3:42

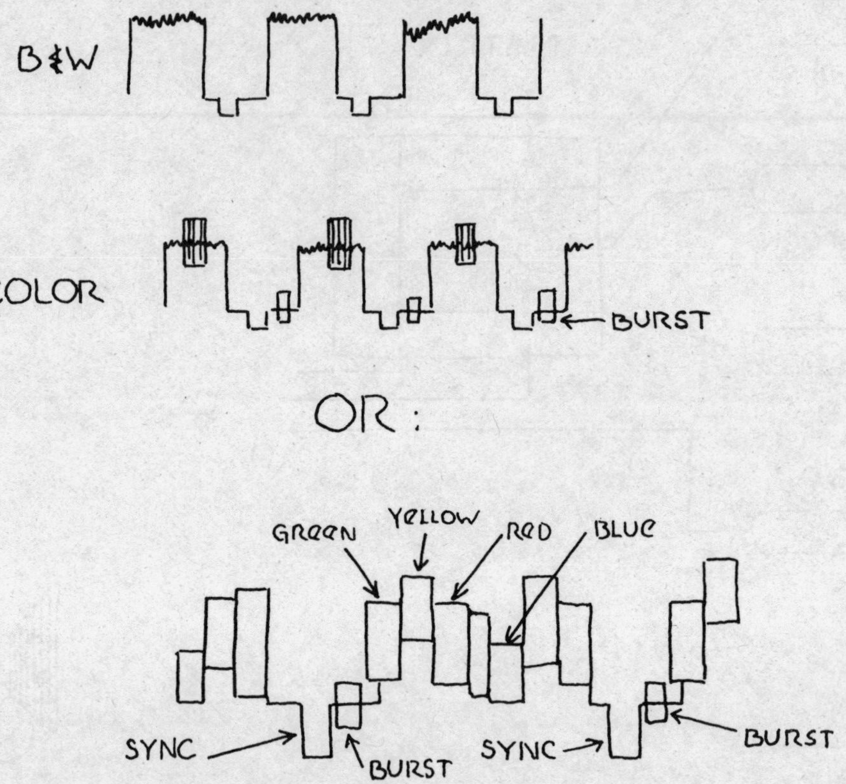

B&W

COLOR

BURST

OR:

GREEN YELLOW RED BLUE

SYNC BURST SYNC BURST

COLOR TRANSMISSION

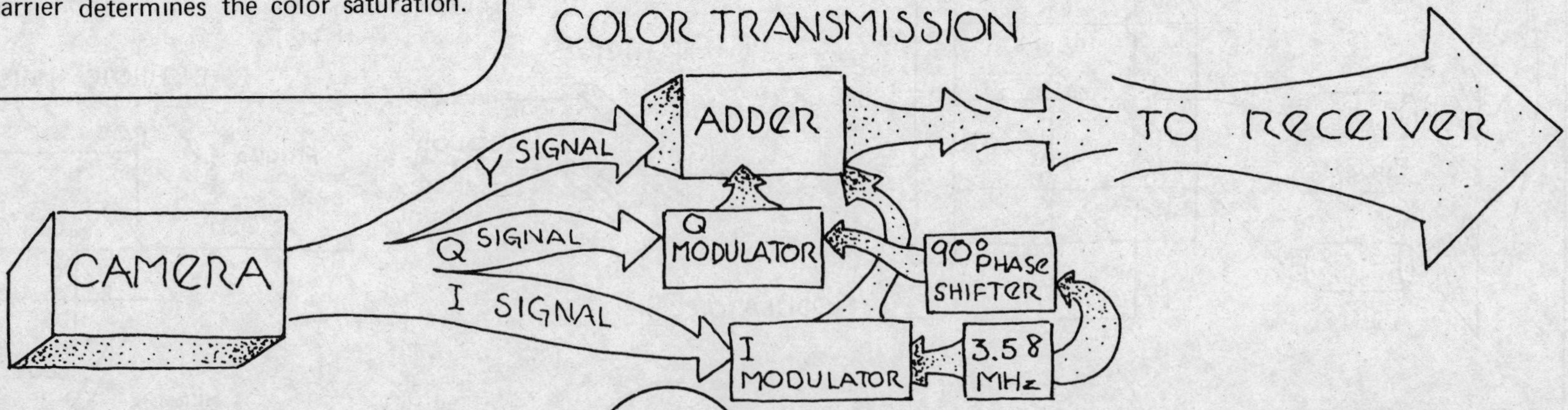

CAMERA

Y SIGNAL

ADDER

TO RECEIVER

Q SIGNAL

Q MODULATOR

90° PHASE SHIFTER

I SIGNAL

I MODULATOR

3.58 MHz

FIG 3:43

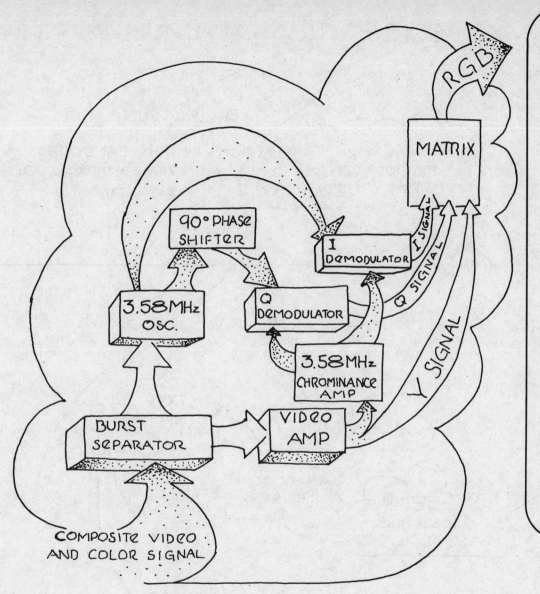

The **burst**—the color sync signal—is carried on the back porch of the horizontal blanking pulse as a reference signal for determining the phase angle—the color—during demodulation of the signals in the receiver. The burst is a sampling of the color subcarrier frequency (3.58 MHz).

In a color signal the horizontal and vertical frequencies are slightly altered. The horizontal frequency of 15.75 MHz becomes 15.734 MHz. The vertical frequency—60 Hz—becomes 59.94 Hz. These changes are necessary to avoid interference caused by harmonic relationships between the carrier, subcarrier, and the horizontal frequency when transmitting a color signal.

COLOR STANDARDS

There are three major standards for color transmission. The one described above is the National Television Standards Committee (NTSC) system of the Electronics Industries Association in the United States. Another is the PAL system which is used throughout most of Europe and utilizes a different subcarrier frequency (4.43 MHz) than does the NTSC system. The PAL system also matrixes the mathematics of the color primaries differently. Still another system is SECAM, used in France. Like the PAL system it operates on a 625-line scanning system. Any color system can be used with any line-scanning system if the equipment is designed or modified to properly modulate and demodulate the signals.

FIG 3·43

COLOR VTRS

In this section (page 73), frequency modulation of the video signal is discussed as the means for storing the picture information on the tape in helical scan recording. The black-and-white signal fed to a VTR is FM coded to reduce its octave range. For color recording, the color signal is phase modulated at its source and fed already coded to the VTR. It must then be reduced to a bandwidth well within the frequency response range of the VTR. It must also be outside and below the bandwidth of the luminance signal. Thus two distinct signals—color and black-and-white—can be simultaneously stored on the tape and easily separated for playback.

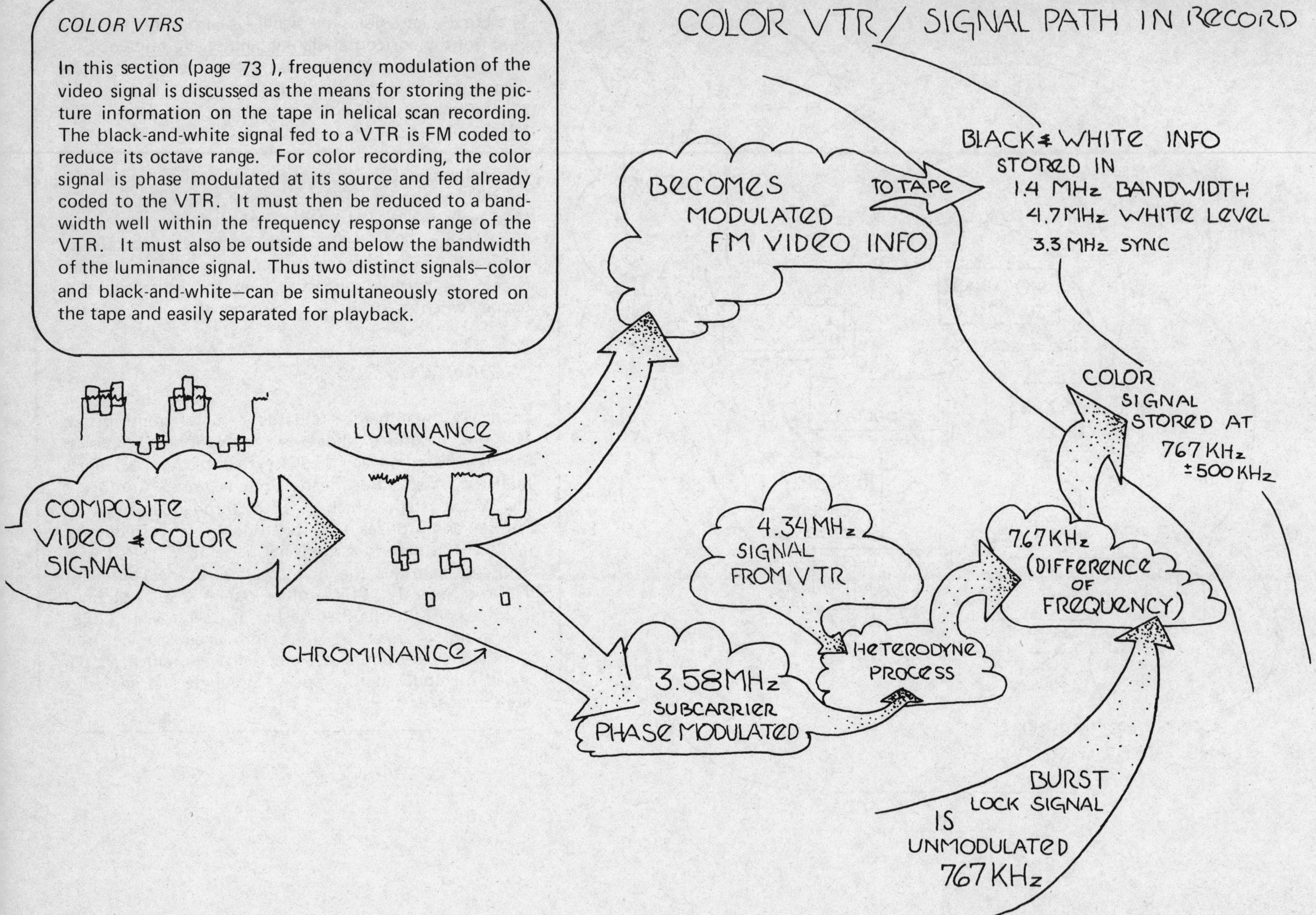

BECOMES MODULATED FM VIDEO INFO

TO TAPE

BLACK & WHITE INFO STORED IN 1.4 MHz BANDWIDTH 4.7 MHz WHITE LEVEL 3.3 MHz SYNC

COMPOSITE VIDEO & COLOR SIGNAL

LUMINANCE

CHROMINANCE

3.58 MHz SUBCARRIER PHASE MODULATED

4.34 MHz SIGNAL FROM VTR

HETERODYNE PROCESS

7.67 KHz (DIFFERENCE OF FREQUENCY)

COLOR SIGNAL STORED AT 7.67 KHz ±500 KHz

BURST LOCK SIGNAL IS UNMODULATED 7.67 KHz

FIG 3:44

The correct convergence of the three electron beams through an aperture of the shadow mask onto a trio of phosphors produces the properly mixed color. Poor convergence results in color fringes which are especially visible in the black-and-white picture on a color set. The **purity** of a picture depends upon each beam hitting its corresponding dot or bar. If the purity is poor, color can be seen on a white screen.

Besides the three-gun CRT there is also a single-gun design. Within a three-gun CRT the guns are arranged either triangularly or in a row. The triangular arrangement accommodates the dot system, and the row arrangement the bar system. A single-gun CRT utilizes three cathodes generating three beams which are fed through a single focusing element to a wire mesh instead of a shadow mask. The mesh serves as a color-switching grid which permits the production of one color at a time. Whereas a three-gun CRT produces the three color signals simultaneously, the single-gun CRT produces each color sequentially. The phosphors in the single-gun CRT are bars which are horizontally stacked: red on top, green in the middle, and blue on the bottom. The mesh is fed a voltage which corresponds to a color. No voltage is green, positive voltage is red, and negative is blue. The 3.58 MHz used for the switching frequency minimizes possible dot pattern interference in the picture.

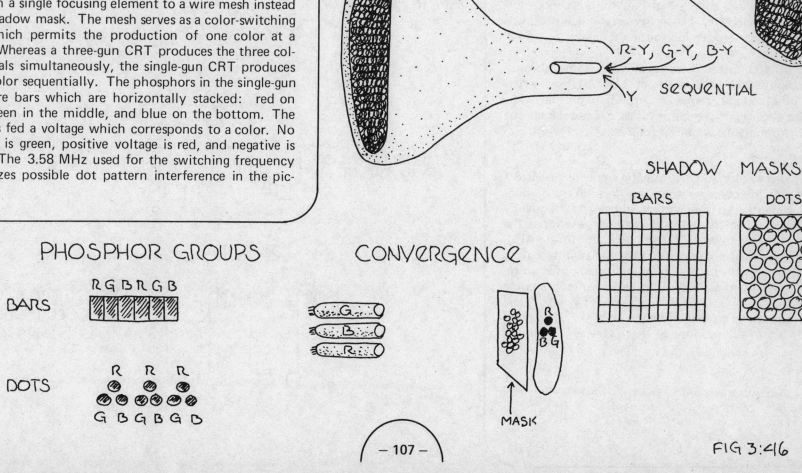

COLOR CRTs

THREE-GUN

SHADOW MASK

ONE-GUN

Y

G-Y
B-Y
R-Y

SIMULTANEOUS

R-Y, G-Y, B-Y

Y

SEQUENTIAL

SHADOW MASKS

BARS

DOTS

PHOSPHOR GROUPS

BARS

RGBRGB

DOTS

R R R
G B G B G B

CONVERGENCE

G
B
R

MASK

FIG 3:46

DEMODULATION

Two modulators are used to decode the chrominance signal. Remember that the I and Q signals are transmitted in quadrature—90° out of phase—modulating the 3.58-MHz color subcarrier. Remember also that the color is transmitted as the phase angle, and that the amount of color is transmitted as the amplitude of the modulated frequency. In the receiver the 3.58-MHz subcarrier signal (which is also the burst, or color sync signal) locks up a local oscillator which feeds both a demodulator and a phase shifter. In turn, the phase shifter feeds the subcarrier signal to another demodulator. Thus two color signals are detected; both are minus Y, and are detected separately. From the combination of the two color signals, the third is decoded in the matrixing circuitry of the receiver which produces the RGB minus Y signals fed to the CRT.

Among other important color circuits is the **chrominance amplifier** which operates at 3.58 MHz and serves as the intermediate frequency amplifier for the color. All color receivers have **color killer circuits** which cut off the chrominance amplifier for a black-and-white picture.

There is also a color **AFC** (automatic frequency control) which holds the color reference oscillator in the demodulation circuitry to the correct phase and frequency (3.58 MHz). The *tint* control on color sets varies the phase of the burst and 3.58-MHz oscillator to the AFC. An **ACC** (automatic color control) is a bias voltage used to control the gain of the chrominance amplifier in relation to the color signal. All other circuits in a color set are the same as in black-and-white TV sets. The color monitor has no demodulation circuitry. The color signal is fed to the monitor in the I, Q, and Y matrixed forms.

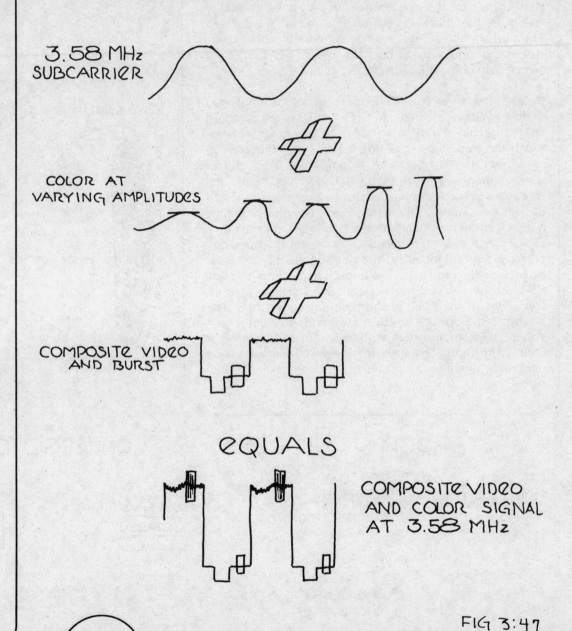

3.58 MHz SUBCARRIER

COLOR AT VARYING AMPLITUDES

COMPOSITE VIDEO AND BURST

EQUALS

COMPOSITE VIDEO AND COLOR SIGNAL AT 3.58 MHz

FIG 3:47

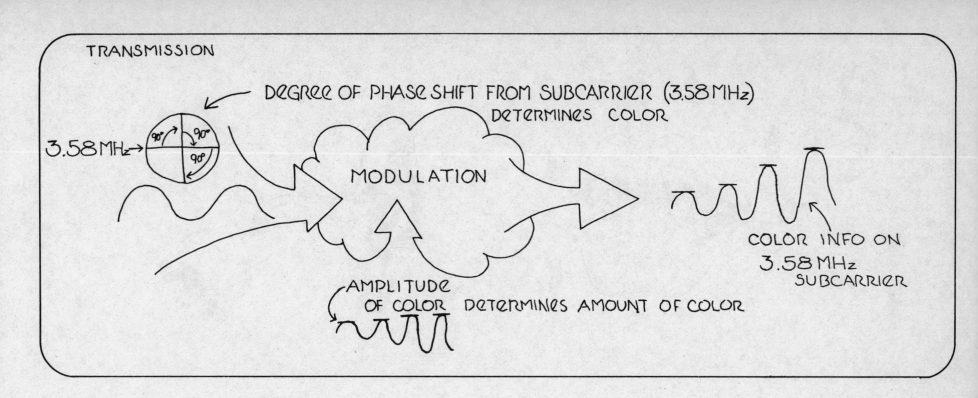

TRANSMISSION

DEGREE OF PHASE SHIFT FROM SUBCARRIER (3.58 MHz)
DETERMINES COLOR

3.58 MHz →

90° 90° 90° 90°

MODULATION

AMPLITUDE OF COLOR DETERMINES AMOUNT OF COLOR

COLOR INFO ON 3.58 MHz SUBCARRIER

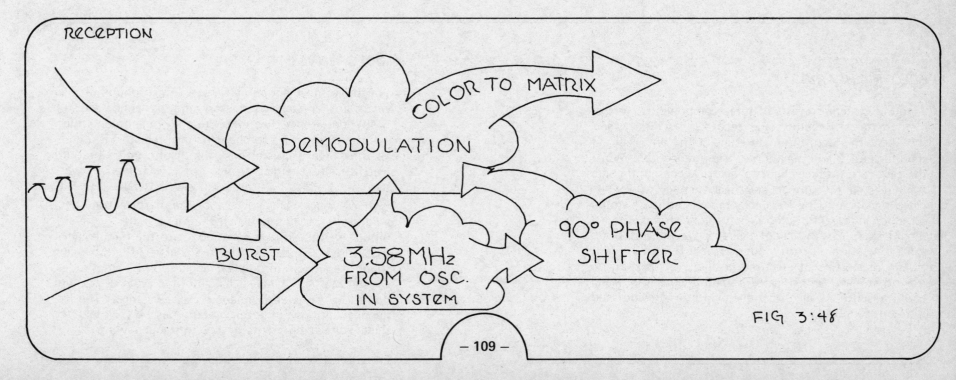

RECEPTION

COLOR TO MATRIX

DEMODULATION

BURST

3.58 MHz FROM OSC. IN SYSTEM

90° PHASE SHIFTER

FIG 3:48

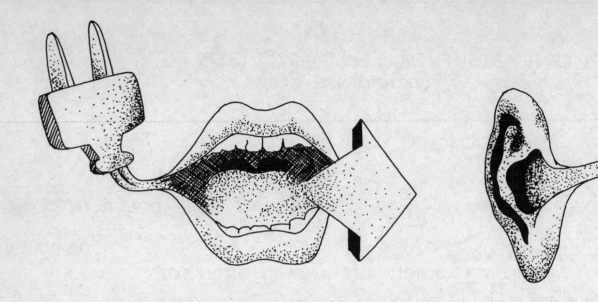

SOUND SYSTEMS
ELECTRIC HEARING

A sound system consists of three components: microphones (mics); audio tape recorders (ATRs); and speakers. In video, the picture and sound are recorded simultaneously and played back simultaneously. While the camera transduces light to electrical energy, the mic tranduces air pressure to electrical energy. In a VTR, video signals must be frequency modulated to be stored on tape; in an ATR, audio signals can be stored without modulation. The display of a video signal depends upon synchronization circuitry to drive a CRT which will transduce streams of electrons to light. A speaker, on the other hand, will receive an amplified audio signal and transduce its electrical energy to air pressure and resultant sound.

MICROPHONES

The three most common types of microphone used in video are **crystal**, **condenser**, and **dynamic** (see fig. 3:49, opp.). A diaphragm (a thin membrane which vibrates in response to changing air pressures) is used in all three. In a crystal mic, the diaphragm's vibrations mechanically energize a piece of crystal held between two metal plates. As discussed in **WORKING THE BIG WORKS** (page 47), because of the piezoelectric effect a voltage is created between the metal plates. The amplitude of this voltage corresponds to the frequency of the sensed sound. An audio signal is AC: Changing sound frequencies produce changing voltage amplitudes. Crystal mics are the cheapest and simplest in design, but do not have a wide frequency-response range. The frequency response of a mic determines how closely the signal voltage represents the sound frequency input.

FIG 3:49

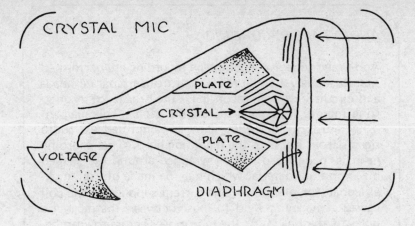

CRYSTAL MIC

PLATE

CRYSTAL →

PLATE

VOLTAGE

DIAPHRAGM

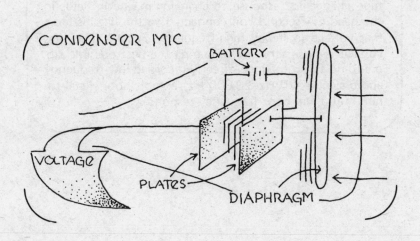

CONDENSER MIC

BATTERY

VOLTAGE

PLATES

DIAPHRAGM

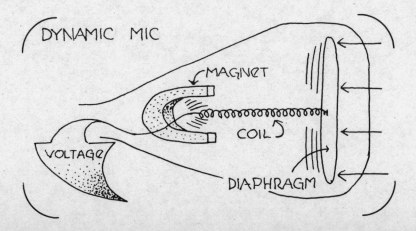

DYNAMIC MIC

MAGNET

COIL

VOLTAGE

DIAPHRAGM

Capacitors are used in the manufacture of condenser mics. The diaphragm in these mics is connected to one of the plates of the capacitor. Remember that a capacitor consists of two metal plates, one with a positive charge, the other with a negative charge, between which electrical energy can be stored. The distance between the plates determines the amount of stored charge. In a condenser mic the vibrations of the diaphragm connected to one of the plates moves that plate and thereby changes the relationship between the two plates. Condenser mics utilize batteries or electrets (miniature charge-storing devices) to supply the electrical charge to the plates. Here, as in the case of crystal mics, voltages corresponding to frequency changes are fed to the ATR as AC audio signals. The condenser mic is a high-impedance device, and therefore a battery-powered transistor is used to produce a low-impedance output signal. For more on impedances, see **VIDEO WORKSHOP** (page 145).

A dynamic mic utilizes a permanent magnet which has a coil placed between the magnet's poles. The diaphragm is connected to the coil, and as it vibrates, it moves the coil within which a current is then produced. That current represents the AC audio signal. Dynamic mics are low-impedance devices—they generate large currents and low voltages. Dynamic mics require no battery. They are less expensive than condenser mics, but have a lower frequency response. However, they are sturdy mics, and supply adequate sound for the monaural audio recording of VTRs.

An important aspect of microphones is their directivity characteristics. The shape of the casing and the manner in which the air hits the diaphragm determines the zone of sound to which a given mic is sensitive. Mics are classified as omnidirectional, unidirectional, cardioid, and bidirectional. Directivity is discussed extensively in **VIDEO WORKSHOP** (page 144).

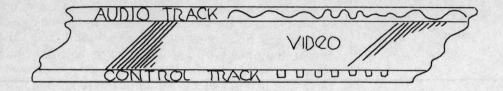

AUDIO TRACK

VIDEO

CONTROL TRACK

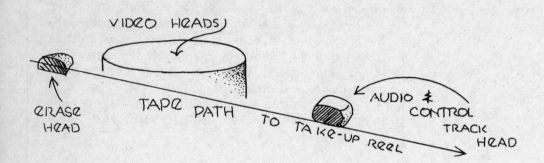

VIDEO HEADS

ERASE HEAD

TAPE PATH TO TAKE-UP REEL

AUDIO & CONTROL TRACK HEAD

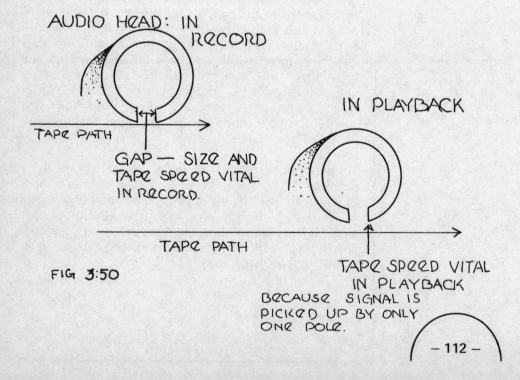

AUDIO HEAD: IN RECORD

TAPE PATH

GAP — SIZE AND TAPE SPEED VITAL IN RECORD.

IN PLAYBACK

TAPE PATH

TAPE SPEED VITAL IN PLAYBACK BECAUSE SIGNAL IS PICKED UP BY ONLY ONE POLE.

FIG 3:50

AUDIO TAPE RECORDING

Audio and video magnetic tape recording are performed simultaneously by the VTR, but utilize separate heads and circuitry. Audio recording is the process of magnetizing minute iron particles on the tape. This magnetizing results from feeding current—amplified AC audio signals from mics—to the recording head. The recording head is made up of a coil wrapped around a C-shaped magnetizable material which may be made of iron, nickel, cobalt, or platinum. The current supplied to the coil causes a magnetic field to exist between the magnetic poles of the head. As the tape moves across the gap between the poles, the domains of iron particles on the tape change in response to changing magnetic fields in the head. A second coil connected to the head is fed a bias voltage (a steady high-frequency signal). This bias voltage is necessary for obtaining the best possible signal-to-noise ratio, since directly recorded low-frequency audio signals (20 Hz–20,000 Hz) exhibit poor signal-to-noise ratio and poor frequency response.

An audio record head in a VTR doubles for the audio playback head. In playback, the recording process is reversed: The magnetic energy which is stored on the tape is moved across the gap of the head and generates a magnetic field between its poles. The changing magnetic energy causes current to flow in the coils.

The erase head functions during recording, wiping out any previously recorded information by placing a steady high-frequency signal on the tape before it passes the record head. Generally, this frequency and the bias frequency are the same—from 60 KHz to 90 KHz.

SPEAKERS

After an audio signal is detected and amplified it can be fed to a speaker. Speakers reverse the process of mics. There are several types of speakers, but here we will discuss only the two most common: dynamic and electrostatic (or condenser). The **dynamic speaker** utilizes a permanent magnet with a coil. The audio signal is fed to the coil which is connected to a cone (a dish-shaped, paper-thin vibrator). As current flows through the coil it generates a magnetic field which interacts with that of the magnet, causing the coil to move. As goes the coil, so goes the cone, and thus air is moved at a corresponding rate, producing sound frequencies.

The **electrostatic speaker** employs a capacitor in the transduction of electrical energy to air pressure. The changing position of the capacitor's plates cause vibrations in the cone. Usually, electrostatic speakers are more efficient at high frequencies. The shape of the box in which the speaker is placed affects its frequency response and directivity.

DYNAMIC SPEAKER

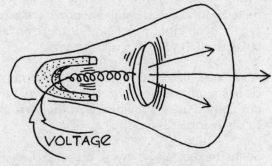

INTERACTION OF MAGNETIC FIELDS CAUSED BY COIL & MAGNET MAKES CONE VIBRATE

eLECTROSTATIC SPEAKER

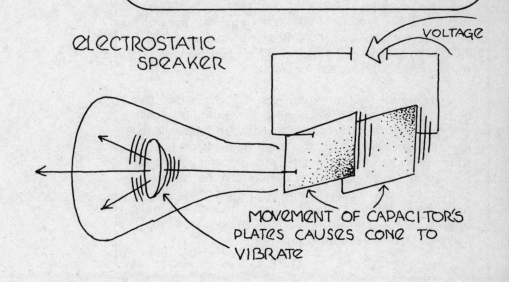

MOVEMENT OF CAPACITOR'S PLATES CAUSES CONE TO VIBRATE

FIG 3:51

AGC

Each audio record system has an **AGC** (automatic gain control) to keep the audio level from becoming too high or too low for accurate sound recording. Prior to recording, the AGC circuitry is fed the audio signals, sensing the extreme levels and compensating for the high ones by lowering them, and for the low ones by increasing them. However, the AGC is relatively slow to respond to sound level changes and so does not respond to or affect the rapid sound level variations normal in speech and music.

EQ (FREQUENCY EQUALIZER)

The **EQ** (frequency equalizer) is a device which controls the range of sound frequencies during playback in order to enhance or cancel their outputs. Sound frequencies can be broken down into any number of ranges. Most commonly, a tonal control (like that on a radio) allows adjustment of the bass and treble. Bass frequencies are low; treble frequencies are high. In a typical inexpensive EQ there are five individual frequency controls: 0–60 Hz for the bass; 60–240 Hz for mid-bass; 240–1,000 Hz for the mid-range; 1,000–3,500 Hz for mid-treble; and 3,500–10,000 for treble.

EQs are useful for limited recovery of voice which has been recorded in an environment with much background noise (like city streets or crowded lobbies). By lowering the power of the bass frequencies—traffic, wind, crowd murmur—and heightening the mid-range and treble—voice—some restoration can be achieved. EQ can be used in combination with a mic mixer during recording to improve noisy live sound, though it is most often used for transferring during editing or for simple playback to improve sound quality.

MIXERS

The mixing of several sound sources for a single recording is accomplished using a mixer. Mixers are varied in design. Some can accommodate only mics; other accommodate mics as well as line inputs from other tape recorders, record players, etc. The difference between the type of signal that comes from a mic and the type that comes from a line source is its voltage level: A line signal is about one volt and up; a mic signal is less than a millivolt (a thousandth of a volt). Both mic and line inputs have impedance levels which can be either high or low. In most ½-inch VTRs, the line inputs are high-level, high-impedance; the mic inputs are low-level, low-impedance. Some mixers have switches for setting the impedance level of its inputs. Mixers also have individual volume controls for each input as well as a master volume control for the total system. Many mixers have **attenuation switches** for decreasing a signal's voltage—for instance, to reduce the signal of a line input in order to match a mic level. Most mixers are equipped with VU meters which indicate the volume level of the mixed sound. Better mixers provide a separate VU meter for each input channel. For more on VU meters, see **VIDEO WORKSHOP** (page 145).

All mixers provide both mic and line outputs for feeding signals from the mixer to the ATR or VTR. Either output can be used, providing that the corresponding input to the recorder is used.

Some mixers also have a pre-amplifier which can increase the level of a mic signal to match a line signal. Mixers with pre-amps require a power supply. Portable mixers with pre-amps run off batteries and are usually also AC adaptable. Mixers without pre-amps are called **passive mixers**. These mixers are inexpensive, but can only mix inputs by decreasing their levels so that all the inputs do not add up to more than the level of the strongest input.

POWER SUPPLIES
AC DC

Essentially, all electronics require DC to operate. Adaptors are available which convert AC to DC so that battery-powered 12-volt systems can operate on 110-volt AC household current. An AC adaptor is made up of a regulator and a stepdown transformer. The regulator guards against extreme surges of power, which can blow the works. The stepdown transformer changes the 110 volts AC to the necessary 12 volts AC, which is then rectified and fed through a filter to knock out the AC ripple, thus rendering the power DC. An AC adaptor is called a **converter**.

AC converters (or adaptors) are used when supplying a normally battery-powered piece of equipment with power from a wall outlet. Most battery-powered equipment, such as a portapak or a portable mic mixer, can be used with an AC converter when AC power is available. The portapak, for instance, is a 12-volt DC system. An AC converter converts the 110 volts AC from the wall to the required 12 volts DC for the portapak.

On the other hand, DC is changed to AC by an **inverter**. Such devices might seem to be a ready solution to the problem of being mobile when using studio equipment, such as a studio VTR requiring 110 volts AC. Unfortunately, they are not. For instance, a 12-volt car battery supplying a studio VTR is emptied of its power in a few minutes. Small, portable gasoline-powered generators, which put out much more power than batteries, can be used with an inverter to run AC equipment. However, since video equipment requires a precise 60-Hz AC signal, a good local oscillator must be an integral part of the system. The inclusion of such oscillators makes these generators somewhat expensive relative to the low power output they provide.

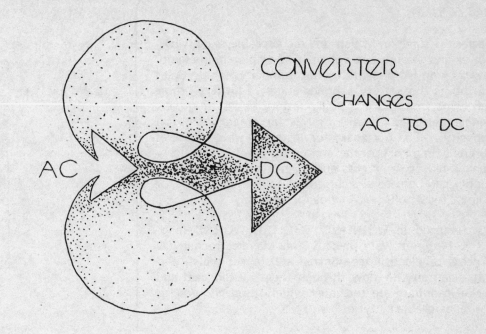

CONVERTER
CHANGES
AC TO DC

AC   DC

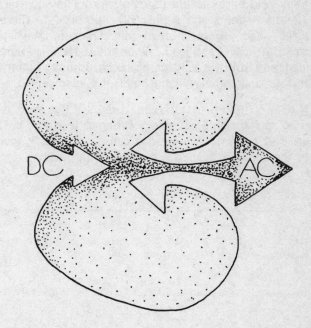

INVERTER
CHANGES
DC TO AC

DC   AC

BATTERIES

Batteries, some of which are rechargeable, supply DC power and are rated in voltage and ampere hours (amp-hrs). Amp-hrs constitutes the number of amps times the hours the battery supplies energy. Battery power can come from either a single battery or a battery pack (single batteries wired in series for greater electrical capacity). The portapak, for instance, which requires about 1 amp to operate, can be powered by a battery pack rated at 4 amp-hrs and 12 volts. Such a power supply can be used at a current of 1 amp for 4 hours, or 2 amps for 2 hours, or 4 amps for 1 hour.

As discussed in **WORKING THE BIG WORKS** (page 48), batteries work because of the electrochemical process of electrolytes—ionized substances which permit electricity to flow through them. Lead acid and nickel cadmium are the most widely used compounds for rechargeable batteries.

Lead acid batteries are used in cars. They can be 6- or 12-volt systems and supply 50 amp-hrs. In these batteries, lead sulfate is electrically charged, converting it to sulfuric acid and lead. When the battery is in use, the lead and sulfuric acid combine, producing water, lead sulfate, and some available electrons—electricity.

Nickel cadmium batteries (ni-cads) are the most widely used rechargeable batteries. Whereas lead acid batteries are **wet cells**, ni-cads are **dry cells**—no water is involved in the chemical reactions of their compounds.

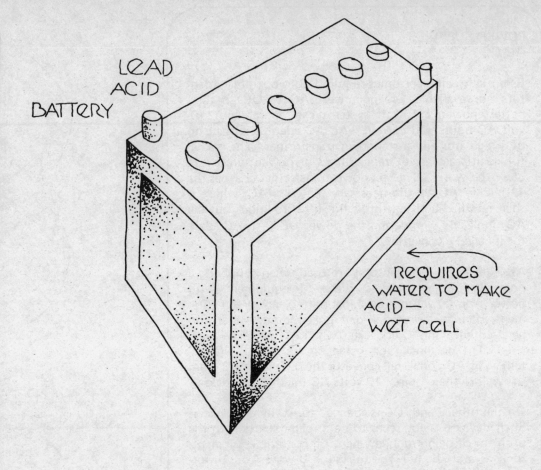

LEAD ACID BATTERY

REQUIRES WATER TO MAKE ACID— WET CELL

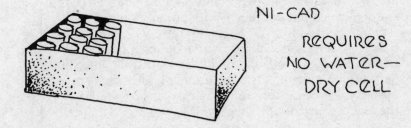

NI-CAD

REQUIRES NO WATER— DRY CELL

FIG 3:52

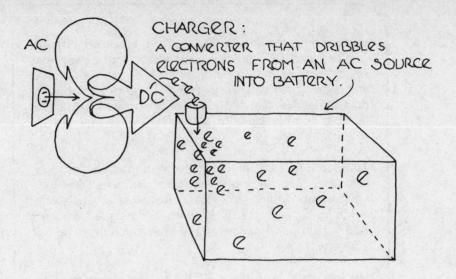

CHARGER:
A CONVERTER THAT DRIBBLES ELECTRONS FROM AN AC SOURCE INTO BATTERY.

AC

DC

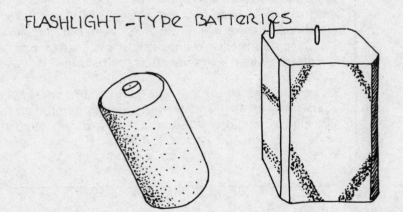

FLASHLIGHT-TYPE BATTERIES

The charger used to charge a battery is simply a converter which slowly trickles electrons from an AC source into the chemicals contained in the battery. Recharging a 12-volt, 4-amp-hr battery pack takes 12–14 hours. Such battery packs can take about 200 to 300 charges before they die. Rechargeable batteries can become chemically sluggish from overuse and then will not accept a full charge. When that happens, battery vitality can be restored by draining the unit of all its charge, either by plugging it into a portapak and letting it run down completely, or by short-circuiting it by bridging its terminals. The drained battery should then be charged for a full 14 hours.

Flashlight-type batteries are used to power mics and portable mic mixers that require a battery supply. Three kinds of these batteries are used most commonly: The first type, constituting the majority, is composed of a zinc shell which contains a carbon rod stuck into magnesium paste; secondly is the alkaline battery; and thirdly, the silver oxide cell. All three supply a small amount of current and are not rechargeable. Magnesium paste batteries continually lose energy even when not in use. Alkaline batteries have more energy and last longer than the magnesium paste type. Silver oxide cells, which are the size of a shirt button, feature long life and sudden death. Most batteries continue to supply power, but ever more weakly—silver oxide cells, on the other hand, show no sign of weakness during operation; when their time comes, they just go. The shelf-life (storage life) of silver oxide cells is much longer than that of ordinary batteries. Storing any batteries in a refrigerator extends their life, since colder temperatures retard chemical processes.

CABLES
THE SIGNAL ARTERIES

Cables—transmission lines—deliver signals from component to component, while incurring minimal signal loss. Cables are either shielded, balanced, or both. **Shielded cable** is surrounded by a grounded metallic braid which protects the inner conductor from stray signals. A **balanced cable** is one in which there are two conductors with the same capacitance to ground. A balanced line usually is used with an input transformer to cancel any stray signal picked up in the conductors.

There are two types of transmission lines, coaxial and two-wire parallel. **Coaxial cable (coax)** is common to all video and audio equipment, and consists of a center conductor encased in an insulator (a dielectric). This dielectric is surrounded by a metallic braid called a shield, which is in turn jacketed by an outer insulator. Coax is unbalanced but shielded, and is therefore best used in noisy areas where stray signals present a problem. Most widely used in video is coax that has an impedance of 75 ohms. Coax has higher signal losses per length of cable than two-wire line: about 4 db per 100 feet at 100 MHz.

Two-wire parallel line can be one of four types: flat twin-lead, tubular twin-lead, shielded twin-lead, and open-wire. **Flat twin-lead line**—common TV antenna line—consists of a ribbonlike dielectric with parallel conductors encased in its sides. It is balanced but unshielded and so should be kept away from power lines since they generate a hum. When wet, its signal losses are higher than when dry—from 1.2 db dry to about 7 db wet per 100 feet at 100 MHz. Most two-wire parallel line has an impedance of 300 ohms, which matches TV receiver inputs.

Tubular twin-lead line is really an improved flat twin-lead line. The flat, ribbonlike dielectric is replaced by a hollow tube which provides a protected air dielectric, reducing signal losses when wet. The signal loss runs about 1 db per 100 feet at 100 MHz when dry to about 2.5 db when wet.

Shielded twin-lead line is similar to other twin-lead line, but has a third wire for grounding. Most twin-lead line must be installed surrounded by special hardware to ensure that it does not rest against walls or poles in which capacitance exists. Shielded twin-lead line, however, can be installed resting against such surfaces since the ground wire negates the effects of the capacitance.

Open-wire line consists of two bare parallel wires held apart by insulating spacers. Its impedance can run up to 600 ohms. Its loss of signal is lowest of all types of line—.2 db per 100 feet at 100 MHz. However, open-wire line is vulnerable to stray signal pickup.

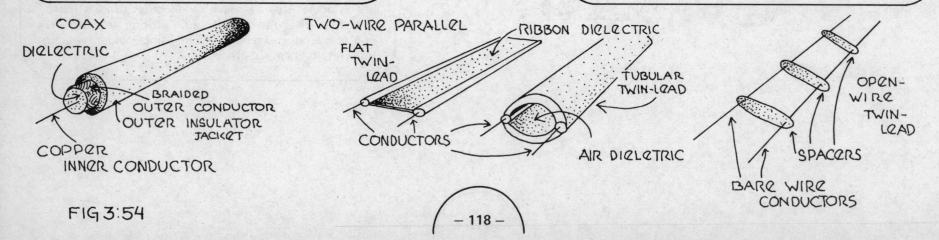

COAX — DIELECTRIC — BRAIDED OUTER CONDUCTOR — OUTER INSULATOR JACKET — COPPER INNER CONDUCTOR

TWO-WIRE PARALLEL — FLAT TWIN-LEAD — RIBBON DIELECTRIC — CONDUCTORS — TUBULAR TWIN-LEAD — AIR DIELECTRIC

OPEN-WIRE TWIN-LEAD — SPACERS — BARE WIRE CONDUCTORS

FIG 3:54

Attenuation (signal loss) is caused by dissipative resistance in the line. The higher the signal frequency, the greater the attenuation in longer lines. Line impedance is the result of the spacing between the two conductors, and it remains the same whatever the length of the line. In practical terms, attenuation means that if a 6-db loss takes place, the signal voltage output at the end of 100 feet of line will be half the signal voltage input. With 200 feet of line, it will drop to a quarter of the input signal. In instances in which long cable lengths are required, line amplifiers are used to boost the signals.

Coaxial cable is made in many sizes, ranging from about 1/8 inch to 1 inch in diameter. Cables used to transmit audio and video signals from a VTR to a monitor, for instance, are often made up of many thinner strands of coax grouped together inside an insulator jacket, each one tied to a particular point in a connector: The most common example is the **8-pin connector** (see drawing below). A 6- or 4-pin connector—**din connector**—is of German design, and is commonly used for power input connections and for studio camera-to-VTR hookups. A ten-pin connector is used in most portapak systems to interconnect the camera and the VTR supplying video, audio, power, and trigger control.

On the other hand, **UHF connectors** are used with coax which carries only the composite video signal. Other types of coax connectors are used with specific kinds of equipment: F and BNC connectors, for instance, are used with cable TV modulators. And of course, there are a variety of made-up cables with different connectors at each end in order to accommodate special situations.

Audio connectors are a breed unto themselves and are pictured for identification in **VIDEO WORKSHOP** (page 144). Audio cable is usually coaxial. Since audio frequencies—about 20–20,000 Hz—are low-level signals, less concern need be given the length of cable than is given for video transmission. Audio cable is relatively high impedance. However, a high-impedance mic cannot be used with a long cable unless impedance transformers are used to lower the mic's impedance level. The signal can then be transmitted along the cable and before it is fed into a high-impedance input, another transformer is used to return the mic to its original impedance level.

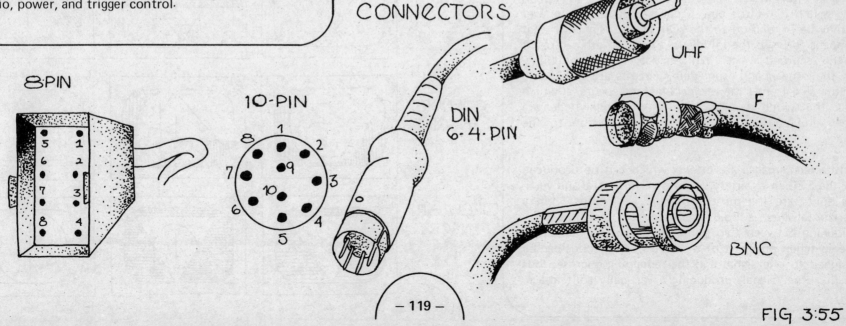

CONNECTORS

8-PIN

10-PIN

DIN 6·4·PIN

UHF

F

BNC

FIG 3:55

VIDEO SWITCHER
SPECIAL EFFECTS GENERATOR (SEG)

A video **switcher** (or mixer) allows for switching from one input to another and for fading two inputs into each other. It can accommodate a number of video signals inputs; usually from 2 to 4 cameras. An **SEG** is a part of a switcher capable of providing the following effects: split-screens, wipes, keying, and negative images. (See figs. 3:56 - 3:57.)

The **fade** produced by the switcher results from adjusting the voltages of two incoming signals. When the fade control is at its middle setting, each of these signals is fed out of the switcher at 50% of its maximum voltage level, so that taken together they make up a single signal and are seen superimposed. Turning the fade control brings up one of the signals to the full 100% voltage level and cuts off the other signal.

Switching among cameras requires that a common sync source be used to drive all the cameras. Some switchers contain 2:1 interlace sync generators, while others require external units. Switching can be either random or vertical interval switching. In random switching, when the switch is hit the new signal is jammed in wherever it may be in relation to the switched-out signal. If that happens to be in the middle of a field, a flash can result in the recorded image. With vertical interval switching, on the other hand, time-delay circuits are utilized to hold a signal until the vertical blanking occurs, at which time the switch is made. In this way, all switches are clean and cause no instability or disruption to the image.

Split-screen images are effects which can be produced by the SEG in a variety of forms. Horizontal and vertical splits are the most common. Remember that a horizontal line is 53.6 microseconds. In time-delay switching between two signals fed from the SEG into the switcher, any part of the 53.6 microseconds can be assigned to one signal and the remaining microseconds to the other signal, producing a vertically split image.

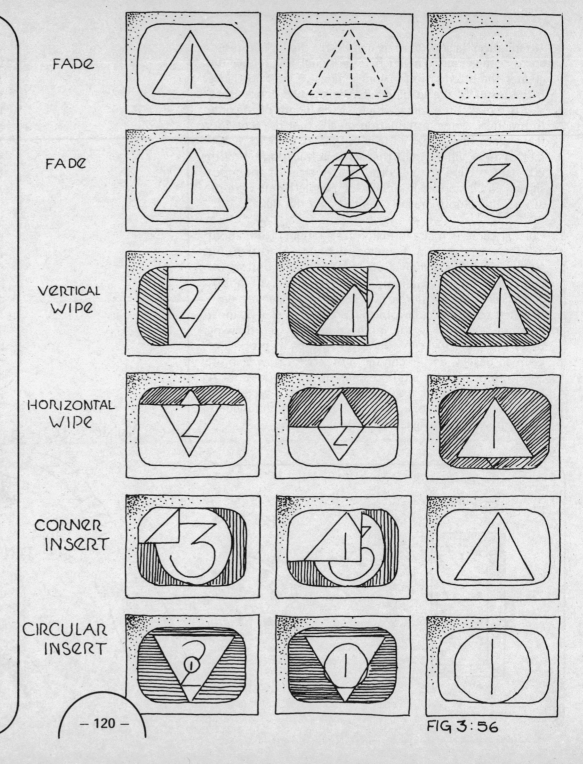

FADE

FADE

VERTICAL WIPE

HORIZONTAL WIPE

CORNER INSERT

CIRCULAR INSERT

FIG 3:56

This image in motion becomes a **vertical wipe** which is controlled by the *wipe* knob on the SEG.

The horizontal split-screen utilizes similar time-delay circuitry controlling the 60-Hz vertical trace. A **horizontal wipe** is a horizontal split-screen in motion, and also is controlled by the *wipe* knob on the SEG. A **corner insert** is produced by combining a horizontal and vertical split-screen. The corner insert can be swept across the screen, increasing in size and wiping out the image into which it is being inserted. More sophisticated SEGs provide for any number of patterns of splits and wipes, including circular and triangular ones.

The **negative image** from an SEG is the result of a switch which reverses the voltage peaks of the black and the white levels of the video signal.

A **genlock** is a circuit which permits the mixing of one prerecorded input with a camera input through an SEG. When the SEG is equipped with a genlock, the sync signals which drive the cameras are taken from the prerecorded input—the signal from the tape of the VTR.

NEGATIVE IMAGE

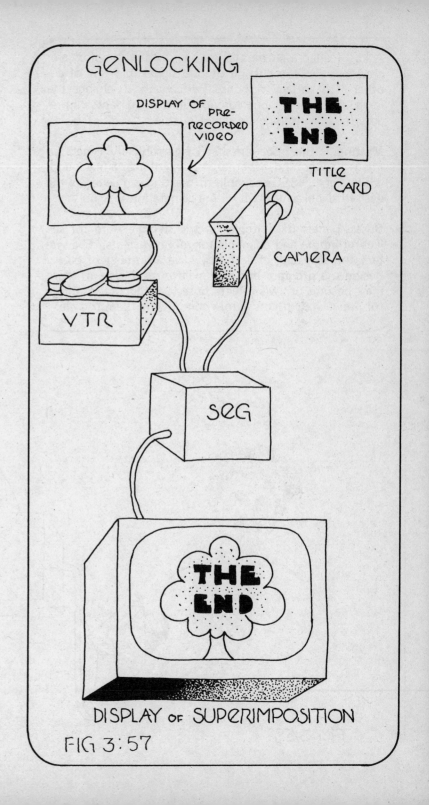

GENLOCKING

DISPLAY OF PRE-RECORDED VIDEO

THE END

TITLE CARD

CAMERA

VTR

SEG

THE END

DISPLAY OF SUPERIMPOSITION

FIG 3:57

KEYING

A **key** (called a **chroma key** when used with color cameras) permits the cutting of one signal in front of another. A voltage response switch acts to change the image from one input to another when it senses a predetermined difference in signal voltage.

Matting is the insertion of an electronically generated image background, whether it be a color or a black-and-white signal. SEGs capable of matting can generate the desired signal and mix it with a camera input signal.

Buses—panels of switches on the switcher—are for selecting inputs and channels for mixing effects. The system for accessing effects may have a number of buses. Beside the **program bus** (the main output system) there may be one or two **effects buses**. Effects buses allow for previewing effects before committing them to tape.

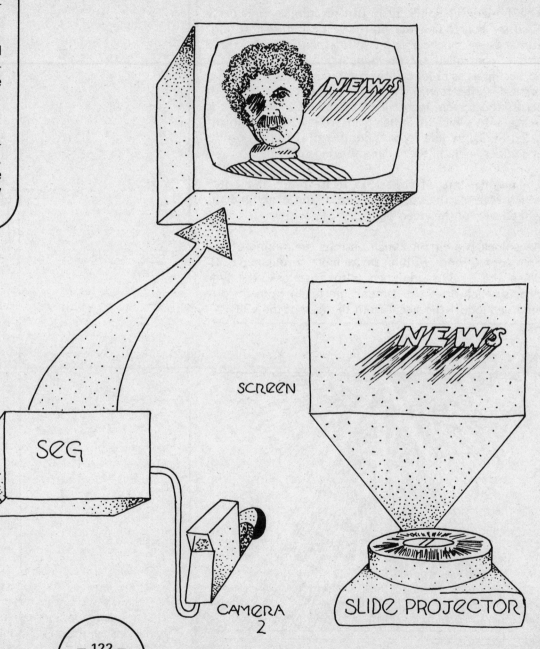

SCREEN

SEG

CAMERA 1

CAMERA 2

SLIDE PROJECTOR

FIG 3·58

SYNC GENERATOR
AN INDEPENDENT DRIVER

As indicated in the introduction to this section, (page 50), some components of video equipment are actually independent circuits grouped together. For instance, the vidicon, signal drive circuits, and viewfinder make up a camera. The **sync generator**, on the other hand, is a separate independent circuit, consisting of an oscillator which generates the horizontal and vertical sync signal at their respective frequencies for 2:1 interlace scanning. An external sync generator is used with cameras that have free-running drive circuits and with camera mixers which require a common sync source to drive a number of inputs.

CAMERA ADAPTOR (CMA)
PORTAPAK-TO-STUDIO

A portapak camera may be used with a studio VTR by fitting it with a **camera adaptor**—a **CMA**. The 12 volts DC power supplied to the portapak camera comes from the same batteries that supply the entire portapak system. The camera's horizontal and vertical drive pulses are also supplied by the portapak VTR. To enable the use of a portapak camera with a studio VTR, the CMA works to step down and rectify the 110-AC voltage and to supply the proper drive signals from the VTR to the corresponding camera inputs. In a manner of speaking, a CMA is a fancy connector.

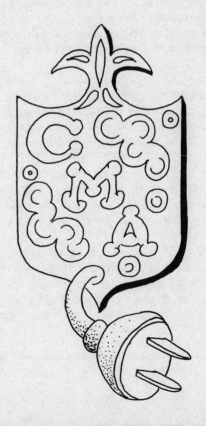

PROCESSING AMPLIFIER (PROC AMP)
BETTER SYNC

A **proc amp** is used to revitalize the picture and sync signals of composite video information just prior to recording. For instance, adjustments to the sync are necessary in some cases to generate exact EIA standard signals. This revitalizing of the sync can be done to a signal from either a camera or another tape. During the process the picture can be somewhat enhanced. A proc amp can be a self-contained unit or can be built into a larger set of circuits which makes up the video recorder.

A proc amp consists of signal amplifiers that feed the composite video signal to a sync-stripper, from which the picture voltage is fed to a filter which knocks off the high-frequency noise of the picture signal. From the stripper, the sync itself is fed to a voltage-level equalizer which reconstitutes the sync signals. Next, the sync and picture signals are fed to an **adder** which recombines them. The signals are then amplified and sent on their way, all spanking new.

A proc amp can do nothing to correct timebase instability. However, it can allow for adjustment of the size of the horizontal and vertical blanking pulse. A **video gain control** allows for raising the amplitude of the picture signal. A **pedestal control** permits manipulation of the picture's black level so that some improvement can be made in an image shot under poor lighting conditions. A color proc amp allows for burst and chroma regeneration and chroma phase adjustments.

Because ½-inch video sync signals have no defined front and back porch within the horizontal blanking period, standard proc amps cannot always handle them. This should be considered when purchasing proc amps, since most are designed to be used with 1-inch and 2-inch systems, in which the specifications for sync are more exacting.

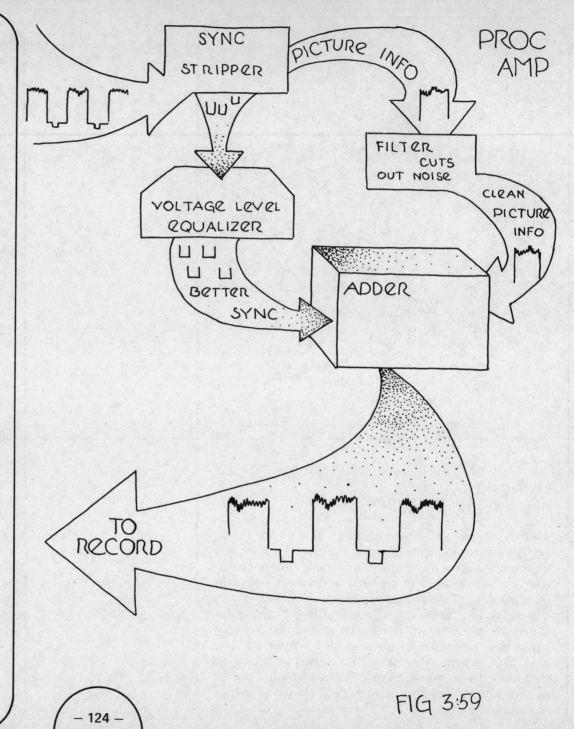

PROC AMP

FIG 3:59

RADIO FREQUENCY MODULATION

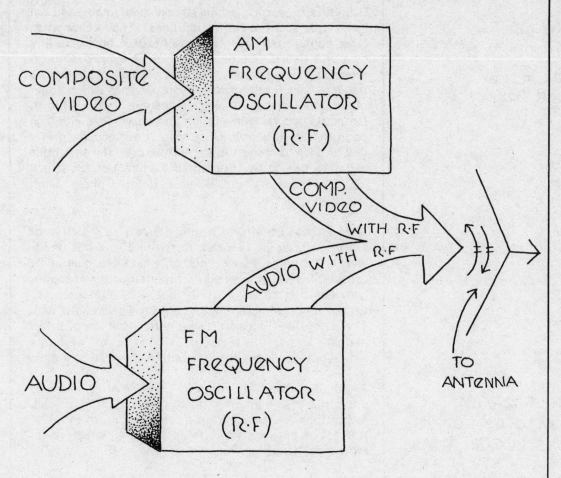

COMPOSITE VIDEO

AM FREQUENCY OSCILLATOR (R·F)

COMP. VIDEO WITH R·F

AUDIO WITH R·F

AUDIO

FM FREQUENCY OSCILLATOR (R·F)

TO ANTENNA

FIG 3·60

RF MODULATOR

As discussed in **WORKING THE BIG WORKS** (page 32), RF modulation is the coding process for transmitting signals through the air for reception by homescreen tuners. Remember that the picture portion of the TV signals is AM, while the sound portion is FM. An **RF modulator** must be used to feed audio/video signals from a VTR to a TV receiver. The modulator contains an oscillator set at a frequency of a specific channel which it is designed to use—most commonly, either channel 2, 3, 4, 5, 6, or 7. For instance, channel 3: The picture carrier frequency is 61.25 MHz and the sound carrier frequency is 4.5 MHz away at 65.75 MHz. The full 6-MHz bandwidth for channel 3 runs 60–66 MHz in the VHF band.

For most ½-inch equipment, the RF modulator is a unit about the size of a bar of soap which connects into the VTR and, via a wire connector, feeds a TV receiver tuned to the modulator's frequency. The signals from the VTR modulate the carrier frequencies of the RF unit and then are transmitted in the wire connector to the tuner of the TV set. A color RF modulator has an additional color frequency oscillator for modulation of the color information at the correct frequency in the bandwidth of the channel. For instance, the color information for channel 3 is transmitted at 64.83 MHz, which is 3.58 MHz—the color subcarrier—away from the picture carrier at 61.25 MHz.

DROPOUT COMPENSATOR

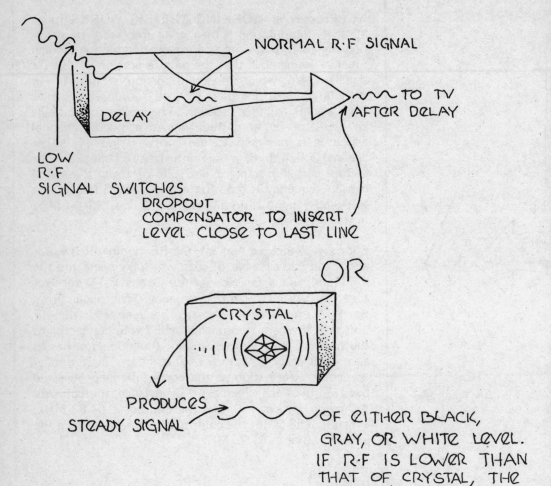

NORMAL R·F SIGNAL

DELAY

TO TV
AFTER DELAY

LOW
R·F
SIGNAL SWITCHES
DROPOUT
COMPENSATOR TO INSERT
LEVEL CLOSE TO LAST LINE

OR

CRYSTAL

PRODUCES
STEADY SIGNAL → OF EITHER BLACK,
GRAY, OR WHITE LEVEL.
IF R·F IS LOWER THAN
THAT OF CRYSTAL, THE
CRYSTAL'S LEVEL IS
INSERTED

FIG 3·61

DROPOUT COMPENSATOR
DROP-INS FOR DROPOUTS

Dropouts appear as flashing streaks in an image, and can be as wide as a few horizontal lines. They occur when close contact between tape and heads is obstructed by dust and debris. Some debris can be ejected through repeated playing of the tape, but permanent damage to the tape can result from foreign particles which either scratch the tape in passing or become imbedded in it. Dropouts occurring in a bright and busy scene with high contrasts are less noticeable than those occurring in a low, evenly lit scene. In the former case, the amplitude variation caused by dropout looks like a match struck in broad daylight; in the latter, it looks like a match struck in a dark tunnel.

Dropout compensators fit into the playback section of a VTR. They are designed to respond to a loss of RF level. When this loss occurs, an alternate signal of an acceptable level is inserted. VTRs that contain dropout compensation circuitry utilize one of several methods. One of these methods employs a delay line and a switch. The delay line holds back one horizontal line of information, and if the signal is below the set level, the switch acts to permit the insertion of the delayed signal.

Another method of dropout compensation depends upon the insertion of a steady signal from a crystal, rather than the signal from a previous line of information. The crystal's signal is set at a level which represents gray, black, or white.

Dropout compensation in ½-inch VTRs equipped to perform it is accomplished by a switch and multiple line delay. The switch is activated by a loss of RF level, which indicates the presence of a dropout on the tape. When the switch is triggered by RF-level loss, it feeds the delayed signals to the TV for display. If the loss of RF level lasts longer than the signal time of the delayed lines, the dropout will be passed onto the TV for display.

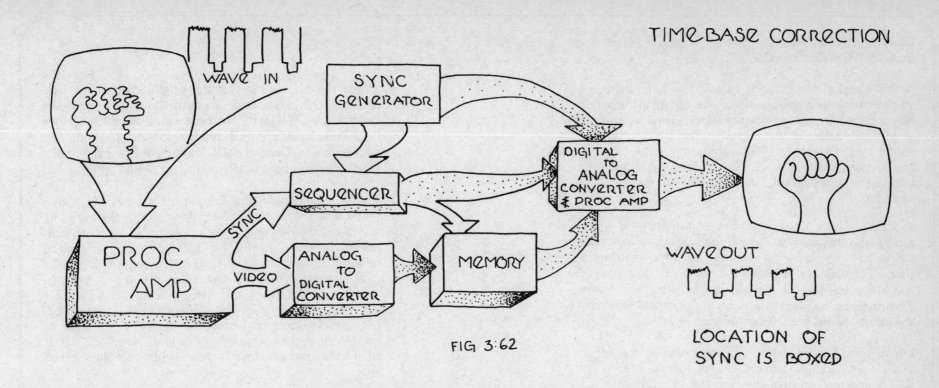

WAVE IN

SYNC GENERATOR

SEQUENCER

SYNC

VIDEO

PROC AMP

ANALOG TO DIGITAL CONVERTER

MEMORY

DIGITAL TO ANALOG CONVERTER & PROC AMP

WAVE OUT

FIG 3:62

LOCATION OF SYNC IS BOXED

TIMEBASE CORRECTION
BROADCAST SYNC

As discussed in **VIDEOWORKS** (page 77), timebase instability in helical scan video recording occurs because of the infrequency of timing references fed to the servo controls of the VTR. It is important to consider timebase correction when transferring from helical formats to 2-inch broadcast standard formats. Being able to accomplish these transfers is the independent video producer's link with Big TV viewers. With the development of timebase correction, even broadcasters are considering using helical scan VTRs because of their economy and portability.

A **timebase corrector** (see fig. 3:62) serves to create a broadcast standard horizontal sync on a recorded composite video signal. A timebase corrector does not affect picture resolution, nor does it correct for any negative qualities of the camera or VTR with which the initial recording was made.

The most significant development in timebase corrector design has been the introduction of A/D (analog-to-digital) conversion. Timebase correctors featuring A/D conversion can change analog signals to digital ones. In a digitized form the signals can be more easily stored and reconstituted for correction. Newer timebase correctors have a correction capability of about plus or minus a line and a half. In other words, within a period of about 95 microseconds (53.5 microseconds is one line), the length of a line and its sequential occurrence in relation to other lines can be adjusted.

DC RESTORATION
BLANKING INSURANCE

As indicated in the drawing below, the sync, blanking, and white level components of the video information are encoded in the composite video signal at specific amplitude levels of that signal: The tip of the horizontal sync pulse is at 100% amplitude; the blanking (black level) pulse is at 75% amplitude; and the white level of the actual picture information is at 12.5% amplitude.

A frame of video has a **relative brightness level** which represents the average amplitude variation from the black level for every 525 horizontal lines of information. The distance between the relative brightness level and the black level is the **pedestal height** of the frame. The distance between the relative brightness level and the white level is the **DC component**.

When two frames have different relative brightness levels, the circuits feeding the picture signal to the CRT's aperture control grid use the DC component to adjust the bias voltage for the brightness changes. Remember, the bias voltage is controlled by the *brightness* control on a TV set. In those cases in which relative brightness levels are quickly changing, manual control is impractical. Thus, the DC component, a part of the video signal, automatically controls the bias voltage.

The DC component originates at the source of the video signal along with the other information. During some instances of video amplification in the TV, the DC component is lost. If this happens and there is no **DC restoration**, unblanked vertical retrace lines will be seen when a scene shifts to a darker background. A suppressor circuit can lessen this effect, but exact brightness levels will not be produced without the DC component. DC restoring circuits reintroduce the DC component in the TV set at the aperture control grid. In color TV, the DC component provides for the correct reproduction of hue.

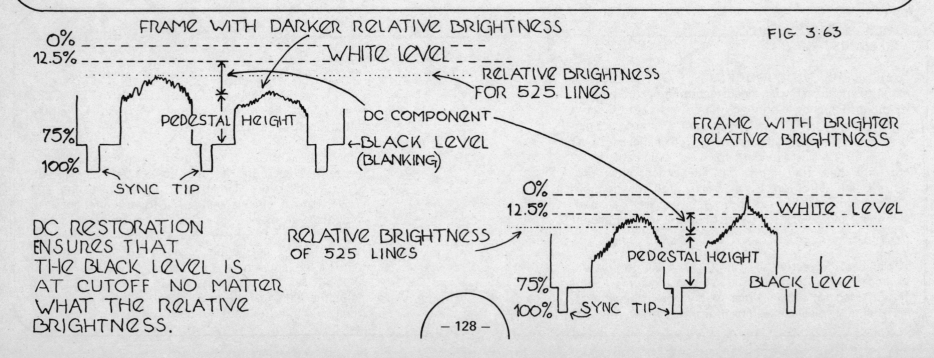

FRAME WITH DARKER RELATIVE BRIGHTNESS

FIG 3:63

0%
12.5%
WHITE LEVEL
RELATIVE BRIGHTNESS FOR 525 LINES
DC COMPONENT
PEDESTAL HEIGHT
75%
←BLACK LEVEL (BLANKING)
100%
SYNC TIP

FRAME WITH BRIGHTER RELATIVE BRIGHTNESS

DC RESTORATION ENSURES THAT THE BLACK LEVEL IS AT CUTOFF NO MATTER WHAT THE RELATIVE BRIGHTNESS.

RELATIVE BRIGHTNESS OF 525 LINES

0%
12.5%
WHITE LEVEL
PEDESTAL HEIGHT
75%
100%
SYNC TIP
BLACK LEVEL

ELECTRONICALLY GENERATED IMAGERY
TV MAGIC

The transduction of light to electrical energy, and vice versa, is fundamental to video systems. Video circuits are designed to use electrons to code light detected by a camera for display on a TV. The development of such systems as colorizers, synthesizers, character generators, and animation computers is based on two variations of typical video systems: the use of electrical signals rather than light as the source of the information to be displayed; and the extensive intermixing of a variety of signals in order to display a totally new image.

Remember, a video signal is an electrical signal—a voltage—so it follows that it would be possible to generate voltages and feed them directly into video circuitry; there would be no absolute need for a camera or any other light-sensing device. Systems to intermix inputs can be built to accept video, audio, and voltage signals simultaneously. As discussed in this section (page 120), timing circuits can be used to display for a selected part of each horizontal scan while inserting another input into the remainder of each scan. Some image generators can be thought of as enhanced SEGs capable of more complex manipulations of signals.

COLORIZERS

Remember that black-and-white signals are comprised of constantly changing voltage levels, ranging from the black level to peak white—from .286 volt (black) to one volt (peak white); and that chrominance (color) signals are also voltages which are superimposed over the luminance (black-and-white) signals. A colorizer generates color signals and mixes them with the luminance signals. A particular color can be set at a particular level of saturation and be generated at a specified voltage level of the black-and-white signal. Every time that voltage level occurs, that color and saturation also occur. Depending on the colorizer, each color (red, green, blue, etc.) has a particular number of saturation levels which can be selected. Some colorizers are capable of keying, which makes it possible to separately colorize areas in close proximity which are also close in voltage level. Realistic color cannot be produced with a colorizer. Instead, colorizing results in a psychedeliclike image similar to that of a solarized color photograph.

SYNTHESIZERS

There are a number of different video synthesizers, most of which have been developed by individuals and small electronics firms. Synthesizers can be found at various college campuses, experimental TV labs of educational stations, and at commercial TV processing houses. Depending on their particular design, they allow for a huge variety of manipulation of input signals. It is beyond the scope of this book to explain all the effects possible with video synthesizing. Such a show as *The Electric Company* on educational TV will reveal an array of such effects—for instance, an image that decreases in size and becomes positioned in a corner of the screen as other information takes over the larger area of the screen, or a logo which emerges three-dimensionally from a twisting, spinning line.

CHARACTER GENERATORS

Such devices, as their name implies, generate letters and numbers which are often seen on Big TV running across the screen like ticker-tape insertions. They usually consist of special announcements or of people's names for identification. The character generator is an electronic typewriter whose keys activate electrical signals which produce the letter or number keyed into another image. Character generators can be designed to present any typeface or set of symbols.

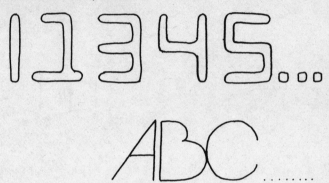

ANIMATION COMPUTERS

In film animation, each frame is individually executed; but in video, the isolating of individual frames is impractical and can be accomplished only with expensive equipment, such as the VR-2000 Editec. Such equipment is not readily available to the independent video producer. However, video animation deserves mention here.

One form of true animation in video is accomplished by using a computer in which information can be stored and retrieved. Unlike film, video animation is a kind of electronic drawing process rather than the assembling of many still pictures. A computer program can be designed from a single image, making it possible to project that image in any of its aspects—position on the screen, size, shape, gesture, and three-dimensional effect. As is indicated throughout **VIDEOWORKS**, the TV image consists of many lines, further broken down to many points. Again, there are about 150,000 picture elements per image. Imagine that during half time at a college football game there are 150,000 rooters assisting in the card-show spectacle. The work done by the card flippers is similar to that done by a computer which can supply individual signals to each and every picture element and thus determine the total image appearing on the CRT. Considering that a computer can supply a great range of signals at extremely high rates of speed, it is easy to appreciate that video animation is unique and expensive.

LARGE-SCREEN DISPLAY
THE BIG PICTURE

There are limits to how large a CRT can be. The deflection angle the electron beam can attain is dependent on the amount of power fed to the CRT, its shape and the size of its neck (where the electron gun is located), and the distance between the gun and the screen. Large-screen CRTs must be long and bulky and they consume much power. At present, the largest TV screens are around 25 inches measured diagonally and are housed in stationary consoles. Another screen size limitation results from the fact that overmagnification of 525 lines will produce an image of poor resolution. If our present system evolves into one of 1,000 or more lines per field, larger TVs could then be developed. Meanwhile, large-format display is possible via video projection and solid-state display.

VIDEO PROJECTION

Video projectors available to the independent producer combine CRT display with light projection similar to overhead projection. Video projectors use a small CRT to which a tape signal, Off/Air signal, or camera signal is fed. With the help of reflectors and projection lenses,

the image is magnified and cast upon a screen, white wall, or sheet. For best viewing, the room in which the image is projected should be darkened.

SOLID-STATE DISPLAY

Currently being developed is another method of large-screen display, one which employs **LEDs** (light-emitting diodes) in large printed circuits. As we know, there are about 150,000 picture elements that compose a TV image. Whereas scanning electron beams smear out the picture elements, LEDs represent each point distinctly— one LED represents only one picture element. The electronics providing horizontal and vertical location can function to produce either an analog or digital signal. In the case of a digitized system, the tape, Off/Air, or camera signals are converted to digital signals, then fed to the LEDs in their proper sequence.

Solid-state display prototypes have been produced in an 8-foot by 12-foot format—wall size. When large-scale production becomes possible the cost of these devices could be in the low four figures. As digital circuitry replaces present circuitry, solid-state cameras and screens will replace the vidicon and CRT.

VIDEO PROJECTION

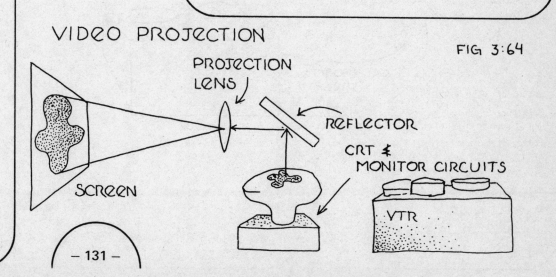

FIG 3:64

PROJECTION LENS

REFLECTOR

CRT & MONITOR CIRCUITS

SCREEN

VTR

SOLID-STATE DISPLAY

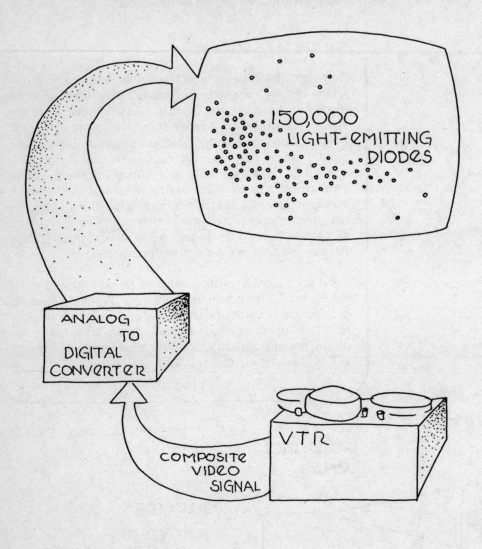

150,000 LIGHT-EMITTING DIODES

ANALOG TO DIGITAL CONVERTER

COMPOSITE VIDEO SIGNAL

VTR

FIG 3:65

CASSETTE, CARTRIDGE, AND DISC
THE HOMESCREEN SCENE

Throughout **VIDEOWORKS**, the discussion of equipment has centered on what can be classified as video production equipment—the camera, VTR, and CRT. Right now we will briefly discuss another type of equipment and purpose: playback systems for home use. Cassettes, cartridges, and discs are TV's answers to radio's tape decks and record players—packaged TV as an outgrowth to packaged sound.

TAPE-TYPE SYSTEMS

Unlike home sound systems, home TV systems have yet to be standardized. Cartridge and cassette systems vary in size. For instance, there are ½-inch cartridge systems that can play back any EIAJ-1 recorded tape, and there are ¾-inch systems which also meet all EIAJ-1 standards, except for tape size. A cassette is a self-contained unit which supplies its own take-up function. The tape in the cassette cannot be removed or replaced. A cartridge differs from a cassette in that the cartridge is a single-reel device which slips into a machine and is automatically threaded to a take-up reel in the system. A cartridge can be opened and supplied with tape. Both cartridges and cassettes ordinarily contain half-hour or hour-long tapes.

Cartridge and cassette systems can be either playback only or record/playback systems which can be equipped with a camera. These systems can be useful in libraries as well as in homes, because of their simple loading process and the protection they provide for tapes.

TV DISC SYSTEMS (TEDS)

Although the home video disc is not yet fully developed, it promises to be the most inexpensive and practical home TV system. A 21-cm (8-inch) video disc usually handles about 10 minutes of information; a 30-cm disc, 20–30 minutes. Such discs, slightly thicker than newsprint, are made of either a piece of polyvinyl chloride foil, or nickel cobalt layered on aluminum. They move on the player at 1,800 rpm. That's about 100 times faster than sound records, and the discs handle about 100 times as much information. They're good for better than 100 plays before any noticeable signal loss occurs.

Video disc recording is accomplished by laser, electron beam, or the mechanical cutting process used in sound recording. Scanning methods can be electrical, magnetic, optical, or mechanical. The signals are either directly recorded or FM. The signal-to-noise ratio is better than 40 db, and as disc surface quality is improved and friction lessened, the signal-to-noise ratio will be increased. In addition to *still* framing, slow- and fast-motion and scene repetition are inherent features of the disc system. Big TV now uses a disc system for instant replay during sports programs.

A playback-only disc system will soon be available for the home user, with video discs costing about the same as sound records.

THE FUTURE
MINIATURIZATION

The future of electronics is already spelled out in an array of three-letter acronyms—FET, MOS, CCD—which are among the primary building blocks of solid-state electronics. The future of video lies in total solid-state circuitry. Earlier in this book is a paragraph about measuring and an introduction to the concepts of analog and digital. Remember that video information is analog: The picture and sound are comprised of changing voltage levels.

When a signal is digitized, a sampling rate and word-size (which is composed of bits) are used to code the information. To convert, for instance, an analog signal (a series of changing voltages) to a digital signal, we need

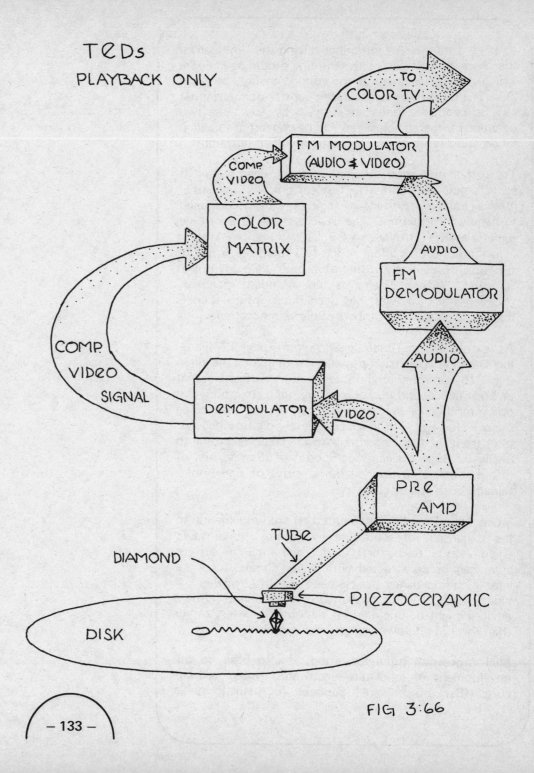

TEDs
PLAYBACK ONLY

FIG 3·66

to have a number of samplings during the timespan of the changing voltages. This sampling should be at a rate which exposes as many of the voltage changes as possible. The bit is the most discrete quantity of change that can be compared between samplings. Via these two parameters, the analog signal can be converted to a digital signal—a series of points having specified notations.

To further understand digital electronics, let's look at some simple logic circuits. In electronics, as in mathematics, universal systems of logic have been developed to handle information. The basic systems of electronic logic are AND, NAND and OR, NOR circuits. A bit of information causes a logic circuit to function or not to function, to be ready to function or to be ready not to function. With such circuits and an added "memory" to keep track of what has been done, information is handled digitally—as numbers of discrete notations.

As is discussed in *Timebase Correction* (page 127), analog-to-digital conversion provides for digitizing the video signal to correct timing discrepancies. Remember that in both helical and quad recording, tape stretching and other mechanical malfunctions can distort the analog signal. However, imagine a completely digital video system, from light-sensing circuit to magnetic recording to display. Digitial signals composed of discrete bits of information could provide for a purity of signal unattainable with analog circuitry.

MOSs (metal oxide semiconductors) are fundamental to the expansion of solid-state electronics. Like **FETs** (field effects transistors), MOSs are small in surface area, can be constructed with fewer circuit stops, are very high-impedance devices, and use little power. A video portapak built with MOSs and other solid-state devices might be operated on a flashlight battery rather than the 12-volt power supply now required.

Microprocessing (miniaturization) is also basic to the development of solid-state electronics. Integrated circuits (ICs), which were developed for ballistic missile

systems, have evolved from small-scale integration (SSI), which integrates five circuits on a 1-inch wafer, to large-scale integration (LSI), which integrates over one hundred circuits on a 3-inch wafer.

Already in existence are a number of **imaging array devices**. One of them, a **CCD** (charge coupled device), consists of light-sensitive diodes which function in the reverse of LEDs (light-emitting diodes). One CCD currently being used is a ½-inch by ¾-inch chip with 60,000 light-sensing elements. That's better than one-third the approximate number of picture elements in a video image. Low-light-level sensitivity will increase with CCD development and the use of more efficient and smaller image-intensifier units.

Op amps (operational amplifiers) are analog processors which deserve note. They are high-impedance devices and have been successfully integrated on a single chip with MOSs, making them useful for analog/digital conversion.

The use of lasers is expanding in video technology. **Laser** (Light Amplification by Stimulated Electromagnetic Radiation) is a means of transmitting information via photons rather than electrons. Lasers have made possible the **hologram**—a laser-transmitted image which appears three dimensionally and may eventually be the means for producing 3-D TV.

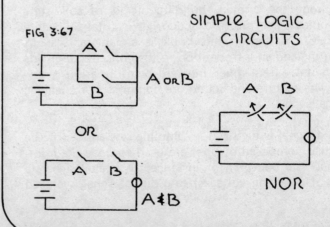

FIG 3·67

SIMPLE LOGIC CIRCUITS

A or B

OR

A≠B

A B

NOR

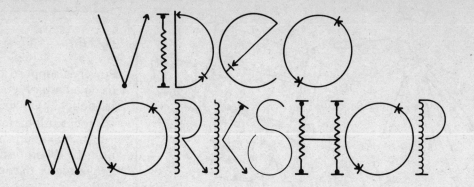

VIDEO WORKSHOP

INTRODUCTION

Video operation can be mastered only with equipment in hand. This section, therefore, presents a guide to taping, producing a videotape, displaying it, and transferring it to other formats for distribution. It does not explain how to operate individual pieces of equipment; that knowledge is readily available in the instruction manuals that accompany all equipment.

We have, for the most part, avoided using brand names and model numbers, which change as new developments are introduced. However, in order to make this book useful in the here and now, we have included a list of the manufacturers and types of equipment on the market today (see page 198).

In the text we will not use equipment brand names. All portable battery–powered camera and deck ensembles will be referred to as *portapaks*; all non–editing VTRs, whether black–and–white or color, will be referred to as *studio VTRs*; all editing decks as *editors*; and cameras, other than portapak cameras, will be referred to as *studio cameras*.

TAPING
EQUIPMENT

It is elementary, but necessary, to state that foremost in the production of a tape is the equipment: that it is working, that you have it with you, and that it is the proper equipment to suit the task at hand.

Your equipment consciousness can be aided by an equipment list (for an example of such a list, see fig. 6:2). This list will help you to get together all necessary equipment for going to and returning from a taping. It's also a good idea to put some kind of identifying mark on all your equipment.

The most important part of the routine of organizing a taping is the selection of proper equipment for the particular job. Knowing where you are going and what action is to occur will help determine what to take. There are eight equipment areas to consider in every case: *power, camera, optics, VTR, lights, sound, monitors*, and *accessories*.

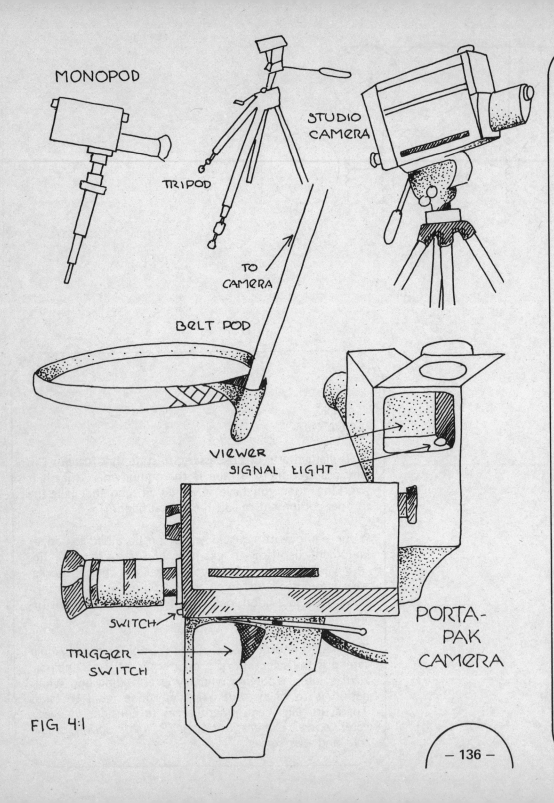

MONOPOD

TRIPOD

STUDIO CAMERA

TO CAMERA

BELT POD

VIEWER

SIGNAL LIGHT

SWITCH

TRIGGER SWITCH

PORTA-PAK CAMERA

FIG 4·1

POWER

Power is supplied by a battery or an AC wall outlet. If using a battery, consider the amount of battery time: Is it enough? Obviously, batteries are almost always needed for outdoor taping. But in an indoor situation in which maximum mobility is desired, batteries are also useful. When using a portapak and wall power, an AC converter is needed to adapt the 110 volts AC to 12 volts DC. Also consider how many power extension cables you might require and how long they need to be.

CAMERAS AND CAMERA SUPPORTS

The choice of camera should be determined by the degree of mobility desired. Since the same light-sensing tube—the vidicon—can be found in most of the cameras available to the independent videomaker, little quality variation exists between studio and portapak cameras. Studio cameras, however, generally have greater horizontal resolution than portapak cameras.

You must also select a device with which to support the camera. Various types of supports are available, among them:

The Monopod. A monopod is a single-leg support which variably extends to the ground or to whatever surface (like a table top) is being used. It is light and therefore easily portable and aids in steadying the camera. A monopod takes up much less space than a tripod.

The Belt Pod. Belt pods are also single-leg supports which extend from camera to waist where they fit into a small pouch on a belt (much like the device used to carry a flag). They are easy to walk with and act to take the weight off your arms which can tire when holding six or seven pounds of camera for lengthy periods. They help prevent up-and-down shakiness of the camera, but do little to eliminate side-to-side shakiness, especially on close-ups. An inexpensive belt pod can be put together by using the main shaft and head of an inexpensive old tripod and a pouch made of gaffers' tape (thick and sturdy cloth tape). Attach the homemade pouch to your belt, and you'll be ready to go.

The Tripod. A tripod is a three-leg support which ranges in price from very expensive to very cheap. Every tripod, whatever its class, has a head and legs. Heads run from hinge-type designs, to spring-action, and on up to fluid heads. Most tripods have telescoping legs which can be easily adjusted. Some tripods come with wheel bases for **dolly shooting** (in which camera and tripod move to follow action).

The Shoulder Brace. A shoulder brace is the ultimate in camera-carrying paraphernalia. This device conforms to your body, placing the weight where your strength is—on your shoulders and back. Using a shoulder brace, you can even perform some "no-hands" shooting. However, a brace limits **tilting** (the movement of pointing the camera up and down). For **panning**, (side-sweeping movements of the camera), a brace is more versatile than a tripod.

For most indoor situations, the tripod is used when the action is fixed, as in interviews. It's also useful for any type of taping, indoor or outdoor, where rock steadiness is needed—for instance, for a close-up nature study or a series of dramatic, slowly zoomed mountain panoramas. On the other hand, if an environment is confined, a better choice might be one of the handheld devices. Selecting a camera support is finally a matter of experience and preference.

OPTICS

Optics refers to lenses, filters, and lens aids. Most cameras come equipped with an all-purpose zoom lens. However, the C-mount adaptor ring allows for interchangeable lenses. When selecting a lens—such as a fish-eye or telephoto—for a particular effect, expect a possible loss in light responsivity, resulting from the slower speed of the lens.

For a rundown on filters, see **VIDEOWORKS** (page 58).

Lens aids can be fitted to regular lenses to provide certain special effects such as split images, extreme close-ups, vignetting, etc. The appropriateness of their use is sometimes questionable, but in some circumstances they can be invaluable aids. For instance, the Spiratone Curvatar, (see chart) can turn the 12.5–50mm standard zoom into a super-wide-angle zoom.

VTR

When it comes to videotape recorders, the choice is between a portapak VTR and a studio VTR (or editor). Only the portapak is battery-powered, so if portability is a requirement, it's your only choice. However, a studio VTR is necessary if you want to do hour-long, continuous recording. The portapak provides only for half-hour reels. A one-hour tape adaptor is available for portapaks, but the portapak cannot be carried when the adaptor is used. A backpack in which to carry the portapak VTR is a helpful accessory.

In this section, (page 156), you can find a discussion concerning the use of VTRs with special effects generators (SEGs). In most cases, a studio VTR is needed.

However, SEGs are available for mobile work with portapaks. It is necessary to use a studio VTR when using a studio camera. Adaptors are available which enable the portapak camera to be used with a studio VTR.

The portapak has a low-impedance microphone input. On the other hand, a studio VTR (when AC power is available) offers the advantage of manual audio volume control and both high- and low-impedance inputs. It is possible to build components into a portapak which provide it with the same sound capabilities as a studio VTR. More on sound, in this section (page 143).

LIGHTS

The first question is: Do you need them or not? If you are using a low-light-level sensitive camera, you will not need light other than what's minimally available, be it artificial or a bit of natural sunlight. Outdoors in the daytime no lights are needed with a vidicon camera, but lights are almost always needed indoors, except where there is *plenty* of outside light coming in from the windows. Lightweight lighting systems are available and it's good practice to carry them with you to be prepared. More on lighting, in this section (page 152).

SOUND

What sound equipment to use depends on the action to be taped. The portapak comes with a mic built into the camera, but external mics can be used instead. The portapak camera mic is good for overall sound but leaves something to be desired when you wish to pinpoint specific sounds. The external mic is a must for taping conversation. Using more than one mic necessitates careful placement of the mics and the use of a mic mixer. These techniques are discussed in this section, (page 143).

MONITORS

The use of TV monitors for either a live feed (simultaneous viewing while taping) or for playbacks is almost exclusively dependent upon the availability of AC power. Some small monitors can be battery-powered, but are impractical to carry if you want to be mobile. A cable which connects the VTR to the set is used to feed signals into the monitor. In most cases, this portapak-to-monitor cable is different from the studio VTR-to-monitor cable.

Another monitoring system utilizes an RF modulator and connector to feed signals on a broadcast channel to the VHF tuner of an ordinary television. For live feed when using the portapak, this RF system is absolutely necessary. If the job is to show tape, the simultaneous use of many monitors is in order. See later in this section (page 164), for a further discussion of monitors.

ACCESSORIES

In addition to what has already been mentioned, important accessories include the proverbial extension cables. In some situations, camera extensions, power extensions, and audio extensions (mic and line cables) are as necessary as the camera itself. Don't forget 3-prong-to-2-prong adaptors, take-up reels, videotape, gaffers' or masking tape, cleaning equipment (usually cotton swabs and isopropyl alcohol), and some tools (such as a soldering iron, Phillips head screwdriver, etc.). Once again, the equipment list reveals all (see fig. 6:2).

THREADING

The method for threading tape on a VTR varies with each type of machine. Every piece of equipment is supplied with a threading diagram in ready view. Remember, for helical scan recording, the tape must pass the erase head, wrap around the head drum, pass the sound and control track head, and be set in–between the pinch roller and the capstan (see fig. 4:2). The threading must be correct. If it is not, the result in playback will be a picture marred by tracking noise or other signal instability.

A portapak presents different threading problems. Since it is mobile, reels can be bounced up and the tape slipped out of its proper path if jarred forcefully. Take care to be threading–sensitive. If by chance you make a mistake, there is a possible reprieve: Misthread in *playback* the same way you misthreaded in *record*. You should then be able to view the tape without any disturbances. Though sufficient for playbacks, this method usually won't work for editing.

CONNECTIONS

Video equipment connections are often designed to fit in only one way. As discussed in **VIDEOWORKS** (page 119), a connector has a number of points which must be exactly aligned to the matching points of the receptor. In almost all cases, the design of the connector will not permit improper use.

In the case of **din pin connectors** (see fig. 3:55) however, the plug can be put in incorrectly if forced. Din pin plugs are commonly used for studio camera–to–VTR connections and for external power inputs on the portapaks. When external power is improperly connected, transistors can be blown out. Make it a practice not to force connections. Use your eyes to see that the fit is correct and test all screw–type connections to ensure that they hold fast.

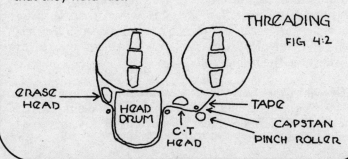

THREADING

FIG 4:2

ERASE HEAD

HEAD DRUM

C·T HEAD

TAPE

CAPSTAN

PINCH ROLLER

MODES OF OPERATION

The portapak camera is equipped with a trigger which activates the VTR for the actual recording. The *record* mode, which readies the system for recording, must be engaged. All switching operations are located on the studio VTR itself. This is so even when using the portapak camera with adaptor and studio VTR.

All VTRs are equipped with the following modes: *forward*, *fast forward*, *rewind*, *still frame* or *pause*, and *sound dub*. There is also a mode selector for the type of input: *TV*, *camera*, or *line*. Portapaks accommodate only *TV* and *camera*. The studio VTRs and editors are equipped with the additional *line* input.

TRACKING, SKEW, AND SOUND AND VIDEO LEVELS

Tracking is best set at the fixed position during recording. When using the portapak on which the tracking control has no fixed position, the center position is best. This is not so much a matter of technicality as it is a matter of convenience. If you always use different tracking settings, you'll find yourself searching for the proper setting each time you play back a tape. So arriving at some kind of standardization will be helpful.

Skew (on studio VTRs and editors) need not be tampered with, either before or during recording. It functions only in *playback*. Remember, skewing has to do with controlling the tension of the tape during playback. To technically understand all the various controls on a VTR, refer to **VIDEOWORKS** (pages 86 & 88).

Generally, all studio decks and editors provide both a manual control and AGC (automatic gain control) for incoming sound. The AGC automatically maintains an audible range of sound levels, ensuring little or no overmodulation. On the other hand, the manual control, accompanied by a volume level meter, enables you to control sound levels in accord with your own judgments. The portapaks generally have only AGC, but can be modified.

AGC and manual controls for video level can also be found on studio VTRs and editors. The AGC maintains a proper range of levels to guard against overmodulation. A video level meter displays the effects of the manual control. When you switch to manual control, it is advisable to keep an eye on the meter throughout the taping. Even changing shadows can affect the overall light level and thus change the video level. Under most circumstances, the AGC should be used.

SHOOTING
RECORD MODE

Once the system is put into *record*, it takes a moment for the picture to appear; the filament in the vidicon needs to heat up so that the electrons can begin to be emitted. An interesting visual effect accompanies the warm-up: The picture blossoms forth from blankness, somewhat like a Polaroid photograph developing before your eyes, but much faster.

Remember, though you see an image through the viewer of the video camera, the image is not necessarily being recorded. In order to record, the VTR must be moving the tape. On the other hand, you may think you are just seeing an image when you are actually recording. This is to merely—but emphatically—point out the possible confusion that can occur in taping.

The viewer of the portapak is equipped with a signal light which is activated by a trigger when the portapak is properly engaged. The signal light goes on when the trigger is activated for actual recording. In the case of studio VTRs or editors, you must develop your own method for determining when the system is actually recording since most cameras do not indicate when recording is activated at the VTR. When using the portapak camera with a studio VTR, remember that the trigger does not function even though the signal light goes on when the trigger is pressed.

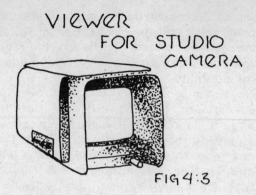

VIEWER FOR STUDIO CAMERA

FIG 4:3

THE VIEWER

The portapak camera's viewer is a 1-inch TV monitor. To me, the most distinctive aspect of video is that what you see in the viewer as you shoot is almost exactly what you will see during playback of the tape on a TV set. No other picture-making medium can make this claim. The final product is there before your eyes as you work. If you see that the light needs adjustment, you can immediately adjust it accordingly. Unlike film, there's no need to fix settings or to calculate light levels and photochemical exposure times.

In the case of studio cameras, which may be equipped with 3-inch viewers, this nearly exact approximation of the end product becomes still more exact. The portapak's 1-inch viewer must be peered at with one eye closed, and is often obscured by light reflections from the magnifying optics in front of it. The larger 3-inch monitors allow for two-eye viewing and have no magnifying optics to reflect light. However, there is always a slight difference in image quality between a live feed and the tape playback, since recording electronics slightly degrade the primary signals.

The viewer is the window to the world of video. However, it's a good idea to occasionally look directly at a scene to determine where to move next, to catch something going on outside the field of view of the camera, or just to rest your eyes while continuing to tape.

Remember, the viewer will not reveal recording problems that might be occurring in the VTR. These problems can only be seen by viewing the tape during playback. It is a good idea to test-shoot before serious taping. Since the portapak allows for playback in the viewer, tests can be made even when mobile.

When powering the portapak with batteries, there will be a sign of depleted power which will show up in the viewer as loss of focus, culminating in a collapsed image. Also, when the portapak runs out of tape, the viewer will go off, as will the whole system. This happens because a spring-type switch along the tape path moves forward when there's no tape to hold it back, thereby turning off the entire system.

Although aesthetics is a highly subjective concern, one should be aware of some standard aesthetic considerations in creating any moving image: clarity, composition, and stability and continuity. Clarity refers to the technical aspects of sharp focus and substantial contrast range, or intended departures from those norms. Composition concerns the arrangement of elements within and related to the frame of the picture. And stability and continuity, particular to moving the camera, refer to the rationale for movement and the interrelating of movements. I include these considerations as keynotes to consciousness in making moving pictures.

STARTING TIME

When using the portapak, be aware that when the trigger is depressed to begin actual recording, there are about 5 seconds of start-up time to allow all the electronics and mechanics to get up to speed. In playback, the first image is only slightly marred by the instability and noise. But for editing purposes, these small segments of tape are useless. For this reason, it is advisable to anticipate triggering the VTR so as not to lose the first few

seconds of a sequence. Or, when possible, hold the action until you know the equipment is up to speed. Also for the sake of editing, try to overextend the end of a sequence so that you won't lose any of the action. Always keep editing in mind.

ZOOM

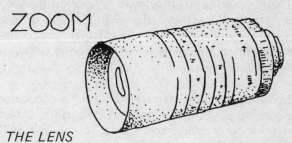

THE LENS

The lens (zoom) provides for focusing, zooming, and aperture setting. The aperture is usually set and left at a particular f-stop unless there are great light variations within a shooting area. On the other hand, when using the low-light-level sensitive camera, which is very responsive to the slightest changes in light, the aperture ring becomes a primary control.

The standard vidicon is equipped with an **automatic gain circuit**. This circuit increases or decreases the target voltage, providing for optimum video image under any given circumstance. Therefore, when the most open aperture setting is used on a bright day, the image, though a bit contrasty, will not be overexposed. Some videomakers claim to use only the most open apertures for all their shooting. The loss, of course, is in the depth of field, and therefore more focusing is necessary. (Conversely, smaller aperture openings allow for greater depths of field, so that less focusing need be done.)

The only cardinal rule in video is *never* to shoot the sun. No automatic gain circuit can protect the vidicon from that intensity of light. It's also wise to make it a practice not to shoot directly at any high-intensity lights. This will avoid what are called *burns* on the face of the vidicon. Shooting the sun can burn out the vidicon: finis. Shooting less intense but still strong lights will result in lingering shadowy streaks or spots which can last the life of the tube.

If by chance you acquire any minor burns, you can remove them by leaving the camera on overnight with the aperture closed, or by pointing the camera at the sky (not the sun) for a few moments with the aperture wide open. These methods create an overall burn on the vidicon face, thereby lessening the obtrusiveness of the spots or streaks resulting from the original burns. Beware of getting slight burns from reflections off windows, metal, water, or snow.

The zoom and focus are interrelated. Given a particular aperture setting, if you zoom to extreme close-up, then focus on your subject and zoom back, the subject will remain in focus—this applies to both large and small aperture settings, as long as the distance between you and the subject does not alter.

Follow focus refers to focusing that is necessitated by zoom changes or by a moving subject. Such changes can be made relatively smoothly by swift and sure-handed lens manipulation. It helps to know in which direction to turn each ring for a particular result. As you regularly hold the camera, the zoom ring turned to the right (clockwise) provides the close-up; to the left (counter-clockwise), the wide-angle view. The focus ring turned clockwise provides focusing at closer distances (usually down to 3 feet on most zooms) and turned counter-clockwise, greater distances out to infinity.

The above directions are standard for most lenses. There are some lenses, however, which turn in the opposite direction or are controlled by knobs or electric buttons, etc. Once again, see the related instruction manual.

CAMERA MOVEMENTS

As mentioned previously, the conventional camera movements are *panning*, *tilting*, and *dollying*. However, such moves which are related to the mobility of a tripod can be expanded upon by the use of a handheld camera

support or no support at all. The camera can get heavy during extended taping but it is actually light enough to handle without support for shorter takes. It is therefore possible to make sideways and upside-down shots, or whatever else might strike your fancy.

RELATING TO PEOPLE

No one is without some sort of picture-taking self-consciousness. For some, there is shyness or fear of what they look like. Others might respond with hostile indignation to someone pointing a camera in their direction. Still others will revel in the attention they are getting. How people react is largely dependent upon the situation in which they find themselves as camera subjects—for instance, they'll respond differently on the street than at home.

The camera can lend itself psychologically to many functions: It can scrutinize, as a microscope with which to probe; it can intimidate, and be a weapon; it can be a telescope, a medium of voyeurism, to invade privacy. It can also be the press—a means for extricating truth or for promulgating propaganda. Of course, it is the operator of the equipment who finally determines the purpose and intended meaning of the end product. Whether used to celebrate or expose, video is a powerful tool.

Again, video has a unique quality which separates it from other picture-making media. Because you can set up a live feed, and play back a tape immediately, the product is available for the subject(s) to see on the spot. As you familiarize people with the processes of the medium, you can ease apprehension, and so gain cooperation and greater participation.

Knowing what you want out of a situation and being able to ask people to do the things that you see need doing are primary requisites for effectively organizing a taping.

SOUND

Since the TV speaker on a home set is a mere three inches in diameter, TV sound leaves something to be desired. Surely, better sound will come, but at present there is little in the way of quality sound from TV. Almost all video sound recording is monaural. Some cassette players and 1-inch VTRs provide for two-track recording, but necessitate the use of sound amplification equipment and speakers of a higher grade than those in the TV set.

The limitations of video sound equipment do not justify lousy sound. In fact, *because* of the limits of the TV set, what you do when recording is critical. Recorded sound and "real" sound are not the same. Our hearing is aided by selectivity, the process by which the brain filters out unwanted sounds and focuses on specific ones. A microphone, on the other hand, is sensitive to a range of sounds and it indiscriminately takes them all in. Further, an ear listening to recorded sound can do little to add any missing sounds or subtract obtrusive ones.

Good sound recording can be achieved by using the *playback* to test and determine the quality of the sound heard through the monitor. In many cases, when carrying even a small TV set is impractical, headsets are in order. As with the picture, for which the camera viewer provides an approximation of the end product, so it is with sound; monitoring the sound through headsets provides you with an approximation of the sound on the tape. If you don't know already, you'll know bad sound when you hear it. The idea is to know why the bad sound occurs and to be able to correct or prevent it.

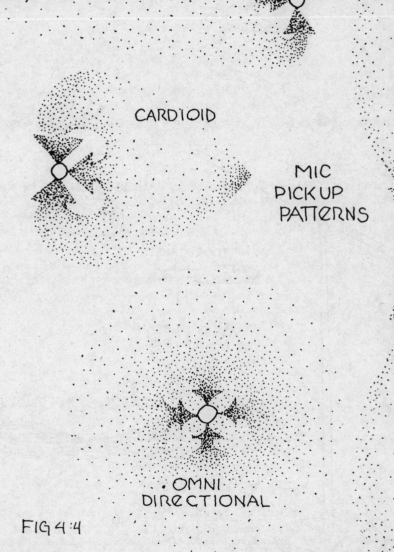

ULTRADIRECTIONAL
(SHOTGUN)

CARDIOID

MIC
PICK UP
PATTERNS

OMNI
DIRECTIONAL

FIG 4:4

BIDIRECTIONAL

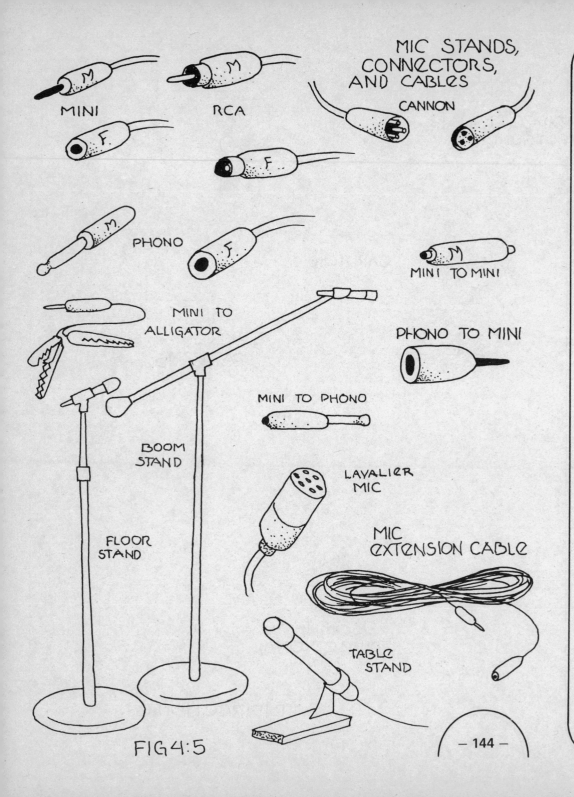

MIC STANDS,
CONNECTORS,
AND CABLES

MINI

RCA

CANNON

PHONO

MINI TO MINI

MINI TO ALLIGATOR

PHONO TO MINI

BOOM STAND

MINI TO PHONO

FLOOR STAND

LAVALIER MIC

MIC EXTENSION CABLE

TABLE STAND

FIG 4:5

EQUIPMENT

In **VIDEOWORKS** (page 110), differences in microphone construction are emphasized. Here, for the purposes of application, the primary distinction among microphones is the directional pickup pattern. It is dangerous to make hard-and-fast rules for mic use based solely on pickup patterns. The other considerations that must be made include room acoustics, overall noise (background, traffic, etc.), and the sound level(s) of subject(s). A pickup pattern is not a fixed border; rather, it is the area of the mic's optimum sensitivity to sound. Microphones include the following types: omnidirectional, bidirectional, cardioid (unidirectional), and shotgun (ultradirectional).

Omnidirectional mics have circular pickup patterns, which means they are sound-sensitive in all directions. They are best used in situations in which you want to pick up allover sound—when you want to hear several people talking around a table, or when you want the all-over atmospheric sound of a country landscape. A **lavalier** mic (worn around the neck or clipped on a shirt), which is designed for a single speaker, may be omnidirectional.

The pickup pattern for a **bidirectional** mic is a figure eight. Useful for stationary in-studio interview situations, it is good for little else. A bidirectional mic used on location will pick up the extraneous sounds coming from the mic's other direction of sensitivity. In most cases, bidirectional mics have been replaced by cardioid mics.

A **cardioid** (unidirectional) mic has a pickup pattern extending in front of it which is roughly shaped like an apple. These microphones are the most generally useful. On-location interviews can be conducted with a cardioid mike, pointed in turn at each speaker. Although they must be pointed in the direction of the desired source of sound, it is this inherent selectivity which makes them the most widely employed mics. Whether placed on a boom, in a stand, or hand-held, cardioid mics enable maximum control over sound.

A **shotgun** (ultradirectional) mic has a narrowed-down cardioid pickup pattern. Because of its mechanical design—long and narrow—it can be used to pick up individual sounds from some distance away. A long, narrow extension tube, like the cardboard center of a roll of paper towels, can be placed on a cardioid mic to turn it into a shotgun-type mic. It's in no way the real thing, but will increase the unidirectionality of the cardioid mic.

Radio (wireless) microphones are also worth mentioning here. They have no cables because the picked-up sound is transmitted through the air to a receiver which connects into the VTR. As good as this may sound, radio mics are prone to nearby broadcast interference, so their use is limited to situations in which there is no possibility of interference.

Microphone impedances are either high or low. The low range, 50–600 ohms, is best suited for video systems. Video sound recording inputs are **low ⤄** (low impedance). Only with low ⤄ mics can you use mic extension cables without loss of high-frequency response. **High ⤄** mics (2,000–10,000 ohms) connected to extension cables of any practical length lose high-frequency response. Some mics have adjustable impedance settings such as 50, 250, and 600 ohms, so you can closely match the impedance of the recording system.

High-level and low-level are terms used to describe signal voltage. A **high-level signal** is one of 1 volt or more. A **low-level signal** is one of less than a millivolt. A high-level signal can have low impedance and a low-level signal can have high impedance. For instance, the *line* input to VTRs accomodates high-level signals which have low (600 ohms) impedance. The *mic* input on a portapak is low-level and low impedance. A crystal mic is low-level and high impedance.

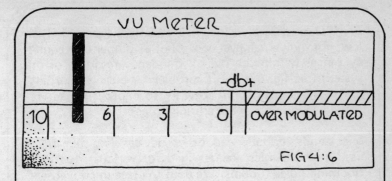

VU METER

-db+

:10   6   3   0   OVER MODULATED

FIG 4:6

MICROPHONE MIXERS

In the monaural video sound system, a **mixer** must be used when working with two or more mics. As discussed in **VIDEOWORKS** (page 114), mixers provide the following: a master volume control; individual volume control for each mic; a VU meter which monitors the loudness of the recorded sound; and high-level inputs for mixing in other prerecorded sources of sound such as records, tapes, radio, etc. (see fig. 4:7). Some mixers also enable you to alter the high- and/or low-frequency response of individual mics or high ⤄ inputs.

The **VU** (Volume Units) **meter** is the most important control in sound recording. As indicated in the drawing (see fig. 4:6), the needle on the VU meter moves back and forth over a scale which measures volume levels in decibels. The zero VU level indicates maximum distortion-free sound level, and can be set for any selected number of decibels. However set, one increment on the VU meter measures a single-decibel increase in sound. The minus side of the scale is where you want to keep the VU needle. The plus side (red) means overmodulation—and thereby distortion. When there's no sound, the needle rests at the extreme minus point of the scale. As the signal is metered, the needle can safely deflect as far as zero VU and still indicate good sound recording.

Accessories to basic sound recording equipment (mics and mixers) are extension cables, stands and booms, windscreens, adaptor plugs, sound equipment connection cables, headsets, and EQs (frequency equalizers).

The **EQ**, as described in **VIDEOWORKS** (page 114), allows for individual level control of a number of frequency ranges within the overall frequency response of the system (see fig. 4:7). It can be used during recording, but in most cases is put to work to improve already recorded sound during the editing process.

Mic stands, booms, and other devices (see fig. 4:5) used to hold mics are designed for various situations. **Booming poles (booms)** are used to place mics overhead and outside the periphery of the action. They are available with extensions, swivel fittings, holders for the mics, etc. You can improvise a boom using a bamboo pole, which is light and can easily be held out over the action to be covered.

Mic stands can be floor- or table-type. When placing mics on a table from which you are going to record a number of speakers, use table mic stands. They prevent the pickup of extraneous noise like fingers tapping, which mics placed directly on the table are prone to pick up. If table mic stands are used, place them on some kind of soft padding to absorb the vibrations of any movements.

Windscreens are useful only outside. They act to cushion the swooshing of wind against the microphone head. Any sponge rubber—but best in thin sheets—can be wrapped around the microphone to serve as a windscreen.

As covered in **VIDEOWORKS** (page 144), several types of plugs are used in sound equipment. It follows that there are adaptors for using certain plugs with different ones. Cables are also available for connecting various sound equipment components into one another—the EQ into the VTR, the mixer into the VTR, etc. The drawing (4:5) illustrates an array of the most common of these devices.

Headsets are important for good sound recording because they are the monitoring tool. Stereo headsets are not needed for monaural video sound recording; in fact,

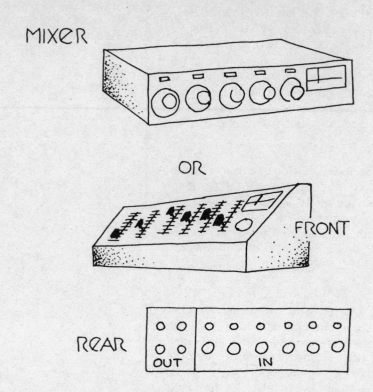

MIXER

OR

FRONT

REAR

OUT   IN

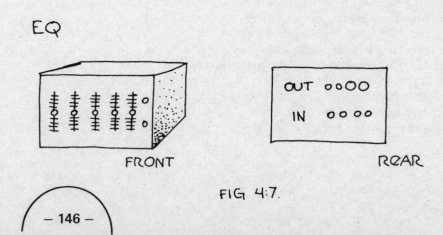

EQ

OUT 0000

IN 0000

FRONT

REAR

FIG 4:7.

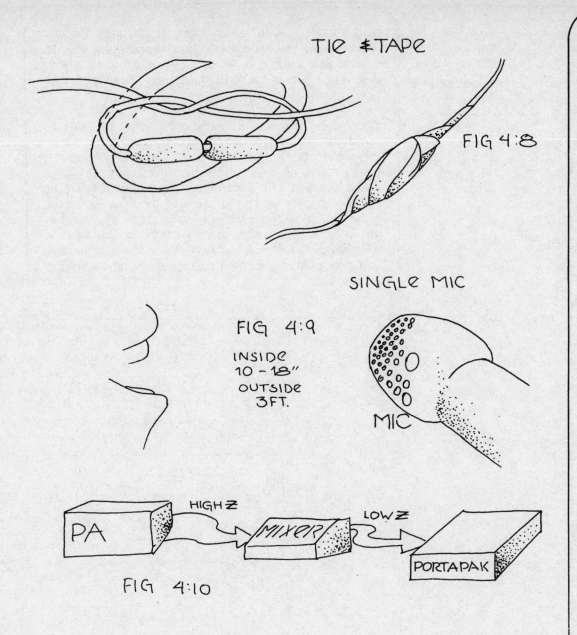

TIe &TAPe

FIG 4:8

SINGLe MIC

FIG 4:9

INSIDe
10 - 18"
OUTSIDe
3FT.

MIC

PA   HIGH Z   MIXER   LOW Z   PORTAPAK

FIG 4:10

if you use them you will hear through only one of the earphones. For recording purposes, a good headset should have an extra-spongy, mufflike cushion to block the outside sound as much as possible. Such a headset enables you to best distinguish the pickup quality of the sound recording system.

The headset should be plugged into the recording system at a point close to where the sound goes onto the tape. It is important to monitor the sound after it has gone through the electronics of the various components in order to best determine the balance among mics, extraneous system noises, and electronic problems.

Extension cable—and for that matter, all cable—has impedance which contributes to losses of signal in cables of great length. This impedance is rated as the number of decibels lost per 100 feet of cable. As stated earlier, when using low Z equipment, longer cables may be employed than when using high Z equipment.

Extension cables are often troublesome at the points of connection. It's a good practice to tie and tape the connections as shown in the drawing (4:8). Although most audio plugs are of a specific size, among the miniplugs there are slight size variations. These variations seem to be determined by the manufacture of the plug—whether it is a German mini or a Japanese mini.

METHODS: SINGLE MICROPHONE

Portapaks are equipped with omnidirectional microphones. These mics function best when aimed in the direction of the source of sound, although as you hold the camera, your own voice is picked up clearly as well. It is therefore possible to have repartee with your camera's subject.

If desired, the camera mic easily can be bypassed by plugging an external mic into the portapak or into the VTR, but the assistance of a soundperson then becomes necessary. This person must hold the mic and, if required, initiate dialogue or conduct an interview. Cardioid mics or shotgun mics are best utilized by a sound-person, since he or she has the mobility to aim the mic in any possible direction.

In order to produce the requisite sound level for talk, a mic should be held anywhere from 10 to 18 inches away from the speaker's mouth. Indoors, in a relatively quiet space, the mic may be placed up to 3 feet away. However, the mic should never be placed less than 8 inches from the mouth, since this will produce too much blast from speech puffs and pops.

When recording live music, the single mic is often the best to use. If there's a public address system (PA), a microphone placed a foot or two in front of the speaker is one good method by which to record the sound. If the PA system has a "to tape recorder" output, by using proper cable you can plug directly into the line input (high-level input) of the VTR. Remember that porta-paks, unless modified, have only a low-level input. If recording from a PA with an unmodified portapak, you must use a mic mixer between them, and the mixer must have both high-level and low-level inputs and out-puts (see fig. 4:10). Usually PA outputs are high-level, and therefore the mixer provides a means for making the proper connection.

Mics must be handled with the utmost care. Nervous flicking or rubbing of the shaft of the mic will result in extraneous scratching noises in the recording. Beware of holding papers in the same hand as the mic. Even paper-crinkling can be picked up as loud, disturbing noises on the soundtrack. Also, always tie mic cables to the equipment into which they are plugged, so if pulled they will not unwittingly be disconnected.

METHODS: MULTI-MICROPHONE

The use of two or more mikes and the mixing of the re-sulting sound is usually reserved for relatively immobile recording situations. Although small battery-powered mixers are available, you can hardly consider yourself

truly mobile as you search some Sunday park for that great moment of tape, with three soundpeople leashed to you like sniffing poodles, all going off in their own direction. Such a display would most likely be its own best subject.

When using a mixer, a soundperson must be there to operate it. Talk shows, town meetings, and other group-show formats are best recorded by several mics strate-gically placed to cover all the possible sources of sound. The individual mic controls on the mixer should be marked to indicate the location of the mics connected into them. Following the previously stated principles of microphone application, the correct mic should be care-fully selected for each location—a handheld shotgun to cover an audience, cardioids to cover several speakers at a table, etc.

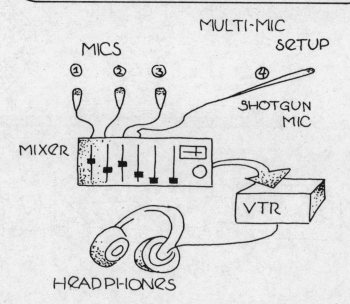

MULTI-MIC SETUP

MICS

① ② ③ ④

SHOTGUN MIC

MIXER

VTR

HEADPHONES

FIG 4:11

MIC PLACEMENT

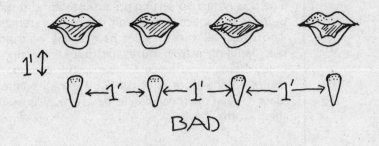

BAD

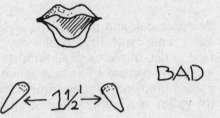

BAD

GOOD

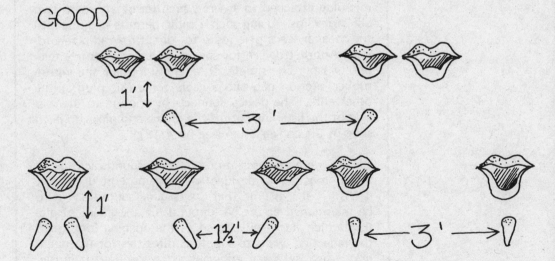

FIG 4:12

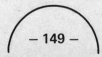

Since the volume range changes in most dialogue sound, it's best to set the VU meter from about -6 to -12 decibels. This setting allows the highest levels of sound to peak occasionally just into the red, but not linger there, which would cause much distortion. It is often wise to turn down the levels of mics which are not picking up desired sound. The mixer operator, using headsets, should be ever-ready to up the level of any of the mics, while downing others. Of course, where dialogue exchanges occur, levels should be kept up.

Unless specially modified, the portapak has only AGC (automatic gain control). The AGC circuit, as described in **VIDEOWORKS** (page 114), serves to limit the input sound level so that it does not overmodulate when recorded. Fortunately, the AGC (sometimes called AVC or automatic volume control) acts just slowly enough so that there is still a range of levels. If it responded immediately, a monotone sound (one with absolutely no level changes) would be produced. All VTRs have both AGC and manual sound level controls. When using the manual control, watch the VU meter on the VTR to control the mic levels.

Mics must be placed to avoid multi-mic interference. Under some circumstances, improperly placed mics will cause voids of frequency response in the recording. (This problem applies to two or more mics feeding into one system and not to two or more mics feeding into two or more separate systems.) Such effects can be avoided if the mics are at least three times as far apart as either one of them is from the source of sound. The drawings on this page give examples of both proper and improper mic placement.

Because of wiring differences among mic plugs, microphones can be out of phase. If, when using a two-conductor shielded cable, wire no. 1 is connected to pin no. 1 of the plug on one mic, but wire no. 1 of the other mic is connected to pin no. 2 of the plug, phase problems will result. All mics and mixer equipment must be consistently wired in order to work properly together.

Out-of-phase problems are detected as loss of sound

level and as voids in frequency response. To determine whether two mics are in phase, aim one of the mics away from a sound source and get a VU meter reading. Then, without changing the level of the first mic, put the second alongside it. If the mics are in phase, the VU meter level should increase 6 decibels. If they are out of phase, the level will drop 6 decibels.

If mics are out of phase, rewiring is in order. The idea is to standardize the wire-to-pin sequence in all mics that are to be plugged into a single mixer. This standardizing will present a problem only if you have a variety of different mics, some of which have already been rewired at some point in their lives.

Multi-mic recording of music necessitates setting the proper level for each instrument or area of sound and knowing the cues of the very high and the very low sound levels. In this way, you'll be ready to adjust the controls to prevent overmodulation or to raise the levels so that the sound remains audible. For instance, percussion instruments should be held down, and vocals should be raised to be heard distinctly among the general din. If you are recording amplified instruments, high Z outputs can be directed from the amplifiers into the mixer. Or, mics can be placed in front of the amplifier speakers. In any case, rehearsals and tests will be necessary. If you're taking the time to record with a multi-mic system, take the time to do it justice.

One more important setup worth mentioning is the sound recording of a group of people situated all over a room, such as a play in the round in which the action and source of sound are constantly changing. Almost an impossible situation; the only solution is to suspend omnidirectional mics overhead—as many as possible—in a grid designed to cover the overall floor space. The additional use of several shotguns in the hands of some quick-draw shooters could possibly do the trick, or at least add to the effectiveness of the hanging mics.

When using a number of mics, it is advisable to ensure that all cable lengths are pretty much the same. Remember that, due to impedances, the longer the cable

the greater the signal loss. This problem becomes especially critical in cable lengths of over 100 feet.

There is an art to setting up a multi-mic situation which permits the space containing the mics to remain usable. Too often all those cables have a way of tripping people, dangling into pictures, getting kicked up, and generally being a nuisance. Tape is the answer. Tape all cables to the floor if possible. Tape all connections in place. Tape overhead cables to whatever is used to hang them from. Tape.

SOUND DUBBING

The portapak and most VTRs are equipped with *sound dub*. This capability enables new sound to be put on tape in lieu of the original soundtrack recorded, without losing the picture. The new sound can be live voice or music; prerecorded sound from a tape, a record, or even the radio; or a combination of sounds if a mixer is used.

One of many types of cables that can be purchased is a mic plug attached to a wire which terminates with two alligator clips. Using such a cable permits hooking into the speaker leads of a radio for direct off/radio recording. Another device for special circumstances is a telephone tap. The simplest is actually a small mic with a rubber suction cup and a cable for a mic plug at the other end. The device connects by suction to the rear side of the listening part of the phone and picks up both sides of the conversation (see fig. 4:13).

Finally, here's a description of several soundtracks being mixed together as a videotape is being edited (see fig. 4:13): Let's assume that the original soundtrack is to be maintained as the background for a segment of picture which has been chosen as the opening footage of the tape. We want to supply audio titles for the opening. Also, let's say we want a low overlay of music. And further, we have a short phone conversation which we want to use as a prelude to the speaking of titles. Each level control of the mixer should be identified with the input it governs. It is also important that

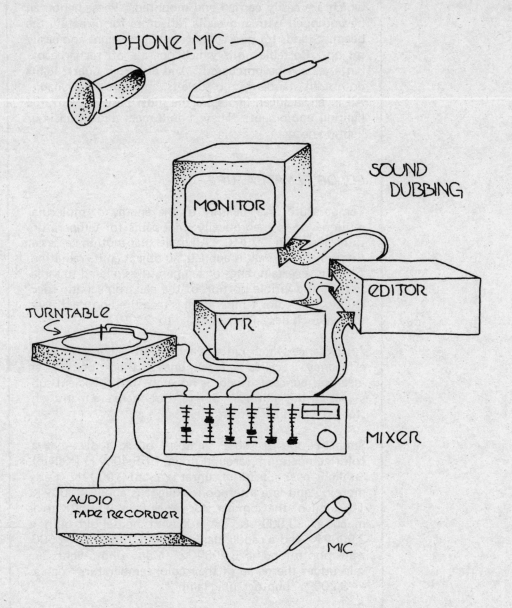

PHONE MIC

SOUND
DUBBING

MONITOR

EDITOR

TURNTABLE

VTR

MIXER

AUDIO
TAPE RECORDER

MIC

FIG 4:13

each level be at the best setting for its particular sound input. Background sounds must be low, yet audible. Key sound, such as the phone conversation and the spoken titles, must be loud and clear. By pressing *sound dub* on the editor before actually doing the edit, you can listen to the sound through the editor on a TV monitor. In this way you can set your levels for each input.

All the sources must be cued up—ready to go from the point from which they are to be used. (The audio tape recorder should be put into *hold*, which upon release will immediately provide the sound.) Start the record (music) quickly, go into *edit*, then bring up the sound from the tape recorder (phone conversation); turn that down, and bring up the sound level of the mic input (spoken titles). After the titles have been spoken, turn down the mic input level and fade out the sound.

Headsets are a necessity when recording with a mic if you are close to a speaker or monitor into which the sound of the mic is fed. Such proximity results in audio feedback—caused by a speaker output being picked up by the mic, which re-amplifies the output. Feedback sounds like a kind of high-pitched howling that changes with the distance at which the mic is held from the speaker. So, whenever you mic-record sound with a speaker nearby, the speaker must be turned down and headsets used. Or, the distance between the mic and the speaker must be great enough to prevent feedback. Prevention of feedback is dependent upon the room acoustics, the mic, and the speaker, and must be determined anew in each situation.

Timing is important. Know the required length of each sound segment (such as the prelude phone conversation above), and after it has passed, turn it down. Otherwise, recording noise will be picked up on the tape. Bringing in and fading out various tracks is often effective. Practice and experiment will help you produce creative and exciting sound. Listen.

LIGHTING

In other picture-making media such as photography and film, lighting techniques are based on careful calculations of light and photo emulsions. In video, since the viewer is a small TV set which approximates the visual qualities of the end product, lighting is mostly a question of a careful eye. Foremost for effective video lighting is to know what quality image you want and to have basic but versatile equipment to achieve that quality.

EQUIPMENT

Halogen lamps (see fig. 4:14) are those which have a tungsten filament surrounded by a gas such as iodine or bromine. The bulb is made of quartz, which can sustain high temperatures without melting. This combination of elements allows the tungsten filament to be placed close to the glass bulb, reducing the size of the unit.

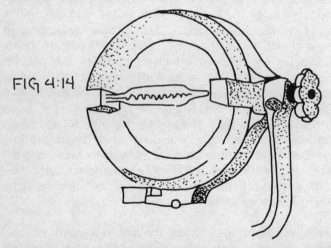

FIG 4:14

Halogen bulbs, or as they are more commonly called, **quartz lights**, are self-cleaning. Therefore the color temperature (discussed shortly) and the light output remain fairly constant. They have a longer life than larger bulbs of equal output and do not produce the filament noise usually associated with large-bulb filaments operated on AC circuits.

Quartz lights are compact and come with housings which are easily carried and mounted. These lights can be equipped with moveable reflectors for directing the beam. Stands for quartz lights are lightweight and easily set up. Portable units which operate off rechargeable batteries can be purchased. And although quartz lights do not fit standard bulb sockets, adaptors are available. All in all, halogen lights are the most basic yet versatile lighting equipment. They should meet almost all your lighting needs.

COLOR TEMPERATURE

Temperature is a measure of the energy of molecular motion. It is theoretically impossible for temperature to be less than -273° C. All molecular motion ceases at that point. As heat is applied, an object emits radiation. There is a certain range of temperatures related to radiation in the visible portion of the electromagnetic spectrum. This **color temperature** is measured on the Kelvin scale, which has a 0°-base equal to -273° C.

A substance which radiates and absorbs light with 100% efficiency is called a **black body**. Black body is an idealized concept; there is no such 100% efficient substance in the universe. Sorry. But there are many substances which act similarly.

Sunlight—one of those "almost" black bodies—has a color temperature, around noon, of 5,400° K (Kelvin). Sunlight near sunrise or sunset is about 2,000° K. Early morning and late afternoon sunlight is about 4,300° K. The light of the summer sky varies from 9,500° K to as much as 30,000° K. A 100-watt household bulb is 2,900° K, and a candle flame is about 1,850° K. A 500-watt photoflood is 3,400° K. Many photo-lights are sold under the name of their color temperature, such as a "3,200° K photographic lamp."

As a black body's temperature increases, it radiates more light in higher frequencies. Thus, temperatures in the range of 5,500°–6,000° K are rich in the blue-violet portion of the spectrum. Temperatures (usually those of artificial illumination) of 3,000° K are deficient in blue-violet and heavy in the red and orange portion of the spectrum.

In color video, color temperature is important. Thus, filters which are attached to 3,200° K and 3,400° K lamps act to provide a natural daylight balance. Such filters, called **dichroic filters**, reflect the red light back toward the lamp and allow the blue light to pass. They are mainly used when quartz illumination is employed outdoors or when a window-light effect is desirable indoors. Keep in mind that filters, though an aid in giving a light balance, decrease a lamp's brightness.

FOOTCANDLES AND CANDLES PER SQUARE FOOT

Another measure of light is **footcandles**. One footcandle equals the intensity of illumination produced one foot away by one candle. **Incident light exposure meters** provide footcandle measurements.

Candles per square foot, on the other hand, is a measure of the brightness of a lit surface, and is dependent on the intensity of light reaching the surface and the inherent reflectivity of the surface. **Reflected light exposure meters** provide candle-per-square-foot measurements.

PHOTOFLOODS

To return to equipment: Besides halogen lamps, there are **photoflood lamps**, which are more like common household lightbulbs. Photofloods are available in various power ratings, from 100 watts to 1,000 watts, and fit standard sockets of several sizes. Their color temperatures range from about 2,900° K to 3,400° K, but decrease with age. They also change in color temperature with changes in line voltage. The higher the voltage the bluer the light, and the lower the voltage the redder

the light. As a rule of thumb, a one-volt change equals a change of 10° K.

Clamps, reflectors, and stands easily can be used with photofloods. Minimal for any basic, versatile lighting equipment are several aluminum reflector holders with squeeze clamps and several 500-watt, 3,200° K or 3,400° K photoflood lamps. In some photofloods, reflectors are built in.

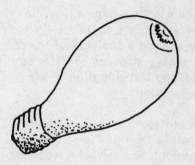

PORTABLE REFLECTORS

The terms *keylight*, *backlight*, and *fill-light* are found in lighting jargon. **Keylight** covers the subject as the primary source of illumination. **Backlight** illuminates the subject from behind. **Fill-lighting** provides an additional light source to soften shadows and decrease contrast.

In the outdoors, the use of reflectors can lessen harsh or contrasty shadows. Simply, a **reflector** is a fairly large white or silvery surface, even a piece of paper, which can be either held or attached to a stand. It is positioned so that the light bounces off it in the direction of the subject and the area that is to be filled. Workable reflectors can be made from white cloth, a white umbrella, aluminum foil stretched over a piece of cardboard, etc. Even a white wall, if in a convenient location, can serve as a reflector.

LIGHTING METHODS: OUTDOOR

Remember the only cardinal rule of video: *Never shoot the sun*; it shoots back, and never misses damaging vidicons. If you are satisfied with what you see in the viewer, then proceed. Once again, the criteria of good picture-making in video are the same as they are in other media: clarity of image (focus and proper light) and composition. As discussed in this section (page 141), a moving picture must also have continuity and stability.

When panning with a camera, keep in mind that an outdoor scene is subject to many light changes. Before taping, try to have a trial run of the camera moves you expect to make, in order to determine which lighting changes will demand alteration of the lens aperture or of the camera position.

Reflectors are seldom used outdoors. The essence of black-and-white taping is to obtain the immediacy of a "real" situation. Conceivably, when in production with a script and having a prescribed scene in mind, more precise lighting than that which is naturally available might be required. However, this has not been my experience, and is mentioned more to suggest alternatives than to pass on a technique.

LIGHTING METHODS: INDOOR

In order to shoot titles or photographs (in fact, anything two-dimensional), use two lights placed at the sides of the camera as indicated in the drawing (4:15). The camera is best set on a tripod at the same height and parallel to the two-dimensional surface plane. It is often advisable to use a live feed so you can more precisely position the title in the frame of the picture tube.

The basic lighting setup (prescribed in all lighting manuals) is to locate the keylight and fill-light on opposite sides of the camera, and in front of the subject (see fig. 4:15). In addition, a backlight can be used to outline the subject. The ratio of the amount of keylight to backlight should be either 4:1 or 2:1. Additional lights can be incorporated to expand this basic formula. Reflectors can be used to soften or direct beams of light. Experimentation is the key to good lighting. It is wise and expeditious to set the lights and then shoot some tape for a quick look at how the setup is working—again, one of the advantages of videotape; it shouldn't be overlooked.

The height of individual lights can vary according to the desired effect. Lights aiming down on a subject will light the subject's topside, leaving shadows on the underside and casting shadows downward. Lights aiming up at a subject will light the underside and cast shadows upward. Again, experimentation is in order.

Fluorescent lighting presents one unique problem: It has no measurable color temperature because of other radiation inherent in it. For black-and-white video fluorescent lighting can provide sufficient illumination, but must be carefully used since it generates a low hum or buzz that is picked up by the audio system. Careful mic-ing can minimize the hum.

Finally, let me emphasize that available light is better to employ than artificial, whether outdoors or indoors. This is admittedly a point of aesthetics, but the natural light of a situation, even if indoors, and even if increased in level but not in flavor, seems to me the best light you can shoot by.

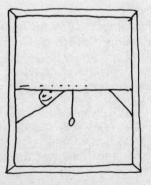

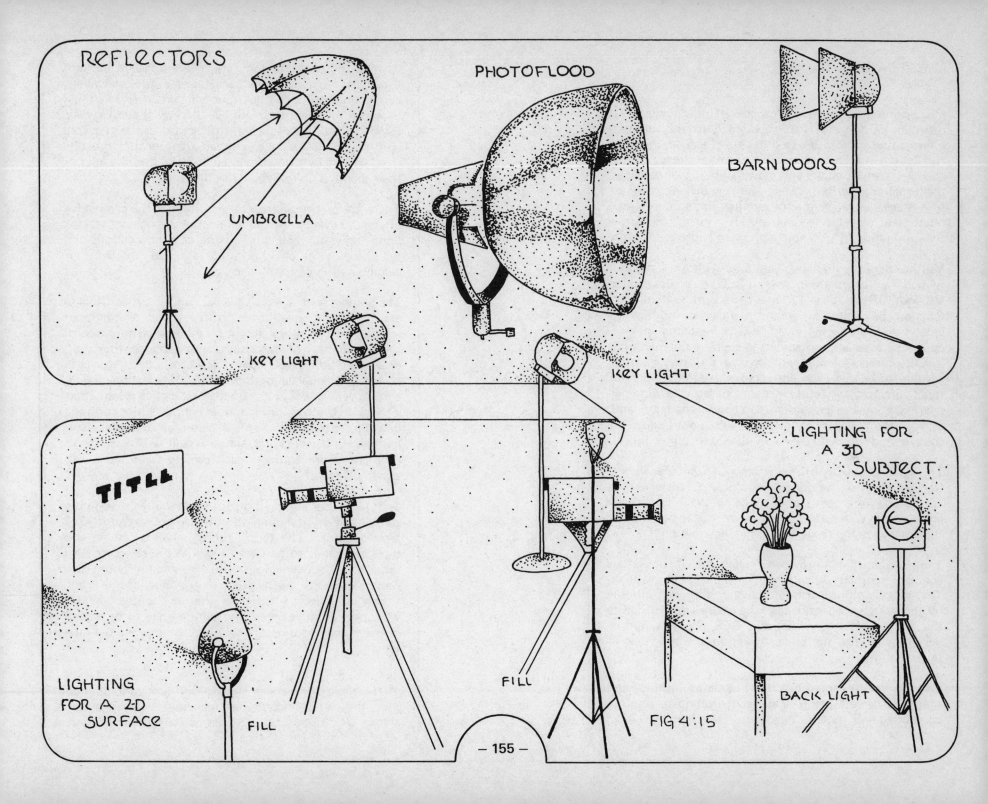

REFLECTORS

PHOTOFLOOD

BARN DOORS

UMBRELLA

KEY LIGHT

KEY LIGHT

LIGHTING FOR A 3D SUBJECT

TITLE

LIGHTING FOR A 2-D SURFACE

FILL

FILL

BACK LIGHT

FIG 4:15

MULTI-CAMERA TAPING
SEAMLESS SHOWS

Multi-camera taping is the process of producing a program in its entirety, from beginning to end, without interruption. It can be used in lieu of assembling shots and lengths of tape to create a video sequence full of changing camera angles and movements. For interviews, theatrical productions, or any events which are confined to a stage, arena, studio, or gymnasium, a coordinated number of cameras feeding a VTR will make possible the production of a complete program without editing.

Multi-camera taping cannot be done without a switcher (which may or may not have an SEG). As discussed in **VIDEOWORKS** (page 120), a variety of switching effects can be used between any two camera inputs. The videomaker producing a single-camera taping may require one assistant to handle the sound equipment, but a multi-camera taping will involve the energies of a number of people: camera people; a switcher operator (tech director); a sound system operator (audio engineer) who may need assistants to handle the mics; and, as is often the case, a director who coordinates the cameras and the switcher via an intercom connection.

The basic problems of multi-camera taping involve setting up the vast amount of equipment (video, audio, lights, and intercom), and orienting the crew to the limits under which they are to work (scene boundaries, camera angles and movements, mic sensitivity, etc.).

The drawing (4:16) provides a schematic of the various connections made in setting up a three-camera system. The preview monitors should be placed for easy viewing by the switcher operator, and the entire setup placed so the director (in some cases the SEG operator him- or herself) can view the scene of action and the video at the same time.

The equipment should be placed as far as possible from the scene to be taped so that mechanical noise from the equipment will not be picked up by the mics. Also,

when using the intercom, voice levels should be kept low. Since the equipment and scene may be far apart, connecting cables can be a nuisance and therefore must be carefully taped down to avoid tripping people. Mic cable laid out across a path of action can be covered with rugs. If mics are suspended, their location must be checked out by camera people to make sure the mics or their shadows do not appear in the scene.

There are several approaches in directing the camera for effective coverage of the action: assigning zones; covering individual subjects; fixing camera locations and type of shots; making no predetermined directives; or a combination of approaches.

The zoning system works by designating a specific camera to cover a specific area of the scene. The number and size of the zones should be established to cover all the possibilities of the action. For instance, four cameras could effectively cover a soccer game, each one covering its quarter of the field. On the other hand, zone coverage would not be the best choice for an interview or talk show—programs taking place in a confined location within which the motion of the subjects is limited. Such programs, static to begin with, would appear still more static if each camera stayed in an assigned place.

The fixed camera method usually requires a **shooting script**—a plan of action for the camera operators and tech director. The script indicates which camera and type of shot is to be used as well as the sequence of a series of shots. It is not unusual to employ two multi-camera systems, each producing a tape of the same action by following different shooting scripts. In this way, post-production editing can be done to cover any mistakes made during the taping, or to improve the final tape.

If the portapak camera is used with a handholding device, the camera people can maneuver with great freedom. Or, tripods can be used to fix camera locations and the types of shots the cameras are to provide. A multi-camera freestyle is often used for taping rock concerts. Everyone and everything gets into the act—colliding camera people, dangling cables, flaring lights, swinging directors, freaked-out switcher operators.

The basic effects produced by the switcher are: cuts from camera to camera; fades from camera to camera; with an SEG, camera-to-camera wipes, either vertical, horizontal, or from a corner; and horizontal and vertical split-screens to display part of an image from each of two cameras.

The vertically split screen can be useful when taping quick interchanges of dialogue. To best accomplish a vertical split-screen effect, one camera should keep its subject on one side of the frame and the other camera should keep its subject on the other side. Make sure that the heads of both subjects face to the center of the frame if they are in profile. If not, your subjects may end up on screen facing in different directions.

A genlock (figs. 3:57 & 4:16) allows a direct camera input to be mixed with a prerecorded signal, an effect often used in titling. With **keying**—the superimposition of one preset signal over another—the genlock can provide combinations of imagery from indoors and outdoors, or from scenes taped on separate occasions. For instance, you could mix a pretaped aerial view of the sea with a couple on a carpet, to produce the effect that the couple is on a flying carpet over the sea. For best results when working with a black-and-white key, the signals of the two inputs must be of distinctly different overall gray tones. Color keying is much simpler, since the signal denoting a particular color is easily distinguishable from others.

As discussed in this section (page 137), a studio or edit VTR should be used for multi-camera taping. Studio and edit VTRs usually have both AGC and manual sound- and video-level controls, *line* and *mic* sound inputs, and *line* and *camera* inputs for video. The *line* input is used to feed the video signal from a switcher to a VTR. Portable switchers are available for use with two portapak cameras and a portapak VTR. Such switchers provide both switching and fading and are battery-powered for field use.

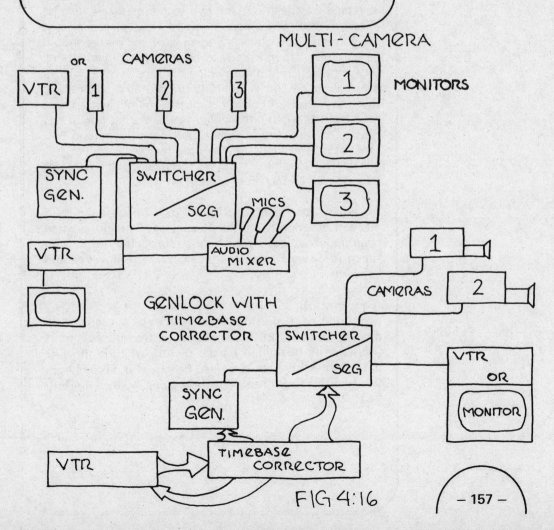

MULTI-CAMERA

FIG 4:16

EDITING
MECHANICAL EDITING

There are two methods for editing videotapes. Most often, segments are butted together by electronically transferring them from original tapes to a second tape—**electronic editing**. **Mechanical editing**—cutting and taping together pieces of the original tapes—is an obsolete method that was widely employed before electronic editing VTRs were available. Although rarely employed now, mechanical editing is worth discussing here, since it is also the process used to repair worn tapes.

A splicing block is used for mechanical editing. It has a groove into which the tape snugly fits. Along one edge of the groove is a set of marks which coincide with the control track pulses printed on the tape. Using an iron oxide solution, which makes the magnetized fields visible on the tape, the control track pulses can be lined up with the marks on the block. Also on the splicing block is a razor-blade guide which intersects the tape groove. The guide ensures that the tape is cut diagonally, precisely between two pulse marks.

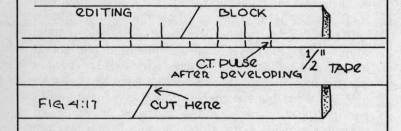

FIG 4:17

The editing procedure begins with marking the videotape at the point at which it is to be cut (see fig. 4:17). If you are cutting for picture, the VTR must be stopped when the picture can be viewed on the screen. If you cut for sound, which is often the case, the VTR must be stopped just *after* you hear the sound. Then the tape should be marked with a white, oil base, felt-tip marker at the appropriate place—for picture at the center of the video head drum, for sound at the audio head. Let the mark dry completely, since oil buildups on the heads can cause dropout and head clogging.

Once marked, the tape should be lifted out of its path and placed—oxide-side up, marked-side down—into the groove with the mark on the blade guide. A small amount of the iron oxide solution should then be placed on the tape and allowed to dry. Once the printed signals are visible, the tape must be slid to either the right or left to align the tape's marks with the block's. With a sharp single-edged blade, the tape should next be cut using the blade guide. Wipe off the excess solution with a soft, clean cloth. Do not rub the tape hard or you may remove the tape's oxide, too.

Say tape has been cut for two segments that are to be joined. Both pieces are clean and are placed on the block, oxide-side down. The ends of the pieces should be carefully brought edge to edge without overlapping. Half-inch-wide aluminum adhesive tape is then placed over the splice and is carefully pressed on the videotape to ensure that no corners stick up. (Any such corners may be snagged by the video heads during playback.) Finally, the aluminum tape should be cut, top and bottom, using the walls of the tape groove as guides. A mechanical splicing kit can be purchased which contains a few blades and a roll of aluminum tape.

Touching videotape contributes to dropout, since skin oils will deteriorate the oxide coating. Therefore, when handling tape, wash your hands thoroughly before you touch it, or wear clean cotton gloves. The gloves should be washed frequently.

A mechanical edit has a unique look. It appears as a horizontal wipe starting at the bottom of the screen and moving to the top. The sound of the preceding cut overlaps the beginning of the picture of the following cut. Remember that the video head is about 6 inches in front of the audio head. If done sloppily, the wipe will flag.

ELECTRONIC EDITING

As covered in **VIDEOWORKS** (page 81), an edit VTR must have capstan servo. It must also have an arming stage that allows the incoming video signal's vertical sync to drive the edit VTR in playback, thereby aligning the edit VTR with the feed VTR. After the edit is made, the edit VTR's capstan servo (in *record*) is driven by the feed VTR's vertical sync.

Remember that the best edit VTRs are capable of **vertical interval** editing, which means that the switch between segments of information occurs not in the middle of a field of information, but only during the vertical blanking. Edits which are not vertical interval are accompanied by a momentary flash or moire pattern which can be disturbing.

The monitors necessary for viewing the tapes must be accompanied by the appropriate cables for connecting VTR-to-VTR and VTRs to the monitors. As to the sound-editing side of things, refer to *Sound* (page 150).

PORTAPAK EDITING

There are a number of alternative editing setups, depending on the equipment available. Though most portapaks have a *playback* mode, the technology of these modes is not highly refined. They are therefore not recommended for editing unless there's no alternative.

In cases in which a rough edit is useful, say, out in the field, two portapaks can be used. They should be plugged into each other, one being the feed and the other the editor. It is necessary to wire a connection between them (see fig. 4:18).

The trick is to use the still control of the portapak as the editor. Wind back the feed VTR from the point to be edited; a few seconds of rewind will do. With *still* in

position holding the reels in place, put the edit VTR into *record*. Then put the feed VTR into *play*; as the point of the tape which is to be edited appears, release the still control on the edit VTR. To cut off the feed signal, use the still control of the edit VTR instead of *stop*. In this way, you can maintain optimum tape tension and gain the best possible results.

The look of a portapak-to-portapak edit is similar to an in-camera edit. Momentary **glitch** (obscured picture) and instability occur, but they are quickly overcome. When taking a lot of time to search out a segment of tape, it is best to cut off the power on the edit VTR so that the heads—because they continually revolve in the *still* position—are not damaged. The revolving head can also wear down the oxide on the tape at the point of contact. When power is turned on again, hold the *still* control in position; the tape tension will be restored and the system will be ready to go.

For viewing when using a portapak, it is necessary to have an RF modulator, a connector, and a TV receiver. Unless modified, most portapaks do not have the connection capability for simultaneous line input and line output.

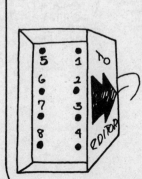

REWIRE 8-PIN AS FOLLOWS FOR PORTAPAK EDIT.

CHANGE PIN 2 TO PIN 4, PIN 6 TO PIN 3, AND CLIP ENDS OF HANGING WIRE. MARK PLUG WITH ARROW TO SHOW DIRECTION OF SIGNAL.

FIG 4:18

The portapak can also be used as the feed VTR in conjunction with an edit VTR. There are two ways to set up a portapak and edit VTR for editing. The most common is a direct line connection between the portapak and edit VTR. The other method is a line connection from the portapak to a monitor, which is then connected to the edit VTR. The edit VTR is set in the *TV* mode which is used for taping broadcast fare off a TV receiver. This method, commonly called *Off/Air* recording, will be discussed later in this section (page 170). It is important to note that this setup is used for editing between two incompatible VTRs; i.e., a pre-1970 Sony CV series VTR with the newly established EIAJ-1 Standard, a Sony AV series VTR.

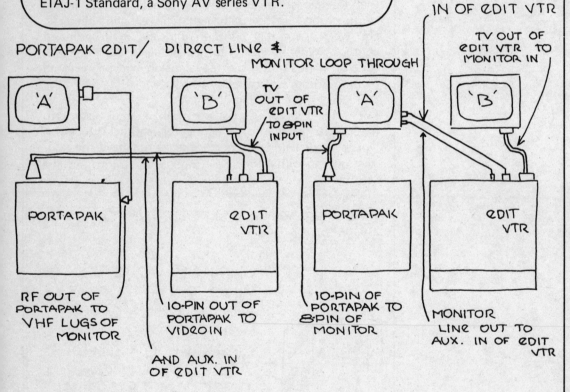

PORTAPAK EDIT/ DIRECT LINE & MONITOR LOOP THROUGH

MONITOR VIDEO OUT TO VIDEO IN OF EDIT VTR

TV OUT OF EDIT VTR TO MONITOR IN

TV OUT OF EDIT VTR TO 8 PIN INPUT

'A'   'B'   'A'   'B'

PORTAPAK   EDIT VTR   PORTAPAK   EDIT VTR

RF OUT OF PORTAPAK TO VHF LUGS OF MONITOR

10-PIN OUT OF PORTAPAK TO VIDEO IN

AND AUX. IN OF EDIT VTR

10-PIN OF PORTAPAK TO 8 PIN OF MONITOR

MONITOR LINE OUT TO AUX. IN OF EDIT VTR

FIG 4:19

COUNTERS FOR BACKSPACING

The most broadly utilized video setups consist of studio VTRs and editors. If both VTRs are capstan servo, the chances for better edits are increased. Monitor connection is preferably made via line rather than RF. The tape counter devices on most ½-inch VTRs are a major stumbling block to easy editing. They count revolutions of the take-up reel, rather than tape length or tape time.

In editing, the idea is to back up both VTRs, put them in *forward* at the same time, and have them both be where you want them at the instant of edit. Some 1-inch VTRs are equipped with counters that provide digital readouts in tenths of a second. They operate by counting pulses which are laid down on the audio track. These pulses can be read in *rewind*, so precision backspacing can be accomplished.

When using the counters on ½-inch VTRs, they are **zeroed up** (set at 000) at that point on the tape where the edit is to occur. The tape is then rewound to about 996 on the counter. Both VTRs must be rewound. Put both machines into the *pause* or *still* position so the heads are up to speed when they are put in *forward*. When both VTRs simultaneously reach 000 the edit is made—the information has been transferred to the edited tape.

Remember that the counter measures revolutions of the take-up reel. If the amount of tape on the take-up reels of both VTRs is the same, the counter reading on the editor and the VTR will coincide. If the amount of tape is different, the counter readings will not coincide, as long as backspacing has been the same for both. In these cases, the thing to do is rewind both VTRs from their zero points to 996. Start them simultaneously, and when 000 shows up on the editor's counter, stop both VTRs simultaneously. You will then be able to see the discrepancy between the two counters. Let's say the feed VTR's counter is at 999 when the editor's counter is at 000. To compensate for this discrepancy, the feed VTR's counter should be backspaced to 997 when the edit counter reads 996.

Ultimately, you must develop the coordination to enable you to watch the numbers and the information on each of the tapes and make quick decisions on whether to edit or not. Mistaken or bad edits can be done over. However, redoing an edit may result in clipping off the previous edit.

Another method for backspacing is to use editing guides. Such guides indicate the number of revolutions the reel makes every six seconds. About six seconds is usually the proper amount of backspacing time. A set of these guides has been designed to fit onto 5-inch (½-hour) reels, and are freely available to videomakers—so here they are passed on to you (see below).

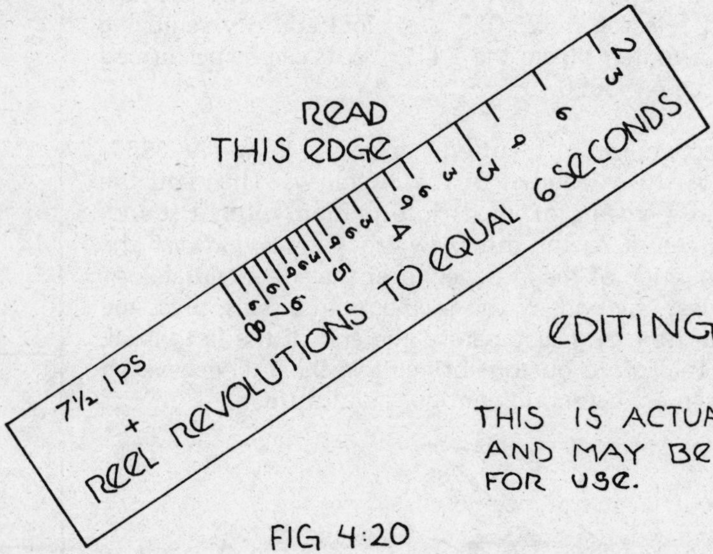

READ
THIS EDGE

7½ IPS
+
REEL REVOLUTIONS TO EQUAL 6 SECONDS

EDITING GUIDE

THIS IS ACTUAL SIZE
AND MAY BE TRACED
FOR USE.

FIG 4:20

A stopwatch can also be used in editing. Backspace to a set number and then time the forward movement to 000. Say that from 996 to 000 on the edit VTR amounts to six seconds. Starting from 996 on the feed deck, try and err until you find the number on the feed deck's counter which equals the six seconds of tape play on the editor. This method is precise, but it can be time-consuming.

SKEW AND UNDERSCANNING

As mentioned in **VIDEOWORKS** (page 86), the *skew* controls tape tension. On ½-inch VTRs, the *skew* is a small knob that adjusts an arm placed at the beginning of the tape path as the tape is fed from the feed reel. Also, remember that tape-stretching is a contributing factor to the timebase instability prevalent in ½-inch VTRs. When editing, using the *skew* makes it possible to lessen the effect of incorrect tape tension (the visual result of which is a bending at the top of the picture). The *skew* should be employed in the playback of the feed tape before the edit.

Underscanning the monitor helps to bring any skew problems into view. By shrinking the size of the scan within the TV tube, you can see the fully scanned area usually obscured by full scanning. Adjusting the skew as a tape is played back allows you to see the effect on the picture. Actually, using an underscanned monitor, you will see that the vertical lines bend at the bottom of the picture. Adjustments to correct this bending result in aligning the bottom of one field with the top of the following field. Thus there is some compensation for stretched tape.

E-E MODE

Remember, a VTR can be put into *record* without running the tape. This mode is referred to as the **E-E mode** —electronics-to-electronics. When it is necessary to set levels before editing (i.e., for video or sound), the edit VTR can be put into *E-E* and the feed information run through the system.

INSERT EDITS

Insert editing, as discussed in **VIDEOWORKS** (page 88), drops a segment of information into an existing edited tape on which you want to replace a segment. In most ½-inch edit VTRs, the insert replaces both the video and audio track, using the existing control track instead. However, it is possible to retain the original sound track when making video inserts by covering the audio erase and record heads with masking tape. Be careful not to mask the video erase and control track portions of the heads.

EDITING PROCEDURES

For editing purposes, it is important to preview and catalog tapes for easy and convenient access to the required information. Previewing is done simply by watching the tapes and cataloging the segments, using the counter provided on the VTR. For instance, zero up at the beginning of the tape. On your catalog sheet, note that 000 to, say, 190 is continuous shooting out window of car driving down country road. Note eye-catching shots or sequences that you'll want to use—056, old barn; 101, Elaine's hair blowing into frame; etc.

The more thorough your notes and the more careful your counter-watching, the easier editing will be. Once into editing, the situation often will warrant the use of a segment from one tape, then another, then back to the first, and so on. To facilitate knowing where you are, place a postage-stamp-size piece of paper in the tape that you are taking off the machine. When that reel is used again, you can easily return to the marked place.

When finishing an edit, instead of putting the edit VTR into *stop*, it is best to overcome the input signal by using the video and sound level controls. Especially when working with sound, you can then stop the incoming information exactly where you want. In order to do so, set the manual sound and video levels to zero signal (so that no signal is passed). During your edit, use the AGC setting for the levels. When you reach the end of an edit, quickly switch into the manual mode (set at zero). It is advisable to allow a bit more picture to pass after the sound has been cut off so you have a recorded signal into which to edit the next segment. It helps to allow the extra bit of picture to pass if your next segment is edited slightly late. You will have a smooth picture transition, though the sound might skip a beat.

An **L-cut** is an edit in which the soundtrack remains constant, while the picture information switches from the source of the sound to other visual material. It can include both the audio and video track of an interview, as well as video cutaways to the subjects being discussed, followed by a return to the original scene, while the audio track continues uninterrupted.

An L-cut can be easily performed by edit VTRs which are equipped with *video only* insert capability. The Sony AV 3650 must be modified to enable it to perform L-cuts, but the modification required is very simple. In the service manual for the AV 3650, under *Record Linkage, Exploded View*, selector 3-604-152 and spring selector 3-625-023 are pictured. By removing these two items from the VTR, L-cuts can be performed with the AV 3650.

To accomplish an L-cut edit using the Sony AV 3650, simply edit a segment of the interview. Then edit the desired segments of visual information without sound. Next, return to the interview tape, and *sound dub* the continuation of the interview over the edited visuals. As you near the end of the segments of visuals, press the *edit* button, and just before the end of the last visual, press the *record* button—bringing in the interview visual as the interview sound continues undisturbed.

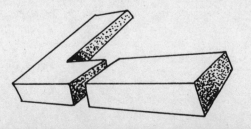

Always make it a policy to check your edits, using the VTR counter. Rewind the tape to a point before 000—the edit—and then roll it through. If it's a bad edit you will see glitch or some other form of instability. For more precise edit checking, an oscilloscope can be used. The oscilloscope makes it possible to examine the waveform of the signal and electronically determine whether the edit is either as good as can be or is really bad. For more on oscilloscopes, see **MAINTENANCE AND REPAIR** (page 179).

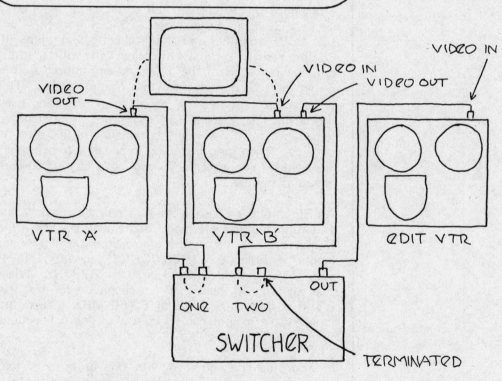

FIG 4:21

SWITCHER EDITING

A video switcher (called an SEG by most ½-inch-video users), can be used in two ways in the editing process: combining taped information with live camera information; or combining two sources of taped information.

Combining a live camera image and taped information can be done with a genlock (see **VIDEOWORKS**, page 121). Genlocking is used for titling. Title cards should have a 3 by 4 aspect ratio. Within the rectangle of the title card is the safe title area—a centered rectangle, which is 75% to 90% as large as the card itself (see fig. 3:57). The safe title area should contain all of the card's information, in order to ensure that the information appears within the area of the screen. The live camera is set on the title cards (as fig. 3:57 indicates). While making edits along conventional lines, using the fade control of the switcher, the title card can be superimposed over the visual information on the tape.

Another mixing possibility is to use the camera to shoot off a monitor instead of a title card. The image from a monitor-to-camera is always somewhat degraded, but varies depending on the quality of the monitor and of the original taped information. Obviously, the combination of high-contrast taped information and a high-resolution monitor will re-record a visually acceptable image. This process is called **scan conversion**, and will be discussed in this section (page 167).

Two separate sources of taped information can be fed through the switcher to an edit VTR. The drawing (4:21) shows two ways in which to set up this process—useful almost exclusively when you have several tapes of the same event, such as a music performance, an interview, a conference, or a play. The tapes must be shot on separate systems which are linked together with the same sync generator. Using the switcher allows for cutting back and forth between any two of the tapes, approximating a live multi-camera taping.

If the tapes are recorded by separate systems sharing a single sync drive source, one tape can be cut into the other to achieve the live multi-camera mixed effect. In this case, the conventional editing setup is used for doing insert edits only. One of the tapes is the edit tape, while the other tape provides the feed information to be inserted into the first.

Camera cuts do not edit cleanly, and should be avoided like the plague. When editing a segment of information, make sure the edit is begun well past the glitch of the camera cut.

As mentioned in this section (page 141), try, when shooting, to anticipate shots and trigger the VTR so as not to lose the opening seconds of a scene during the editing process.

The art of electronic editing in ½-inch and 1-inch video has definite limits. Very quick cutting cannot be satisfactorily achieved. Freeze-framing lacks signal stability and should be avoided. The use of lap dissolves, fades, and wipes for editing transitions is not possible without a video synthesizer and a 2-inch editor—both relatively expensive. For the most part, the art of editing is confined to assembling segments of information in sequence. Length of individual edits, sequences of edits, and the overall duration of the tape are critical aspects of producing good videotapes.

SHOWING

Using a VTR for playback, videotapes can be shown either on monitors or receivers. A single VTR can feed any number of TV sets if proper amplification is provided. Or, a showing can consist of an array of TVs, each fed by its own VTR. Unlike film, TV can be viewed clearly in the light, so situations for showing are many—on the street, in galleries, lobbies, living rooms, etc.

As discussed in **VIDEOWORKS** (page 96), a receiver is a tuner which selects RF TV signals from the air. Using an RF modulator, a TV channel frequency can be modulated by a VTR's video signal, and in this way any home TV set can become a means for showing tapes. The RF modulator is an essential tool for cable TV programming.

MULTI-MONITOR

A **splitter** is a device used to distribute a video signal from an RF modulator to more than one TV receiver. Utilizing a splitter, up to four sets can be fed from a single VTR without signal loss. (To feed more than four sets an RF amplifier must be used.) Coaxial cable with 75-ohm resistance is used to connect the splitter to the antenna terminals of the TVs, and any unused splitter outlet must be terminated with a 75-ohm resistor. This termination prevents the signal from reflecting back down the line, causing bad reception. The standard impedance for TV antenna terminals is a 300-ohm resistance. Therefore, matching impedance transformers are needed to connect the 75-ohm cable to the 300-ohm antenna terminal.

An RF amplifier is also necessary when the coaxial cable extension is extremely long. Remember, the higher the frequency of a signal, the greater the signal loss per length of cable (see **VIDEOWORKS**, page 119). In ½-inch VTRs the video signal is about 2.2 MHz. When that signal is RF modulated, on channel 3 for instance, it's at a frequency range of 60–66 MHz. Therefore longer cable lengths can be used with line connections than with RF connections.

Monitors can be equipped with one or both of two types of inputs: 8-pin and UHF connectors. Many monitors also have video outputs for feeding signal to other monitors. When connecting a line of monitors it is necessary to use a 75-ohm resistor to terminate the signal at the last monitor in line. If there are more than ten monitors being fed by a single VTR, a video amplifier must be used to compensate for signal loss to those extra sets.

RF DISTRIBUTION

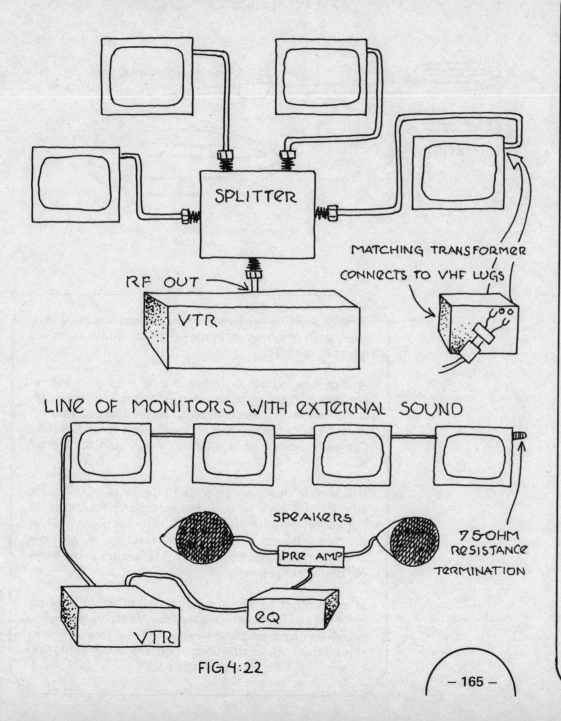

SPLITTER

MATCHING TRANSFORMER
CONNECTS TO VHF LUGS

RF OUT

VTR

LINE OF MONITORS WITH EXTERNAL SOUND

SPEAKERS

PRE AMP

75 OHM RESISTANCE TERMINATION

VTR

EQ

FIG 4:22

To enhance sound quality, external speakers can be used. The sound from the VTR must be run through a pre-amplifier before being connected to the speakers. The TV speakers should be turned down completely when using external speakers. Using a pre-amp alone will enable some tonal control, and using it with an EQ will permit still more precise tonal control.

MOBILITY

Using battery-powered equipment allows for mobile showings. Small monitors or receivers can be battery-powered, as are portapaks. If a car is handy, power can be obtained from its 12-volt battery either by a direct tap or by using a car battery cord which plugs into the car's cigarette lighter. Taping or showing while in a moving car or while it's idling can cause interference in the picture and sound, due to ignition noise. Ignition noise suppressors are available which can be put over the spark plugs to eliminate this problem. Street showings are generally done with power borrowed or bought from a nearby store or house. However, streetlamp bases are frequently equipped with usable outlets, and if you plan ahead you can request permission from the municipality to plug into a conveniently positioned lamppost.

VIDEO THEATRE

Video theatres have no specific forms. They can be places for entertainment, meetings, forums, etc. A theatre can be established in a loft, a basement, a church hall, or any space large enough to accommodate the desired audience.

Video theatres can often be set up to encourage interaction among people. Comfortable and intimate seating, for instance, in groups around totems of TVs stimulates exchanges among the viewers. Live recording and instant playback of an audience's reaction to and discussion of tapes can be a distinguishing addition to the video theatre experience. Audience-assisted productions -in-process are another possibility unique to video theatre.

Since VTRs are not very noisy, they can be concealed or left in sight, depending on your preference, when setting up the theatre. The number and placement of monitors; the sitting, reclining, and standing arrangements; the light level; volume of sound; and even the temperature of the space are all elements to be considered in setting up the environment. Equipment resources, size of space, and budget for alterations need be the only limitations.

VIDEO PROJECTION

A video projector can direct an image onto a screen, a wall, a suspended white sheet, or any large, flat surface. However, inexpensive models can only project low-resolution images which can be viewed only in the dark. Remember, the image is no longer the result of the transduction of electrical energy to light from a phosphor-coated tube. Instead, it's a projected beam of light reflecting off a surface.

Large images can enhance certain situations. For instance, in a gallery they can be wall-size video artworks; or at a rock concert a live-feed projected image of the performers can be used as a backdrop.

Specific video projection units are discussed in **VIDEOWORKS** (page 131).

DUPLICATING AND TRANSFERRING
DUPLICATING

One simple and direct method of copying tapes is available to anyone who has access to two VTRs. One VTR plays back the **master** (original) tape; the other VTR records the **slave** tape. It takes the length of the tape to copy it; there's no expediting the process. The imperfections of the master are passed onto the slave, and are

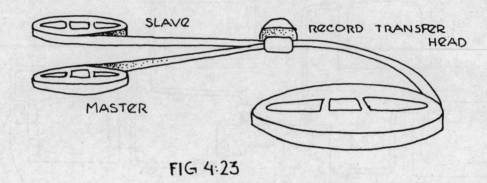

BIFILAR DUPLICATION

SLAVE

RECORD TRANSFER HEAD

MASTER

FIG 4·23

compounded by whatever imperfections the slave contains, such as dropouts in the tape, instability, or record errors in the VTR.

A copy made from an original tape is called a second generation copy, and so on. Since picture resolution and signal quality decrease with succeeding generations, it is best to copy from originals whenever possible. Copies of edited tapes are best made from the master edit.

It is best to duplicate an edited tape by playing it back on the VTR on which it was recorded. Any slight instability in the edits are likely to be less noticeable when the tape is played on its "mother" machine. Any of the VTR combinations covered in this section can serve for duplicating as well.

It is also best to begin copying before actual information begins, in order to allow the VTRs to get up to speed and lock into each other. If the lockup occurs during the transfer of information, signal instability will be seen when the tape is played back.

DYNAMIC DUPLICATION

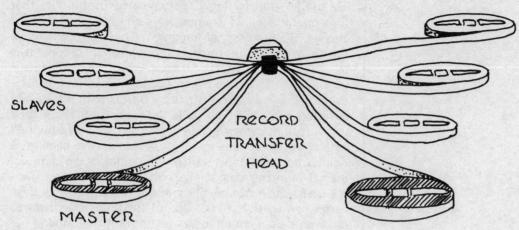

SLAVES

RECORD

TRANSFER

HEAD

MASTER

FIG 4:24

A duplicating method which can be used at home is one in which a camera and monitor are used. This method is called **scan conversion**. Sometimes faint horizontal bars moving upward on the screen are picked up by the camera from the monitor. These bars in fact represent the vertical sync, and they appear if the vertical sync timing differs in the playback VTR and the recording camera. Though picture quality is lost, signal strength and stability are gained. (In VTR-to-VTR copying, a definite loss of signal strength occurs.) A fresh recording from the camera has all the advantages of an original. In instances in which signal strength is more important than the excellence of the picture, use the camera-to-monitor method. Take care to adjust the monitor's contrast and brightness controls in order to obtain an optimum through-the-camera picture.

Not so readily available for home use are AC transfer and thermal duplication processes. Both are methods for quick, multiple duplicating which are offered by video labs serving Big TV operations.

In the first phase of **AC transfer**, a special high-coercivity tape is used. The coercivity of this tape measures 900 oersteds, compared to the 300 oersteds of normal ferric oxide tape. (For more information on coercivity, see **VIDEOWORKS**, page 97.) A VTR must be specially designed to drive such high-energy tape. Such VTRs must also be able to record a mirror image of the original recording. This double recording is necessary since duplication is achieved by oxide-to-oxide contact of the master and the slave tapes.

When the two tapes are brought into contact, they are exposed to a high-frequency AC field. This field acts to agitate the low-coercivity tape, while barely affecting the high-energy tape. When the field is removed, the domains of the copy tape fall into the pattern of the domains of the master. The mirror image of the master produces a ready-for-play image on the copy.

The AC transfer process works poorly at low frequencies and therefore requires that the audio and control track pulses be recorded on the copy by the conventional high-speed transfer method. AC transfer copies also suffer a loss of FM signal. This signal loss is due to the fact that during transfer the ferric oxide tape maintains its full magnetic properties, and these properties inherently oppose the transfer process.

There are two methods for winding the tape in an AC transfer system: dynamic and bifilar. Using the **dynamic** method, three or five 1-hour-long tapes can be copied simultaneously in six minutes. The **bifilar** method duplicates only one tape at a time and delivers an hour-long tape copy in two minutes.

The **thermal duplication** process exploits the characteristics of high-energy chromium dioxide tape. The **Curie point** of this tape (the temperature at which the magnetic properties of the tape are lost) is lower than that of ferric oxide tape. A ferric oxide master is put in contact with a chromium dioxide slave. They are then heated to 125º C—the Curie point of chromium dioxide —and cooled. Due to the proximity of the two tapes, as cooling occurs and the magnetic properties are restored to the chromium dioxide tape its domains fall into the magnetism pattern of the master ferric oxide tape.

The above process produces a mirror image of the original which can then serve as a master for further duplication. A new chromium dioxide slave is heated before contact with the original. Only during cooling are the two tapes brought together. Thus, a chromium dioxide master can duplicate chromium dioxide slaves. The quality of such copies is almost as good as that of the ferric oxide originals. Mirror-image recorders are not necessary when the thermal duplication method is used.

The big problem associated with thermal duplication is that the tape length can be altered by the heating process. Critical tension for each of the tapes must be maintained in both the heating and cooling operations in order to guard against the tape stretching and contracting. Other than that, thermal duplication offers many advantages—a high-performance copy, no need for a high-energy master, simultaneous transfer of audio and control tracks with no need for other heads, and the elimination of the need for a mirror-image recorder.

TRANSFERRING

There are four video transfer processes: TV-to-film; film·to·tape; tape-to-tape; and Off/Air. TV-to-film transferring—**kinescoping**—dates back to early broadcast TV, prior to the existence of videotape. TV shows were recorded on film off monitors. Kinescoping was then the only method for storing and distributing programs. Film-to-tape transferring is accomplished by using a **film chain**—a device originally designed for the broadcasting of kinescopes. Tape-to-tape provides the best results, since it is done by direct manipulation of electronic signals. Broadcast-to-tape—more commonly called Off/Air recording—is simply accomplished with almost any VTR.

TV-TO-FILM

TV-to-film transferring is complicated by the fact that film operates at 24 frames per second, while TV operates at 30 frames per second. Therefore, an image filmed off a TV monitor without special equipment is traversed by some partial frames, which cause the image to flicker. The frames-per-second discrepancy can be overcome by shooting off the monitor with a specially designed camera which pulls the film down faster than ordinary film cameras. These cameras are also equipped with very good lenses. For shooting, the camera is rigidly mounted 1–3 feet from the monitor which measures 3–5 inches diagonally. Special kinescoping films are used which can be black-and-white or color, and reversal or negative. The face of the monitor is read to determine the light-exposure settings for the camera.

Electron beam recording (EBR) is another commonly used (but expensive) process for TV-to-film transfer. In this process the transfer is effected by directly exposing the film to a scanning electron beam. There are two steps in color electron beam recording: First, three film frames are exposed during one video frame, producing one film frame each for red, green, and blue. Second, the three separated color exposures are combined on another film to reconstitute the color image.

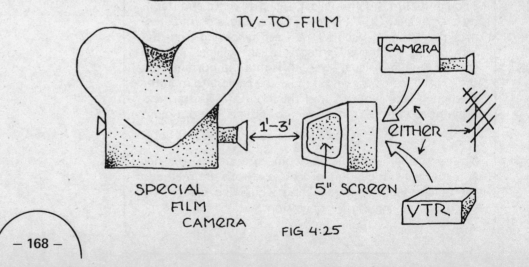

TV-TO-FILM

SPECIAL FILM CAMERA

1'–3'

5" SCREEN

CAMERA

EITHER

VTR

FIG 4:25

FILM-TO-TAPE

Film can be transferred to tape by using a video camera focused on the projected film image. The smaller and more finely resolved the film image, the better the video image. Better results can be obtained by using a rear-projected film image in combination with any video camera and VTR. The film image should be projected small (about 9 by 12 inches) and the video camera placed on a tripod for stability. To ensure proper framing of the film image by the camera, use a monitor with a live feed.

It is preferable, however, to transfer film to tape via a film chain—a film projector directly connected to a TV camera (see fig. 4:27). The projector used in a film chain must be equipped with a five-blade shutter. Often available for use at cable TV studios, film chains are somewhat expensive for the independent videomaker.

TAPE-TO-TAPE

Transferring from format to format, such as ½-inch to 1-inch or ½-inch to 2-inch, is a process much like editing with two VTRs. Connections can be made between the two VTRs, or else the signal from the original-format VTR can be fed to a monitor which then feeds the new-format VTR. Direct line connections can be made from ½-inch to most 1-inch VTRs. Proc amps are often used in the transferring process to improve sync-signal quality. In this way, the 1-inch copy tape can be as good as the original ½-inch tape.

Whenever broadcast standard signals are required, a proc amp and timebase corrector must be used when transferring to a 2-inch quad system. The necessary equipment is expensive and is owned only by cable companies, educational TV facilities, schools, and commercial video labs.

FILM -TO-TAPE

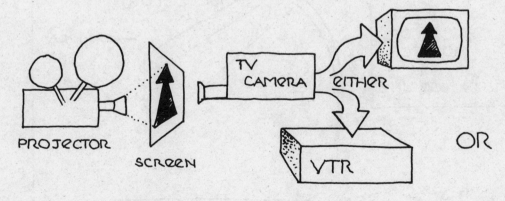

FIG 4:26

OR

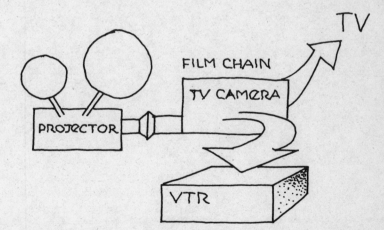

FIG 4:27

OFF/AIR

A broadcast video signal fed to a TV set can easily be connected into any VTR for Off/Air recording (see figs. 4:28–4:29). The TV set must be both a monitor and receiver, and can be connected to the VTR by either UHF or 8-pin connectors. Such monitor/receiver combinations have *air* and *line* switches which determine how the set is to be used. If the monitor is connected to the VTR with an 8-pin connector, and the VTR is in *record* with its mode selector on *TV*, the image on the TV screen will be the same whether the monitor is switched to *air* or *line*. However, it is best to use the *line* setting so that you can monitor the image through the electronics of the VTR—electronics-to-electronics. If a UHF connection is used, the VTR mode selector must be on *line*.

If you wish to stop an Off/Air recording temporarily, for instance, to leave out a commercial, put the VTR into *pause*, while keeping it in *record*. You can start up again whenever you like, obtaining only slight signal disturbance during playback.

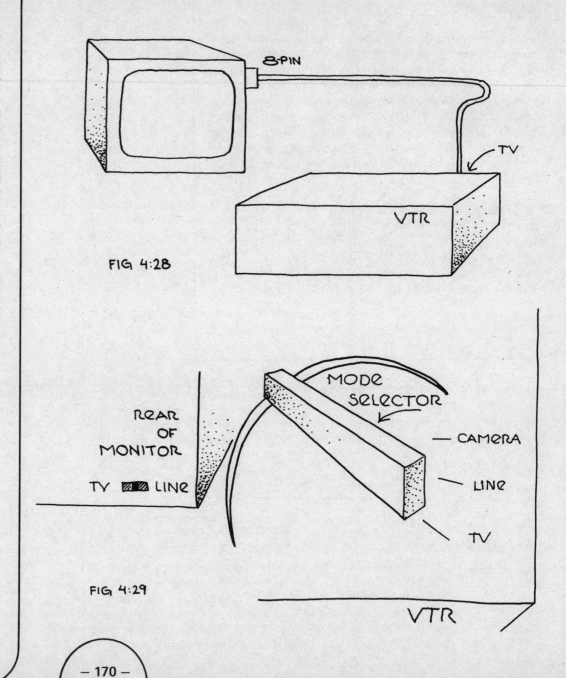

FIG 4:28

FIG 4:29

MAINTENANCE & REPAIR

CARE AND CLEANING
CARE

The automobile is probably one of the most popular machines around. At one time or another, most of us have coaxed, kicked, shyed away from, or felt great pride in a car. Video machines elicit similar responses from their users. Feelings toward such machines can run from reverence to contempt. Our curious reactions to machines can sometimes result in even more curious behavior—petting a camera or clobbering a VTR. But machines don't need emotional relationships; they need care.

Care starts with considering the conditions in which the equipment is to be used. Extremes in humidity, heat, and cold inhibit the proper functioning of electronic circuits. The cold makes tape brittle, and high humidity loosens its oxide coating, which contributes to clogging heads. Dust and smoke (even cigarette smoke) dirty heads and tape.

When using a portapak in extremely cold temperatures (around 32º and below), a blanketlike covering around the VTR will help to keep it operating. On the other hand, in extremely hot (90º and up) and humid (75% and up) climates, frequent cleaning is the only answer. Loosened tape oxide builds up on the erase, video, audio, and control track heads. Control track head clogging is a specially pesky problem since the head can clean itself and clog up again intermittently. Frequent checking of the recorded material via playback can save you from wasting an afternoon of useless taping.

One must also consider the presence of RF signals, which can cause interference patterns in the image. RF signals may come from nearby radio or TV transmitters, and the radiation of these signals can reach the interior of the camera through any openings on it. The interference these signals cause can be seen through the viewfinder. When working in situations in which there is RF radiation, wrap aluminum foil around the camera body. The foil will act as a shield, absorbing the RF radiation.

Care of equipment also includes thorough periodic checkups for missing or loose screws in the camera, mics, VTR, cables, etc. And remember, never point a vidicon camera at the sun or any other intense source of illumination; the light-sensing tube can be irreparably damaged.

CLEANING

The areas of the equipment that must be cleaned frequently are: the tape path; the brushes; the optics; and (though less often) the belts.

The tape path consists of the capstan, the head drum, and all the guides, heads, and rollers which come in contact with the moving tape on the VTR. The two major types of dirt are dust and tape oxide residue. Cleaning is accomplished by applying isopropyl alcohol, freon, or carbon tetrachloride with a cotton or chamois swab (a small piece of cotton or chamois on a flat plastic stick). Aerosol-spray head cleaner is also available. Do not use acetone or any other cleaner that is a plastic solvent. Plastic solvents damage tape and rubber rollers, and can loosen any plastic bonding that may be used in the assembly of parts. Also do not use freon on the rubber rollers since it can dry out the rubber.

Each metal, plastic, and rubber guide should be lightly scrubbed with a swab soaked in the cleaner. When a swab becomes dirty, discard it and use a clean one. Thoroughly clean the erase head and the audio and control track heads. When cleaning the head drum, take care not to nick the video heads. The video heads must be carefully cleaned without leaving any lint residue in the gap of the heads. (See fig. 5:1.)

When using spray cleaner, a thorough spraying of the tape path can be accomplished even while a tape is moving on the machine. If the video heads should need to be cleaned when you don't have your cleaning equipment with you, place the pad of your index finger lightly, for a few seconds, against the head drum over

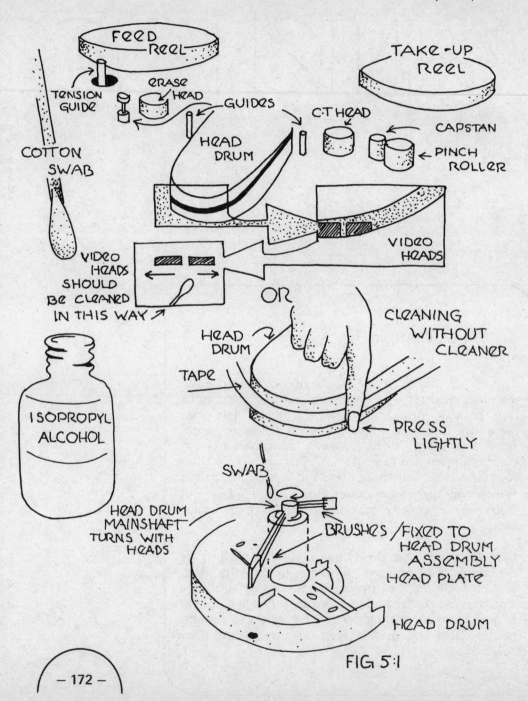

FIG 5:1

the tape as it passes. The slight abrasion of the tape against the moving heads will act to clean them, but be especially careful not to nick or chip the heads with your fingernail.

Brushes are the small metal contacts (which look like miniature Afro-combs) which feed the signal current to and from the moving heads. They are fixed within the head drum assembly and rest on slip rings fitted around the main shaft of the head drum motor. Dirt can collect in the rings and prevent contact between the brushes and the heads. Poor brush contact or lack of brush contact appears in the TV image as a continual line of dropout in the same place on the screen. Brushes need be cleaned only when this **brush noise** (slip ring noise) is noticed. To clean the brushes, remove the head drum top plate. Insert a soaked swab between the brushes and the slip rings on the main shaft. Take care not to leave any cotton lint entwined in the brushes, and make sure that each pin of the brushes is in contact with the proper ring. (See fig. 5:1.) If cleaning does not elim- inate the brush noise, new brushes may be needed.

Lens-cleaning should include the inner and outer optic elements as well as the viewfinder, lens, and monitor. It is best to use lens paper to wipe lens surfaces, since it will neither leave lint nor scratch the surfaces. Any photographic lens-cleaning liquids may also be used. It is important, too, to clean the vidicon face. You can get at it by removing the lens from the camera. Dust and lint can collect on the vidicon's surface, and when the aperture of the lens is closed down and the depth of field is maximum, small blotches may then be seen on on the TV image. These blotches can look like small light burns on the vidicon. The vidicon face can be cleaned by applying a drop of lens cleaner to it and then carefully wiping it off with lens paper.

Large, rubberbandlike belts are used in the mechanical operations of the VTR. They are accessible only by removing the VTR from its case. A residue of rubber dust can collect on the pulleys which the belts turn, causing slippage. Though it is best to replace the belts and clean the pulleys, some improvement can be made by cleaning the existing belts and pulleys with isopropyl alcohol and swabs.

The magnetic recording heads should also be **degaussed** (demagnetized) about once every ten hours of use. A permanent magnetic charge can build up in the heads, preventing them from responding exactly to the signal currents fed them. The effect on the TV image is noise and grain, and in the sound, a low hiss and a weak sig- nal. Head degaussing is accomplished by using a **degaus- ser**—a device which generates a high-frequency signal to break up built-up magnetism. To use a degausser, turn it on, hold it very close to (but not touching) the head, rotate it slowly for a minute, and then very slowly pull it about six feet back from the head, then turn it off.

Another possible cause of a noisy and grainy video image can be an improper record current level in the VTR. Each manufacturer prescribes its brand of video- tape and sets the record current level of its VTRs for optimum functioning with that tape. However, record currents are adjustable and when an unprescribed tape is used, the record current should be reset. Adjusting the record current is not a simple procedure, so frequent changes of brands of videotape that have varying re- quirements is not recommended. If it becomes neces- sary to adjust the record current, refer to the VTR service manual for instruction. Standardization may someday provide a simple switch on the VTR for select- ing the record current levels for a number of types of videotape.

A new set of printed symbols has been developed to help clarify electronic systems and devices for their users: the spec sheet; the block diagram; and the circuit schematic. These items tell you what a piece of equipment is and how it works by describing its components and how they interconnect.

THE SPECIFICATION (SPEC) SHEET

Spec sheets are found in instruction manuals that come with electronic equipment, and are also included in pamphlets and ads used to sell the equipment. The specifications and data concerning a piece of equipment indicate its vital statistics—its power requirements, signal system, input and output levels, etc.

For example, let's examine the spec sheet of the Panasonic NV 3130 ½-inch color VTR: At the top of the sheet is the *Power Source*—AC 120 volts, 60 Hz. *Power Consumption* is next, and is about 90 watts (.75 amps). Then comes the *Video Recording System*, which is helical scan, USA standard (525 lines, 60 fields). The *Video Modulation System* is described as "both sideband FM." As discussed in **VIDEOWORKS** (page 73), a composite video signal must be frequency-modulated to narrow its frequency range for recording. Both sideband FM means the information is carried in both sidebands of the frequency-modulated signal. If the spec sheet is more specific, it will note the various frequencies used for modulating the signal.

Continuing with the sample spec sheet, *Tape Speed* is 7½ inches per second and *Tape Width* is ½ inch. Remember that these specifications are an important part of the EIAJ-1 standard. The *Heads* are listed as follows: Video—two rotary heads (some spec sheets indicate what the heads are made of); Audio/Control Track—one stationary; Erase—one for both video and audio and one for audio dubbing. The *Recording Time* is 63

minutes for the manufacturer's specified brand on a 7-inch reel (2,400 ft.).

Horizontal Resolution is given separately for black-and-white and color. For black-and-white, it's more than 300 lines and for color, more than 240 lines. Remember, the horizontal resolution is the approximate number of picture elements in a single horizontal line. The color horizontal resolution is never as high as the black-and-white horizontal resolution.

The *Active Elements* are described as fully transistorized. If tubes were used, that too would be indicated, and in more detailed spec sheets the number and types of components would be listed. *Frequency Response* for video is greater than 2.5 MHz and for the audio, it is 80–10,000 Hz. Frequency response is the range of frequencies in which signals are optimally handled by the system. The *Signal-to-Noise Ratio* is only given for the black-and-white video and is better than 40 db. Better than 40 db means that there is 10^4 times more signal than noise. For audio, the signal-to-noise ratio is also better than 40 db.

Input Levels are for video (.1 volt peak-to-peak) and for audio, both mic and auxillary. Remember, the video signal is a series of changing levels within a specified range having a top peak and a bottom peak. The mic input level is .001 volt (-60 db) and the auxillary input level is .1 volt (-20 db). The -60 db and -20 db indicate base levels on a VU meter. The *Input Impedance* for the video is 75 ohms unbalanced. For audio, it's 20 kilo-ohms unbalanced for the mic and 1 mega-ohm unbalanced for auxillary.

Output Levels for the video are 1 volt peak-to-peak and for audio, .1 volt (-20 db). *Output Impedance* for the video is 75 ohms unbalanced and for audio, 600 ohms unbalanced. *Dimensions* and *Weight* are given, as well as a list of *Standard Accessories*. And that's the average spec sheet, give or take an item or two. It is necessary to have information such as the audio input and output levels when selecting the correct mics and other sound equipment to use with the VTR.

INSTRUCTION MANUALS

Operating or instruction manuals come with every piece of equipment you use. They tell you (sometimes in an overcomplicated manner) how to use the equipment. They identify all the dials, levers, buttons, knobs, plugs, switches, meters, etc. They also explain what each does. Various uses of the equipment are explained and, when necessary, diagrams illustrate connections, processes, and parts. These manuals should be read cover-to-cover and kept handy while you are getting familiar with a new piece of equipment.

REPAIR MANUALS AND SCHEMATICS

Repair (also called service) manuals are prepared by manufacturers to explain how to service their equipment. A set of manuals, for instance, for the Sony AV 3650 VTR, costs about ten dollars and includes specifications; operating instructions; circuit descriptions; mechanical maintenance procedures; alignment instructions for video, servo, and audio systems; power-supply alignment instructions; diagrams of printed circuit boards; schematics; an electrical parts list; and exploded views of various assemblies that make up the equipment.

Unfortunately, not all service manuals are complete and comprehensible. They are written for repairmen and, therefore, contain abbreviations and codes. However, many needed repairs can be made by a conscientious lay person. Throughout the manual, there are block diagrams which illustrate the circuit components that make up the particular systems within a piece of equipment.

The audio block, (see fig. 5:2), for instance, shows the pre-amp, buffer, AGC, line and rectifier amp, and the bias/erase oscillator of the audio system, as well as how they are connected and fed signals through the various sound inputs. Notice the letter/number groups above each component block. They indicate the electronic part(s) used in that component. In the electrical parts

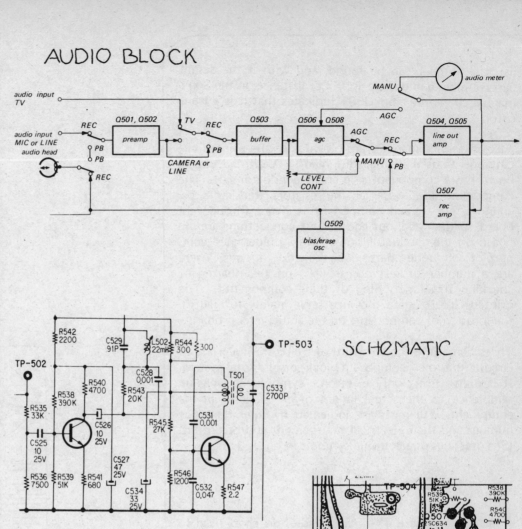

AUDIO BLOCK

SCHEMATIC

PRINTED CIRCUIT BOARD

FIG 5:2

list, the number can be found, and with it the actual parts number and description. For instance, in the Sony manual, their pre-amp Q501 indicates that it is a transistor.

Also in service manuals are blowups of the printed circuit boards used in the equipment. A printed circuit board has a component side and a conductor side. The component side houses all the resistors, transistors, oscillators, etc. Each component is fitted through the board so that its input and output connections are exposed on the conductor side where a predesigned complex of conduction paths does the work of wires. There are a number of test points (TP) on the boards for checking the functioning of their components. The printed circuit board blowups serve mainly to identify the location of components on the actual circuit board.

The schematic is the blueprint of a circuit, of a group of circuits that may compose a block, or of a total system. It is drawn using only electronic symbols, and has no semblance to the actual layout of components in the equipment. All parts are indicated by their reference number and their electrical requirement and/or output. (See drawings of electronic symbols in fig. 5:2 .)

READING A TEST PATTERN

A test pattern is a TV image resolution chart used to check contrast, linearity, and picture resolution on a TV or from a camera. (See sample test pattern, fig. 5:3 .) Test patterns can be of various designs, usually with some kind of figurative center image for checking the quality of gray tones in the TV picture. Diagonal lines in the pattern which display a slight moire effect indicate good interlacing. The aspect ratio (3 by 4) is set by using two large circles on the test pattern. The height of the picture is equal to the inner circle and the width is equal to the outer circle. Linearity of the scanning movement can also be checked by the circles once the aspect ratio is set. If the circles do not appear round, the linearity needs adjustment.

Alternately black and white lined wedges in the test pattern, both vertically and horizontally oriented, determine the picture resolution. Such wedges also serve as an alternate means of judging linearity. Each pair of wedges is of equal length. If the horizontal pair appears the same in length, the horizontal scanning is linear. If each wedge of the vertical pair appears equal, the vertical scanning is also linear. Resolution is determined by the number of lines discernible in the wedge on the TV screen. Horizontal resolution is determined by the vertically oriented lines, and the vertical resolution is determined by the horizontally oriented lines.

SAMPLE TEST PATTERN

FIG 5:3

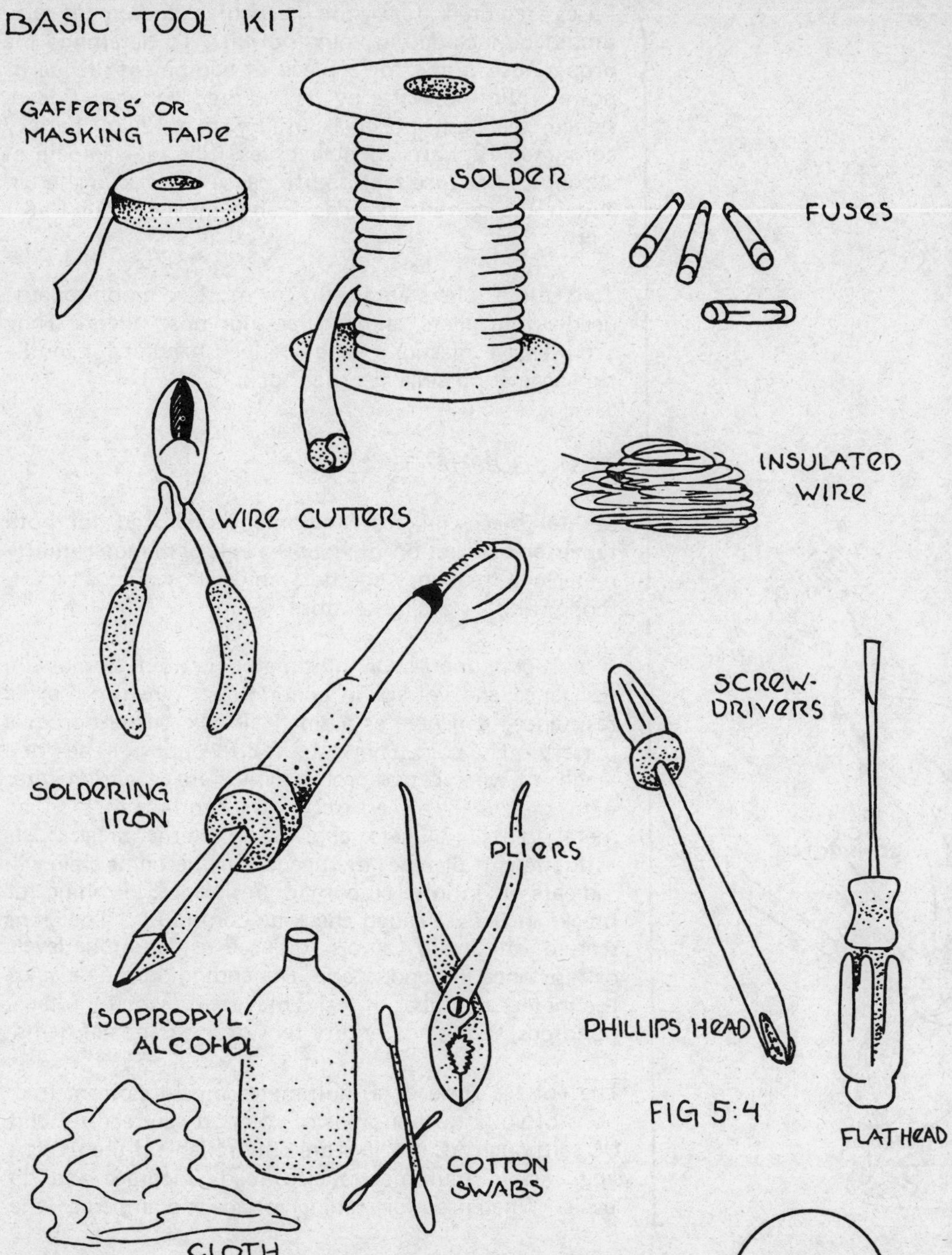

BASIC TOOL KIT

GAFFERS' OR MASKING TAPE

SOLDER

FUSES

INSULATED WIRE

WIRE CUTTERS

SOLDERING IRON

SCREW-DRIVERS

PLIERS

ISOPROPYL ALCOHOL

COTTON SWABS

PHILLIPS HEAD

FIG 5:4

FLATHEAD

CLOTH

TOOLS AND TEST EQUIPMENT

Every trade has its tools and test equipment, and video is no exception. The tools are used to repair wires, circuits, and individual components, and the test equipment is used to determine what the electrons are doing inside them. In order to tune circuits and perform many of the alignment procedures outlined in service manuals, test equipment is a necessity.

TOOLS

A set of tools includes the usual electrician's paraphernalia: a roll of electrical tape; solder and a soldering iron; some insulated wire; wire cutters and splicers; screw drivers; fuses; pliers; and cleaning equipment.

Since most of your own repairs will be for cables and connectors, soldering know-how is a must. Rosin core solder is made of tin and lead and has a relatively low melting point. Using a soldering iron, this solder easily can be melted and applied to a metal surface, providing an excellent bond that will conduct electricity. Most soldering is done to attach a wire to the connection point of a plug, connector, or other electrical part.

If the wire is made of many tiny strands, it must be twisted into a single strand in preparation for **tinning**—a process of coating both a wire and a connection point with solder prior to the actual joining. Tinning produces the compatible bonding surfaces on the wire and the connection point necessary to achieve a good bond. To tin a wire, place it against the iron with the solder on top of the wire. As soon as the solder begins to flow, the iron and solder should be removed. The wire will then have a shiny silver coating. The connection point should be tinned in the same way, and the two will then be ready for joining.

Next, the wire and the connector should be held together and the iron and solder applied. As soon as the solder begins to flow and a solder bead of sufficient size has collected at the connection point, the solder and iron should be removed. (See drawing below.) Care must be taken not to jar the connection as it is being made. Although solder hardens quickly, the solder will crystallize and make a *cold-solder connection* if jarred. Cold-solder connections are weak and are poor conductors. If the bond appears shiny, the solder has not crystallized and the connection is good. If the bond appears dull, the solder has crystallized and the connection must be redone. To undo a botched connection, simply melt it with the soldering iron.

It is important to keep some insulated wire among your tools. It can be any type of thin wire capable of making connections between parts and splices in wires. Also, a number of screwdrivers are necessary for working with electronic equipment: several flat head screwdrivers of intermediate sizes; a Phillips head screwdriver of small or intermediate size; and a set of jeweler's screwdrivers (which include very small Phillipses and flat heads) for working with the tiny screws used in cable connectors.

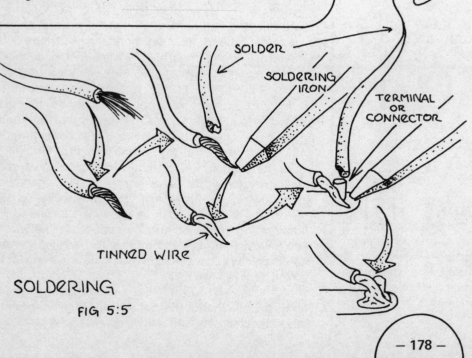

SOLDER

SOLDERING IRON

TERMINAL OR CONNECTOR

TINNED WIRE

SOLDERING
FIG 5:5

Fuses required for your particular equipment also should be included in your tool kit. To determine the proper fuse rating for a piece of equipment, divide its power rating in watts by its required voltage. For instance, the Sony portapak used with a 12-volt battery consumes 12 watts of power, resulting in 1 ampere of current. The fuse required to cause a break in the circuit if the current exceeds 1 amp must be rated at 1 amp.

Two sets of pliers are useful for most common repairs: needle-nose pliers, and regular snub-nose pliers. They should have plastic or tape-wrapped handles for insulation against possible electric shock.

TEST EQUIPMENT

Several pieces of test equipment are used for both repair and operation of video: a volt-ohm meter (multimeter); a frequency counter; an oscilloscope; a vectorscope; and a signal generator.

A **volt-ohm meter**, or **multimeter**, is used to measure resistance and voltage in conductors. When measuring resistance, it generates a small electric current from a battery. The current may be fed to opposite ends of a length of wire via two probes, which are extension wires with pencillike pieces of plastic terminated by long metal points or alligator clips. If an internal break exists in the length of wire, the needle on the ohms scale will indicate an infinite amount of resistance. Probing for breaks in lines is called checking continuity. The ohms scale of the meter can also be used to determine levels of resistance in conductors. Depending on the range of the meter, a number of scales may be provided: in tens, hundreds, thousands, and/or tens of thousands of ohms.

The voltage scale of a multimeter measures from fractions of volts to thousands of volts. It can read AC and DC, although AC readings are only reliable if the AC is a sine wave. Multimeters also read amperage and db levels. When used for reading voltage and amperage, the

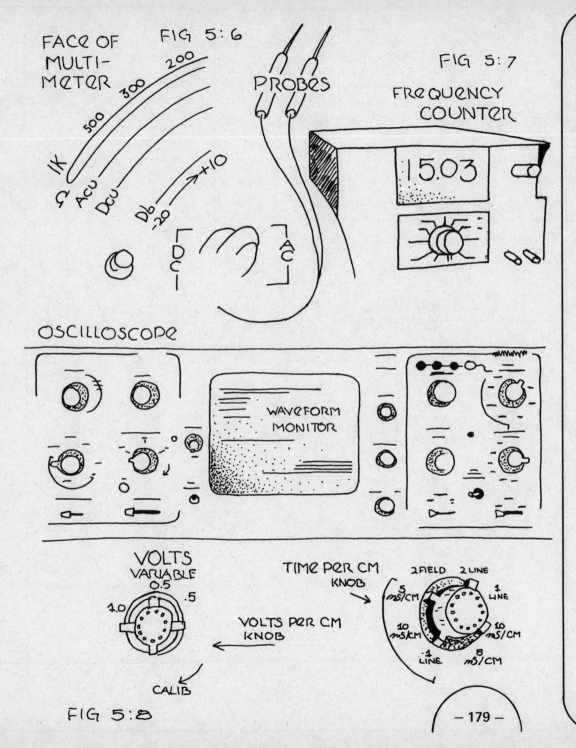

FACE OF MULTI-METER FIG 5:6

200
300
500
1K
Ϛ
ACU
DCU
Db
-20
+10

DC

AC

PROBES

FIG 5:7
FREQUENCY COUNTER

15.03

OSCILLOSCOPE

WAVEFORM MONITOR

VOLTS
VARIABLE
0.5
.5
1.0

VOLTS PER CM KNOB

CALIB

TIME PER CM KNOB

2 FIELD   2 LINE
5 mS/CM
1 LINE
10 mS/CM
10 mS/CM
.4 LINE
5 mS/CM

FIG 5:8

meter's probes are of opposite polarity—one negative, the other positive. Some amount of electricity is drawn from the conductor being measured and is passed through the meter for reading. Every meter has an impedance rating. This rating consists of the impedance the meter adds to a circuit by drawing the current it needs for a measurement. Most meters are designed with a transistor amplifier which allows for tapping very small currents which are then amplified in the meter before they are read. The FET (field effects transistor) that serves as the amplifier is powered by a battery.

A **frequency counter** gives a digital readout of the frequency of electrical signals in circuits and conductors. It is equipped with probes to draw current to computing circuits which count hertz and display the result via LED (light-emitting diode) arrays or vacuum tubes that have **nixie tubes**—filaments shaped like the numbers 0–9.

An **oscilloscope** provides a visual rendition of a signal waveform and can be used for any measurement involving voltage. The visual display represents a plotting for voltage along the vertical axis, and a plotting for time along the horizontal axis. An oscilloscope is used to observe waveshapes, to measure peak-to-peak amplitude, and to check frequencies. The *bandwidth* of an oscilloscope determines its frequency responsiveness, which for video work should be a range of about 10 MHz. The minimum voltage with which the oscilloscope can work is called its *sensitivity*, which for video should be at a variable range of .1 volt to 10 volts.

The signal is displayed on the face of a small CRT (waveform monitor). The CRT's surface is covered with a graph divided into square centimeters. Variable vertical and horizontal oscillators can be driven by signals fed to the scope. The beam of the CRT's electron gun travels along one horizontal line at a rate determined by setting the *time per centimeter* knob on the scope. The time ranges from fractions of a second to one second. The beam moves vertically off the scan line as the voltage changes. A *volts per centimeter* knob on the scope allows for selecting the scale of vertical deflection. For instance, 1 volt spanning 2 centimeters would result in a kind of magnification of 1 volt per 1 centimeter. There are also dual-beam scopes which have two electron guns for simultaneous display of signals for comparison.

Frequency checks using an oscilloscope are usually performed with a signal generator which can produce any set frequency in order to reference an unknown signal. The unknown signal is first fed to the scope's vertical input. The scope's beam can then be adjusted to display two cycles of the unknown signal. Next the signal generator output is fed to the scope's vertical input in place of the unknown signal, and is adjusted to display two cycles by turning the frequency control on the signal generator. (The frequency control on the oscilloscope should not be touched.) The frequency of the signal generator will then be equal to the unknown signal since both are producing the same beam scan motion.

Frequency comparison and phase angle measurements of sine waves can also be made with an oscilloscope. Two sine waves can be compared by connecting one sine wave voltage to the horizontal input of the scope and the other sine wave voltage to the vertical input. The oscilloscope will then produce *lissajous patterns*, which are visual renditions of frequency and phase comparisons of sine waves.

The oscilloscope is also used to monitor signals while equipment is being operated. During editing, for instance, signal monitoring provides a sure way of determining the quality of the edits. Often the VTR on which an edit has been performed plays back a flawless signal, while other VTRs shows its weaknesses. For this reason, critical editing requires a scope for inspection of the waveform.

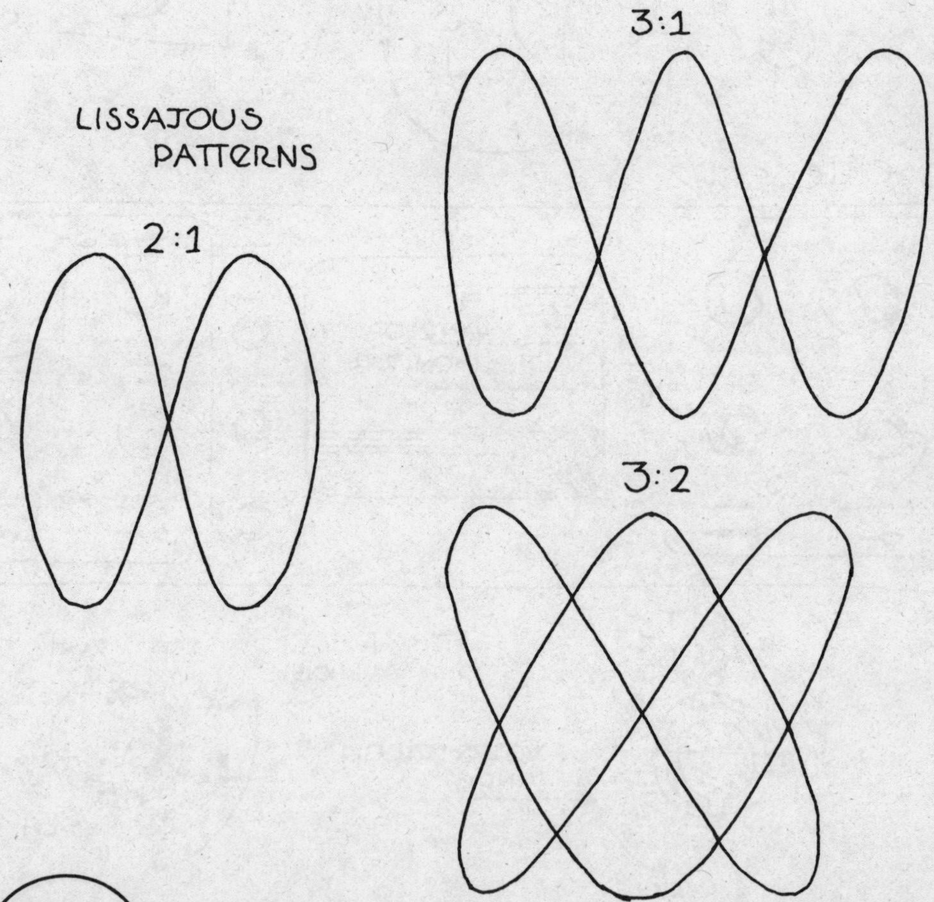

LISSAJOUS PATTERNS

2:1

3:1

3:2

FIG 5:9

A **vectorscope** provides a visual rendition of the color signal. A polar graph is used; each color has a specific location on the graph (see fig. 5:10). A vectorscope is used to determine luminance amplitude and chrominance phase and amplitude. Color saturation is represented on the graph in terms of displacement from the center. The farther away from the center, the greater the saturation.

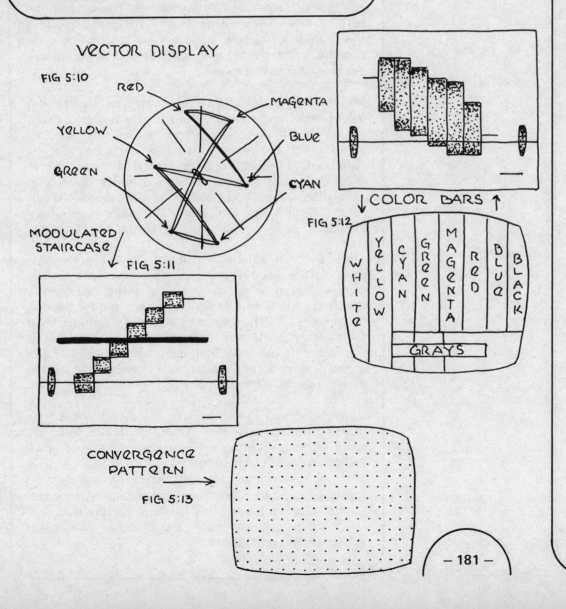

VECTOR DISPLAY

FIG 5:10

RED
MAGENTA
YELLOW
BLUE
GREEN
CYAN

MODULATED STAIRCASE

FIG 5:11

COLOR BARS

FIG 5:12

WHITE | YELLOW | CYAN | GREEN | MAGENTA | RED | BLUE | BLACK

GRAYS

CONVERGENCE PATTERN →

FIG 5:13

Linear, rather than polar, display can also be used to examine differential gain and phase. **Differential gain** is the amplitude change of a color subcarrier as a function of luminance. **Differential phase** is the phase modulation of the color signal by the luminance signal.

A **signal generator** provides specific test signals such as sync, color burst, color bars, or convergence patterns. Signal generator equipment must often be used with an oscilloscope for certain maintenance procedures. The electronically generated signals are used for reference during alignments.

The following list indicates the most common test signals and their uses (see figs. 5:11–5:13):

color bars: Used to check color-circuit alignment. A color bar generator produces five or ten color bars. Every sixth bar is a complementary, 180° away when plotted on a vectorscope. Some color bar generators provide the simultaneous generation of a range of black to white bars for comparing chrominance and luminance levels (staircase).

modulated staircase: Used for measurements of differential gain and phase, luminance signal linearity, and burst phase errors. The staircase signal is a series of uniform changes in signal amplitude, progressing from white to black.

convergence pattern: Used for checking monitor-picture linearity or camera-scanning linearity, aspect ratio, and geometric distortion. Convergence signals provide for display of white crosshatch, vertical lines only, horizontal lines only, white dots only, and crosshatch plus dots.

audio frequency signals: Used to check signal frequencies within the audio range (20–20,000 Hz), in which are found the vertical sync (60 Hz) and the horizontal sync (15,750 Hz).

TEST TAPES

Most manufacturers provide **test tapes** (also called alignment tapes) which can be purchased and used for many alignment procedures performed in the maintenance of equipment. The various patterns and signals on a test tape, recorded under optimum conditions, are a good measure for determining the proper functioning of a VTR. A test tape signal is used as a standard to which the VTR is adjusted. Adjustments can be made on the video playback level, the tracking control, noise killer circuitry, etc.

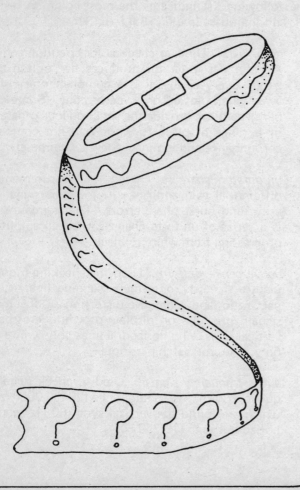

REPAIR PEOPLE
REPAIR WHERE

Repair people are in business to make money by providing a service. They are paid by the hour for their time, and are reimbursed for the cost of parts and for overhead. A repair person must have access to test equipment. And the better the test equipment, the better a repair person can perform. Routine to repair is the probing of circuits to locate malfunctioning components, so the quality of a repair shop's test equipment can save or cost you money.

Manufacturer-authorized service centers can be found in most large cities in which video equipment is sold. Manufacturers also maintain factory service centers at regional office locations from where parts can also be purchased. In most cases, the authorized service center is operated in conjunction with an authorized dealership —the place where you bought the equipment. Repair personnel working in these service centers usually have attended training courses operated by the manufacturer.

There are two schools of thought regarding the best place to have equipment repaired: One opts for the factory service center; the other, the authorized dealer's service center. The cost for repairs is often the same at both places. The factory service center is equipped with some highly specialized tools which are not available to the dealer. Repairs requiring such tools need to be done at the factory service center, and if sent there by the dealer, you pay a handling charge.

However, if you live in an area in which there is a reliable authorized service center and dealership, there are some distinct advantages. Since the purchase of video equipment and its maintenance involves substantial time and money, a friendly relationship with a dealer and its repair people can result in special discounts, over-the-phone help, service people's familiarity with your particular equipment, and contact with other local video producers and general goings-on.

MAKING A DIAGNOSIS

Before going to the repair people, it is important to have some idea of what's wrong with your equipment. Diagnosing equipment problems can save you time and money. All too often, a piece of equipment is lugged to the repair shop only for its operator to find out that he or she had not set a certain selector knob properly, or that just a cleaning was needed. A complete knowledge of how to use a piece of equipment is a prerequisite for determining the type of problems it may have.

Following is a list of symptoms and problems associated mainly with the display circuitry and the CRT found in monitors, TV receivers, and camera viewfinders.

When the TV is on with no picture signal:
- if the raster has weak brightness, the CRT or high voltage in the system needs work;
- if the raster is too small the power supply needs work (weak batteries also cause a collapsed raster);
- if the raster is not wide or tall enough, the horizontal or vertical deflection output circuitry needs work;
- if only a bright horizontal line is displayed, the vertical deflection circuit needs work;
- if the raster is tilted, the deflection yoke is twisted;
- if the raster displays pincushion or barrel distortion, the deflection yoke needs adjustment;
- if there is a blossoming of the high brightness levels, the high-voltage system needs work.

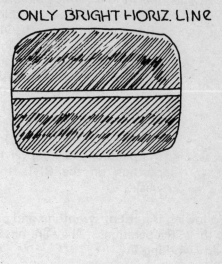

RASTER TOO SMALL

ONLY BRIGHT HORIZ. LINE

TILTED RASTER

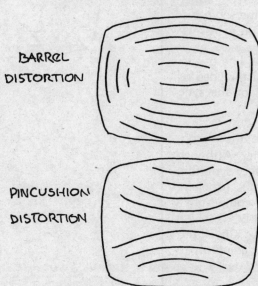

BARREL DISTORTION

PINCUSHION DISTORTION

VERTICAL ROLL W/HORIZ. SLIP

FIG 5:14

When the TV is on with a picture signal:

    -if the picture is weak and low in contrast, the CRT needs work, or the video signal is insufficient;

    -if the picture rolls vertically and slips horizontally, the sync circuits of the set need work, or the sync of the incoming video signal is weak;

    -if a picture bends, the horizontal sync is weak (timebase instability);

    -if a picture is locking vertically in the wrong position on the CRT, the vertical sync is weak.

Following is a list of symptoms and problems associated with VTR operations. They are observable using a properly working TV.

When the TV displays a video signal from a VTR:

    -if the picture is snowy, the recording heads are dirty or broken;

    -if the picture displays a line of continuous dropout over one-third of the screen, either the tracking needs adjustment, the servo systems need work, or the head drum is misaligned;

    -if the picture displays a blipping line of picture noise, either the tape is misthreaded or was misthreaded for recording, or the sync circuits need work.

These lists can help you identify only some of the problems that may arise with your equipment. Although keeping an eye out for trouble can help, every symptom does not necessarily mean there's a serious problem. Remember that the problem could actually come from a cable with a loose connection, an improperly set switch or knob, dirt, the cold, or your batteries. Check out these possibilities a couple of times before going off to the repair shop.

BENDING PICTURE

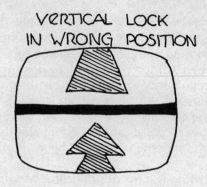
VERTICAL LOCK IN WRONG POSITION

SNOW

LINE OF PICTURE NOISE

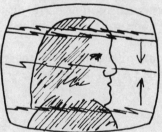
BLIPPING LINE OF PICTURE NOISE

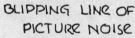

FIG 5:15

CABLE TV
COAX

TV picture and sound signals can be transmitted via cable. **Cablecasting** is accomplished using coaxial (coax) cable—an inner conductor of copper wire surrounded by plastic foam, together with an outer conductor of aluminum covered with protective sheathing. Coax can carry signals up to billions of cycles per second. The standard cable used in cable TV systems accommodates a range of about 300 MHz, from about 1 MHz to 300 MHz. If proper amplification is provided along the line, a single cable can carry about thirty 6-MHz channels.

TV air transmission is often interferred with by mountains, buildings, and atmospheric conditions. Coaxial cable provides interference-free transmission, since signals traveling in cable are protected from the elements. Rural communities originally received TV programs by hooking their sets into an antenna placed on some nearby hilltop. These early cable TV systems were called CATV—community antenna TV—systems. They were either privately owned or collectively owned by a group of viewers.

Today, many cable TV systems are owned and run by corporations with systems across the country. With the attraction of better reception and additional channels of programming, cable TV is growing in the urban areas. Cable TV has become a major communications industry with a future promising not only more TV in your sets, but also two-way TV, meter-reading by TV, doctors, lawyers, and firemen by TV, and even government by TV.

APPENDIX

Whatever its future, present-day cable technology provides the independent video producer a ready means for disseminating programs to sometimes small but very particular audiences. To understand this potential, let's look at a cable TV system from hilltop antennas to living room receivers.

THE CABLE SYSTEM

The antennas which pick up signals coming from various directions must be situated at a height and location where reception is best for that general area. A **field strength meter**—a device for determining the quality of reception—enables a cable system designer to determine how well TV air signals are received at any given spot.

With the antenna site established, the location of the **headend**—a shelter for housing the signal processing equipment, the brains of the system—is next determined. This equipment basically consists of an amplifier and modulator for each channel fed into it by the antennas. If need be, the antennas and headend can be considerably far apart. Usually they are located close to each other and are easily accessible for maintenance.

Incoming signals fed to the headend equipment are cleaned up, boosted, and cablecasted down the line. In some cases, one frequency must be shifted to another frequency in order to be received at the home set. For instance, when the antennas pick up two channel 6s, each from a different location, one of the channel 6s can be converted and cablecasted on a channel for which there is no received signal—channel 10, perhaps.

Three types of coax lines are used in wiring a system: trunk, feeder, and drop. **Trunk line** is the heaviest and is used as the main distribution cable. If proper amplification is maintained along the line and the number of taps to homes does not exceed about 50 per mile, present technology permits a system to utilize about 15 miles of trunk line in any direction without significant signal loss. The prevention of signal loss demands the use of at least two amplifiers for every mile of cable. The more taps to homes per mile, as in urban areas where there are sometimes as many as 700, the shorter the overall trunk line length can be.

The **feeder lines** are used to distribute signals from the trunk lines to the **drop lines** which feed subscriber TV sets. Feeder lines can be hooked into the trunk lines at amplifier locations; drop lines are tapped directly off feeder lines wherever needed. Most cable systems attach their lines to existing utility poles. The cable company pays a rental fee to the utility company for pole use. Poles for the exclusive use of the cable company can be installed where no other poles are available.

A matching impedance transformer is used to hook the cable into the VHF antenna terminal of the receiver. Systems with more than 12 VHF channels provide the subscriber with a convertor box for tuning in the extra channels that are offered. Cable TV is not free. There is a charge for installation as well as a monthly subscription fee.

Although two-way cable is a technological reality, it is still costly. Two-way amplifiers can be placed in the system, and modulators for cablecasting can be located in every subscriber's home. The first two-way systems are not so extensive, and do not provide every subscriber with his own home audio/video channel. Most are simply some type of home audio reply mechanism (not usually voice) which can be monitored at the headend or at some designated studio location. Although telephonelike two-way TV communication is technologically feasible, the cost of such a system is prohibitive. Some experimentation is being conducted with point-to-point two-way cable TV, in which a limited number of designated locations are connected for intercommunicating—a laboratory in a downtown hospital with a university research center at an uptown campus, for example.

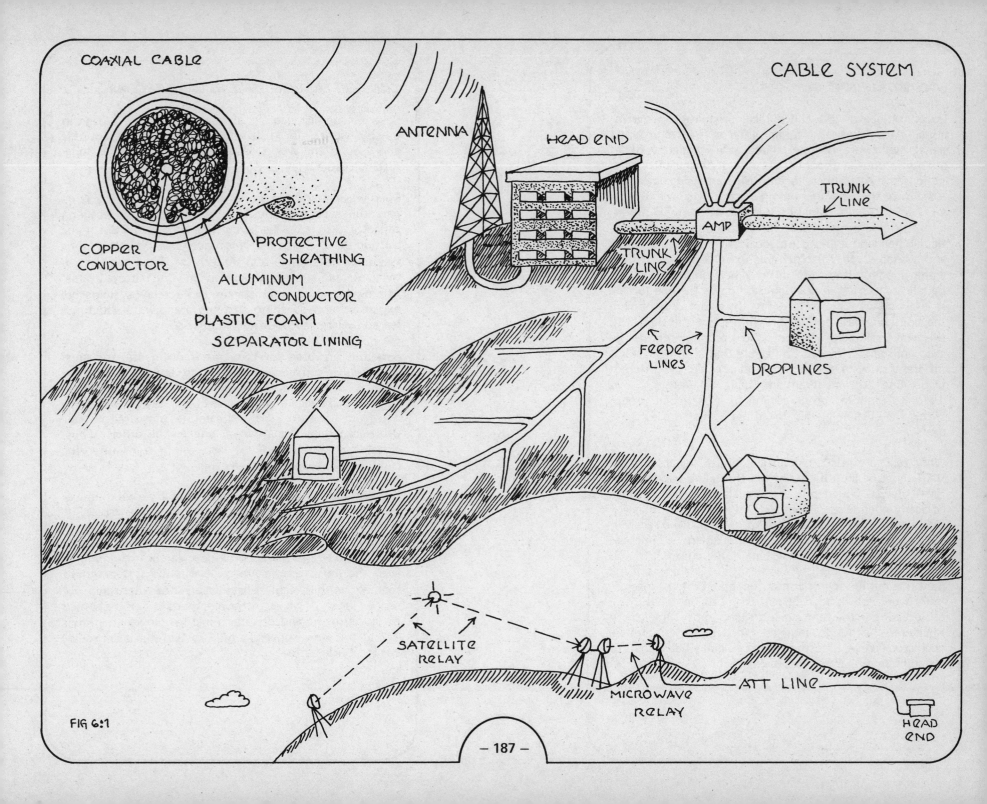

COAXIAL CABLE

CABLE SYSTEM

ANTENNA

HEAD END

TRUNK LINE

AMP

TRUNK LINE

COPPER CONDUCTOR

PROTECTIVE SHEATHING

ALUMINUM CONDUCTOR

PLASTIC FOAM

SEPARATOR LINING

FEEDER LINES

DROPLINES

SATELLITE RELAY

MICROWAVE RELAY

ATT LINE

HEAD END

FIG 6:1

LOCAL ORIGINATION

Local cablecasting is called **local origination programming**. At the headend, an amplifier is fed live or taped signals which are RF modulated at a frequency of an otherwise unused channel. As with TV signals from the air sensed by antennas, locally originated signals can be fed down the line to home TV sets. Using a ½-inch VTR (even the portapak) equipped with an RF modulator and the proper cable for connecting into the particular headend equipment, local origination is possible and available. It is also possible to hook into one of the trunk line amplifiers. In this case keep in mind that the signals are carried in one direction down the line (unless it is a two-way system). Only those subscribers from the point of the amplifier on will receive the signal. In this way, selective neighborhood programming can be accomplished. However, be aware that in some systems different sides of the same street are fed by different feeder lines from different amplifiers. Therefore, if you desire to pinpoint programming to a particular group, check the system layout for those kinds of discrepancies.

When plugging into an amplifier, the RF signal from the VTR must be amplified and fed through a **bandpass filter**—a device which prevents signals from leaking into adjacent channels. Generally, cablecasting ½-inch RF modulated signals creates some problems at the receiver, depending on the TV set's age and quality. Timebase instability of the ½-inch system is the culprit. In this case, timebase instability can result in a shakiness of the picture or inferior horizontal lockup. Edited tapes are more troublesome to cablecast than original tapes. Live cablecasting is the best since no tape idiosyncracies can interfere. Although somewhat expensive, a timebase corrector can be used to upgrade ½-inch video signals to a standard comparable to broadcast.

LONG-DISTANCE SIGNAL RELAY SYSTEMS

Several long-distance signal relay systems have been in use by Big TV for distributing TV across the country and around the world. They include **microwave, long-distance cable relay**, and **satellite** transmissions.

Microwave transmission is achieved by spacing large parabolic reflectors about forty miles apart. A receiving reflector dish must be in the line of sight of the transmitting dish. Signal carrier frequencies are increased to the microwave range—ten billion Hz. Thus, the electromagnetic radiation is generated in very narrow beams. Microwave and long-distance cable relay systems are expensive and so these systems are owned and time-leased by large corporations like AT&T.

Satellites are used for those intercontinental transmissions which can be seen on almost any TV news program. Communications satellites are sky-loft relay stations which receive and transmit microwave signals to and from the earth. Several satellites staggered in their orbits can relay signals from one to the other. Thus, signals from one side of the earth can be transmitted for simultaneous viewing on the other side.

Domestic satellite is the twinkle in many a communicator's eye, since it is an alternative to costly cable TV. With regional placement of transmitters and receivers, a domestic satellite network could serve as a sky-loft communications terminal to provide clear programming to even the most remote areas. A satellite system would require neither cable installation nor monthly subscriber fees. Its cost of development is being assumed by government and private industry. However, it does not at this time appear to be a system that will provide for local origination.

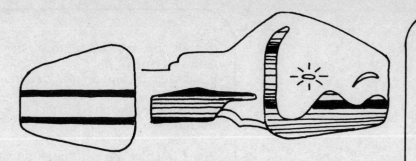

WOODSTOCK COMMUNITY VIDEO
A BRIEF HISTORY

In 1970, two years after TV making became accessible to people outside the TV industry, an alternate media movement emerged and the decentralizing of media resources began. Using ½-inch video systems, independent organizations produced programs about people and events either not covered or unfairly treated by the mass media. Unable to negotiate with the media establishment and denied access to broadcast TV, they set up video theatres, using schoolrooms and even living rooms as local information centers to show tapes on such subjects as alternate life styles, communes, liberation activities of various communities, as well as raps with artists and educators.

Woodstock Community Video (WCV) is an outgrowth of one of those centers—People's Video Theatre (PVT)—which was set up by Elliot Glass and myself. When first setting up PVT in a New York City loft for viewing tapes, and in turn taping views, we defined the following objectives which we believed to be essential to a community video resource: to provide people with a medium for exposing their goods, services, and ideas; to stimulate community dialogue; to develop community video journalism; to provide a public-access production facility; and to establish a video library.

Four newly-begun video groups—Videofreex, Raindance, Global Village, and People's Video Theatre—demonstrated new ways in which media could function in the hands of people who felt either cut off from the viewpoint of mass media, or who were attempting to control their own information to prevent its distortion. In the latter part of 1970, the movement received some publicity from a not overly sympathetic press. An article in *New York Magazine* dubbed the movement "guerilla TV." Within months, *Newsweek* reported on some of the more sensational aspects, which included a British video group's (TVX) takeover of the David Frost show.

The New York State Council on the Arts (NYSCA) provided grants to the four video groups operating in New York during that time. People's Video Theatre had been functioning successfully in Greenwich Village, drawing tourist audiences during weekend nights. But attempts to reach the local community were not successful. Cable TV with its public-access channels was beginning to provide a means for the dissemination of independently-produced TV, but those systems' penetration in the city was uneven and minimal. The essence of alternate media, programmer/audience interaction, appeared to me to be unrealizable in the big-city context. So in the fall of 1971, Elaine Milosh and I moved to Woodstock, New York to set up a community video resource there.

Woodstock is a community of about 6,000 people located in the Catskill Mountains of the mid-Hudson region of New York State. It has had an operating cable system since 1965, supplying about 1,500 subscribers with reception of mainly New York City TV. A relatively small system (but with a potential to double), Woodstock's cable, then owned by NBC, is a part of Kingston Cablevision, a system with over 10,000 subscribers. Local origination programming was being provided for the Kingston system, but Woodstock with its separate headend received no local fare. Woodstock has a low population density with an approximate average of 25 homes along every mile. The cable industry takes the position that economically they cannot survive with too many under 40 homes along every mile. Thus, the cable system has only been developed in the high-density areas of the town.

The town has a sizable population of longhairs, a bedroom community for IBMers working in nearby Kingston, a rural citizenry with roots in the early Hugenot-Dutch settlements, and an artist colony established over 75 years ago. It has two weekly newspapers and is connected to the larger region by AM radio originating in Kingston and by that city's daily paper.

Our arrival in Woodstock coincided with the local elections, and so our first project involved taping all the candidates running for local office, playing those tapes back on the streets, and in turn taping the reactions and comments of the voters on the issues. For some eight days before the election we set monitors on trashcans in front of various stores along the main street (from which we obtained power) and made and displayed tapes. The candidates of all but one party readily participated, while it took a vocal request at a public meeting for those of the holdout party to finally agree to join in.

Within a few months of that event, we published a pamphlet to inform people about cable TV in general, the local system in particular, and about the potentials of community video:

". . .community programming is a tool for vitalizing communications. . .in a time of complex and varying social values and problems. Our local TV. . .can provide the town with its own message-making facilities. . .a community cable channel. . .low-cost advertising for local businesses. . .video programs in schools, churches, social groups, etc."

The pamphlet also outlined a plan of action requesting that the town government help citizens obtain cable service where there wasn't any, and that it provide space for a community channel studio in Town Hall. Other

institutions were asked to participate in creating programs as part of their activities. And the public at large was asked to support the development of community video by letting the cable company know that they wanted a community channel as well as support for its operations.

The pamphlet was distributed in early 1972, prior to a project which included a 12-week series of video shows held in cooperation with the Woodstock Artists Association, in its gallery in the center of town. Each show consisted of a half-hour-long video magazine on local events and issues, followed by a live forum discussion and taping of the audience. During this period, we were approaching Kingston Cablevision and the Town Board to start the ball rolling. And in some instances, the weekly show served as a public meeting to deal with our campaign. For example, at one show attended by a member of the Town Board and the cable company's program director, the initial arrangements were made to test our ½-inch equipment to see if it could be used for cablecasting. Within three months the company completed the tests and by the end of May 1972, WCV did its first two-hour, once-a-week (a limit set by the cable company) cablecast from the system's headend located on a nearby mountainside.

Patience and persistence are prerequisites for working with town governments and cable companies. The local government took until January 1973 to act. It set up a committee on cable TV to study and make recommendations for a new cable franchise to be negotiated in the fall. Also at that time, as a result of months of urging, the cable company offered to install an origination line at Town Hall so that programming could be cablecast from the center of town. With operations based in town, programming could be expanded, and cablecast at any time of day. It then took some eight months to come to an agreement. The cable company took three months to prepare a document it wanted the town to sign, three more months for the town officials to consider and reconsider whether they really wanted it, and another couple of months redrawing the document so it was agreeable to both parties. Meanwhile, every week on Wednesday night at 7:30 PM, WCV Channel 6 has gone on cable with live and taped programming: mini-documentaries, news, talk shows, Town Board meetings, election information, and occasional outside productions from other communities.

Some interesting questions emerged during the Town Board's deliberations on the desirability of a town-government-based community cable channel. Valid concerns were expressed regarding programming content, access, and responsibility for these things. With sensitivities directed toward their electorate, the Board members looked dimly on possible association with the expression of extreme political views, or the exposure of off-beat life styles which could offend the more conservative viewers. Our response to this took two forms: In setting up Woodstock Community Video as a non-profitmaking, tax exempt, educational organization, it was decided that it have a board of directors composed of the broadest possible spectrum of interests represented in the town. One of its major responsibilities would be to guide the selection of content and to ensure fairness in access. Secondly, Marco Vassi, a writer working in video, provided us with a written document which has been accepted as the guideline for operating the community channel by our Board and the local government:

". . .Responsibility for a full-time open channel requires total commitment to the principles of accurate information, technical competence, artistic integrity, and good taste.

"Our aim is to produce and exhibit tapes and live programming which is vivid and coherant; the goal is a multiplicity of voices, each distinct and strong, rather than an imposed conformity. We believe that the purpose of local origination is to give the community the opportunity to look at itself from the inside, thus coming to terms with its complexity of values and problems.

"As a channel we have no mandate or desire for censorship. In fact, we will be. . .beneficial to the community only to the degree that we are free to experiment with form and content. . . .

"We recognize, however, three areas of influence and restraint: legal requirements, broad community feedback, and the variety of sources of program material.

a) Legal requirements: These involve the regulations of the FCC and other governmental agencies, the stipulations of the town-authorized cable operator(s), and the general laws involving libel; through our attorneys we will remain informed about these jurisdictions;

b) Broad community feedback: We will exercise sensitivity to general reactions to individual programs and types of programs; . . .we are pledged to keep the channel from engendering alienation in the community;

c) Sources for program material: As moderately priced, easily operated equipment becomes more prevalent in schools, churches, special-interest groups, and among individuals, the base of our programming will spread to allow participation by everyone in the community, although, at the core of the station will remain a nexus of managers, producers, and WCV Board members, who will be responsible for quality control.

"We shall maintain a weekly schedule to be announced several times each broadcast day, and to appear in the local newspapers. The programs will be described in enough detail to afford viewers full discretion in their choice of program material.

"Ultimately, there is no substitute for good faith. A local channel, operating almost entirely from local resources, and available twenty-four hours a day, is an invaluable means for processing the information flow which keeps the town vital. In addition, it is a forum for teachers, artists, politicians, merchants, and the general citizen. To keep this channel open in such a way that aids us all in the problems of survival, that serves as a valid means of relaxation, and yet follows the highest individuation of viewpoint presupposes a thorough understanding of the nature of the medium and mutual trust between those who operate the channel and the community they serve.

"To maintain that understanding and that trust is our basic guideline."

PRESENT AND FUTURE

Involvement of local people has been integral to every project since the first, when Bob Dacey, a local artist/filmmaker, headed up the elections program. However, funding has so far provided support for only a director, an assistant, and maintenance of the facility. Sustained, active participation has therefore come only from those with their own resources. There are a number of independent video producers working in the area who have contributed programming to the channel. Other people too, not so media-occupied, have produced programs. For instance, the chairman of the town cable committee (an insurance salesman by trade) produced an interview show; and teenage members of a WCV workshop have produced tapes on the streets of Woodstock. Other programs have been made by a couple of artists who are exploring the video medium; several women who have participated in producing tapes on rape, breast cancer, women performers, etc.; and a teacher working with elementary school kids who has produced improvisational pieces for tape.

With a second grant from the NYSCA, we are now setting up an Artists' TV Lab to explore the creative applications of the medium for the arts. With the community channel soon to be installed at Town Hall and so

allowing more time to cablecast, community organizations are beginning to plan programming. For instance, the town's Narcotics Guidance Council is considering a series dealing with drug abuse; a youth center has proposed a video workshop from which shows would come, made by and about youth; some clergymen have discussed religious shows; and The Family, a social services organization, is considering using local TV to extend their programs. Programmers are asked to support their own productions by paying low fees to cover the cost of tape, equipment maintenance, and depreciation. Since most groups have publicity and educational activities items in their budgets, many of them can support low-cost production activities. Further support is anticipated from viewers as our programming gains more appeal and value to them. And local industry and business support most likely will increase as audience size increases.

The existence of Woodstock Community Video, like so many other fledgling community media groups throughout the country, represents the need and desire for locally responsive media to meet local needs and values. Hopefully, some of the information here will both encourage and reinforce similar efforts by providing a model from which to expand. Still in the early stage of development, we all need support.

Ken Marsh, WCV, March '74

GLOSSARINDEX

GLOSSARY

This Glossary consists of terms not defined within the text of the book. They are included here to help you gain a more thorough comprehension of electronics. For access to definitions of terms used in the text, refer to the page numbers listed in the index after each term.

A- (A negative): Symbol used to indicate the negative terminal of a filament's source of voltage.

A+ (A positive): Symbol for the positive terminal of a filament's source of voltage.

accelerating electrode: The internal element of an electron tube which increases the speed of a beam of electrons.

admittance: The reciprocal of impedance, measured in *mhos*.

angle of lag or lead: The phase angle by which voltages, currents, or impedances precede or follow one another.

anode: The element of a tube to which the beam of electrons flows; called the *plate*.

attenuator: A device used to reduce the amplitude of a signal.

audio-frequency oscillator: A device which generates audio frequency signals.

autotransformer: A single-coil transformer whose primary and secondary connections are made to the one coil.

B- (B negative): Symbol used to indicate the negative terminal of the supply of energy to a plate.

B+ (B positive): Symbol for the positive terminal of the supply of energy to a plate.

ballast resistor: A type of resistor used to compensate for fluctuations in AC voltage. The resistance in this resistor rises with increases of the current through it, thus maintaining a constant current in spite of voltage fluctuations.

beat frequency: The frequency derived from combining two different frequencies. It is equal to the sum or difference of the combined frequencies.

broadband: Ability of a circuit to operate over a relatively wide range of frequencies. Cable TV is often referred to as broadband communication.

buffer: Any part or circuit used to minimize interaction between circuits.

C- (C negative): Symbol for the negative terminal of a grid's bias voltage source.

C+ (C positive): Symbol for the positive terminal of a grid's bias voltage source.

Cable Television Information Center: A part of the Urban Institute; established as an information clearing house for cable TV to assist locales in the growth of the medium. 2100 M Street NW, Washington, DC, 20037.

capacitive coupling: Coupling in which a capacitor is used as the signal path between two circuits or stages of a single amplification circuit.

carbon microphone: A microphone in which the pressure of sound on a diaphragm is mechanically transmitted to carbon granules, thus altering their resistance in accordance with the sound pressure.

cascade: In series, as in amplifier stages which are connected to one another in a line.

cathode: The negative or electron-emitting electrode of a tube. In some cases, the cathode is the filament; in others, a filament heats the cathode which emits the electrons.

coupling: The means by which signals are transferred from circuit to circuit; it can be direct, electrostatic, or inductive.

current-limiting resistor: A resistor which protects circuits from voltage surges.

decoupling circuit: A circuit in which resistors and capacitors separate and bypass unwanted signals.

distortion: Poor-quality reproduction of signals, resulting from alterations of the original signal wave form.

dropping resistor: A resistor which decreases the voltage in a circuit.

electric degree: 1/360 of a cycle of AC amperage or voltage.

electrode: The combination of elements in a vacuum tube, such as the cathode, anode, and grid.

envelope of a wave: A smooth curve which is drawn by plotting the positive and negative peaks of a modulated wave, and which thereby outlines the modulating wave.

Federal Communications Commission (FCC): A commission responsible for regulating all electronic communications systems originating in the United States. The FCC has a board made up of Presidential appointees. Address: 1919 M Street NW, Washington, DC, 20036.

filter: A resistor, coil, capacitor, or combination of such parts for blocking or attenuating AC at certain frequencies, while leaving it unimpeded at other frequencies.

harmonic: A sine wave that is a multiple of a fundamental frequency, referred to as the first harmonic. A complex wave is made up of a number of secondary frequencies referred to, for example, as the second or third harmonic.

harmonic content: The degree or numbers of harmonics in a complex frequency.

inductive coupling: A coupling process whereby energy is transferred by induction from a coil of one circuit to a coil of another circuit.

isolation transformer: A transformer with independent windings which is used to isolate AC/DC components from the power line.

jumper: A short length of wire used to make a temporary electric hookup.

Kirchhoff's current law: A law of electricity which states that the sum of all currents flowing to a point in a circuit must be equal to the sum of all the currents flowing away from that point.

Kirchhoff's voltage law: A law of electricity which states that the sum of all the voltage sources in a complete circuit must be equal to the sum of all the voltage drops in the same circuit.

linear: A relationship in which any change in one of two quantities is reflected by an exactly proportional change in the other.

linear amplification: Amplification in which the signal is reproduced exactly, but magnified.

line filter: A filter which blocks noise in power lines, preventing it from entering a component.

magnetic flux: The sum of all magnetic lines of force in a magnetic field.

matching: Coupling two circuits so that the impedance of either one will be equal to the impedance existing between them.

mho: A unit of admittance (as opposed to impedance), derived from the word ohm spelled backwards.

New York State Commission on Cable Television: A state regulatory body which oversees cable TV. Located in the Alfred E. Smith State Office Bldg., Albany, New York, 12225. Check state government listings for a cable TV regulatory commission in your state.

nonlinear: Not directly proportional, and thus producing a curve instead of a straight line when plotted on a graph.

output: Useful energy delivered.

rated output: The wattage, voltage, or amperage a device will provide, operating under normal conditions.

rheostat: A resistor with a moveable terminal for altering its value.

root-mean-square (rms): The heat energy content of a sinusoidal AC signal which is determined by multiplying the peak-to-peak AC value by .357. Most volt-ohm meters have rms and peak-to-peak scales.

shunt: A part connected in parallel to another part.

slug: A moveable iron core in an inductor which, when moved in or out, varies inductance.

trap: A tuned circuit used to eliminate or block a signal from a circuit.

tuning: Adjusting the inductance and/or capacitance in a coil-capacitor circuit. Or, adjusting circuits for optimum performance.

vacuum-tube voltmeter: Testing equipment which measures voltages without affecting the circuit being measured by using the high-input impedance of vacuum tubes.

vibrator: A device which electromagnetically converts a DC voltage to pulsating DC or AC.

voltage divider: A resistor with one or more contacts along the length of its resistance element.

voltage doubler: A rectifier which doubles the output voltage of a conventional rectifier.

wire recorder: A magnetic recording device, similar to a tape recorder, which uses round stainless steel wire instead of tape.

TV STANDARDS

	BRITISH	SOUTH AMERICA, US CANADA, JAPAN	FRENCH	GERMANY, HOLLAND, ITALY	SOVIET
No. of scan lines	405	525	819	625	625
Horizontal Frequency MHz	10.125	15.750	20.475	15.625	15.625
Frame rate	25	30	25	25	25
AC Hz standard	50	60	50	50	50
Video Bandwidth MHz	3.	4.	10.4	5	6
Channel Bandwidth MHz	5	6	14	7	8
Composite Video Voltage	1	about 2	1	1	1
Pict. Signal Voltage	.7	about 1.5	.75	.75	.75
Picture carrier modulation	AM	AM	AM	AM	AM
Sound carrier modulation	AM	FM	AM	FM	FM

COLOR SYSTEMS

	NTSC	PAL	SECAM
SUBCARRIER FREQUENCY	3.58	4.43	4.43
MODULATION SYSTEM	AM 2 color signals in quadrature	AM 2 color signals in quadrature	FM one color per signal line
SCAN SYSTEM	525	625	625

EQUIPMENT LIST / LOCATION

DATE / /

Equipment	CONDITION OUT	CONDITION IN	MODEL #	SERIAL #	NUMBER OF ITEMS
PORTAPAK CAMERA					
PORTAPAK VTR					
MONOPOD					
BELT POD					
SHOULDER BRACE					
TRIPOD					
LENSES					
AUXILIARY LENSES					
CAMERA EXT. CABLES					
TAKE-UP REELS 5" 7"					
AC ADAPTER CABLES					
BATTERIES—INTERN., EXTERN., CAR BATTERY CORDS					
MICS					
MIC EXTENSION CABLES					
MIC MIXER					
AUDIO CABLES—VTR TO MIXER, PA TO MIXER, ETC.					
HEADSETS					
ADAPTER PLUGS FOR INTER-CHANGABILITY OF INPUTS					
STUDIO VTR					
EDITOR					
AC POWER CABLES					
STUDIO CAMERA					
CAMERA TO VTR CABLES					
EXTERNAL SYNC. GEN.					
SYNC. GEN. CABLE TO VTR					
PORTAPAK CAMERA ADAPTER					
SWITCHER/SEG					
SEG CABLES					
VTR TO MONITOR CABLES					
MONITORS					
MONITOR TO MONITOR CABLES					
DISTRIBUTION AMP					
LIGHTS					
LIGHT STANDS					
AC POWER EXT. CABLES					
GAFFERS' OR MASKING TAPE					
HEAD CLEANING EQUIPMENT					
VIDEO TAPE—1/2 HR OR HOUR					
TOOL KIT SOLDERING IRON SOLDER SCREWDRIVERS PLIERS WIRE CUTTERS METER					

FIG 6:2

MANUFACTURERS' EQUIPMENT LIST

The following list is composed of major manufacturers' models readily available on the market. It does not reflect the complete line of equipment offered by each and every company. Addresses are included and it is advised that you periodically write for up-to-date catalogs. In the sections dealing with monitors, audio equipment, lights, and miscellaneous manufacturers, only names and addresses are listed. It should also be noted that most of the major manufacturers produce or distribute a complete line of accessories, such as mics, audio mixers, cables, sync generators, RF modulators, etc.

VIDEOTAPE RECORDERS AND CAMERAS

Akai America Ltd., 2139 East Del Amo Boulevard, Compton, CA 90220

VTRs	VTS-100S Portable VTR 1/4-inch B/W
	VTS-110DX (complete Portapak unit)
	VT-700 VTR 1/4-inch B/W
Cameras	VC-115 2/3-inch Vidicon B/W
	CCS-150 two 2/3-inch Vidicons NTSC Color (to be used with Color Control Unit)

Ampex Corporation 401 Broadway, Redwood City, CA 94063

VTRs	VR 420 VTR 1/2-inch Color and B/W EIAJ-1
	VPR 5800 VTR 1-inch Color and B/W
	VPR 7900-7903 VTR 1-inch Color and B/W Editing
	VPR 7950-7953 VTR 1-inch Color and B/W with Timebase Corrector
	VPR 5200 VTR 1-inch B/W Editing
Cameras	CC 500 3-Tube Color
	CC 452 2/3-Vidicon B/W

Audiotronics Corporation, 7428 Bellaire Avenue, North Hollywood, CA 91605

VTRs	PVR 707 VTR 1/2-inch B/W EIAJ-1
	PVR 708 VTR 1/2-inch Color and B/W Editing EIAJ-1
Cameras	PVC 808 2/3-inch Vidicon B/W with 3-inch Viewfinder
	PVC 818 2/3-inch Vidicon B/W with no Viewfinder

Cohu Inc. Electronics Div., PO Box 623, San Diego, CA 92112

Cameras	Series 1200 1-Tube NTSC Color

Concord Communications Systems, 46 Smith Street, Farmingdale, NY 11735

VTRs	VTR 800 VTR 1/2-inch B/W EIAJ-1
	VTP 310 Video Player 1/2-inch B/W EIAJ-1
	VTP 360 Video Player 1/2-inch Color EIAJ
	VTR 460e Portapak 1/2-inch B/W EIAJ-1
	VTR 1120 and 820 VTR 1/2-inch Color and B/W EIAJ-1 Editing
Cameras	CTC-30 2/3-inch Vidicon B/W
	CTC-36 2/3-inch Vidicon B/W with External or Internal Sync
	TCM-50 2/3-inch Vidicon B/W with Viewfinder

Hitachi Shibaden Corporation of America, 58–25 Brooklyn-Queens Expressway, Woodside, NY 11377

VTRs	SV-510U VTR 1/2-inch B/W EIAJ-1 Slow Motion
	SV-510D VTR 1/2-inch B/W EIAJ 1 Editing
	SV-512 VTR 1/2-inch B/W EIAJ-1 Time Lapse
	SV-550 w/ FP-707 Portapak 1/2-inch B/W EIAJ-1

Cameras	HV-405 2/3-inch Vidicon B/W
	HV-15 1-inch Vidicon B/W
	HV-155 1-inch Vidicon B/W 2:1 Inter-lace
	HV-1100 three 2/3-inch Vidicons Color (to be used with Color Control Unit)

International Video Corporation (IVC), 990 Almanor Avenue, Sunnyvale, CA 94086

VTRs	IVC 700 VTR 1-inch Color and B/W Editing
	IVC 760 VTR 1-inch Color and B/W Editing
	IVC 870 VTR 1-inch B/W Editing
Cameras	IVC 90 and 150 Color
	IVC 500A B/W with Tivicon

Javelin Electronics Company, 6357 Arizona Circle, Los Angeles, CA 90045

VTRs	X-400 VTR 1/2-inch Time Lapse and Slow Motion
	VTR-200 VTR 1/2-inch B/W EIAJ-1
	VTR-300 VTR 1/2-inch Color and B/W EIAJ
Cameras	CC 500 2/3-inch Vidicon B/W
	CC 700 2/3-inch Vidicon B/W

JVC Industries Inc., 50–35 56th Road, Maspeth, NY 11378

VTRs	KV 350 VTR 1/2-inch B/W EIAJ-1
	FV 1500 Video Player 1/2-inch Color EIAJ
	FV 3500 VTR 1/2-inch Color and B/W EIAJ
	PV 4500/GS 4500 Portapak 1/2-inch B/W EIAJ-1
	PV 4800U/GS 4800U Portapak 1/2-inch Color EIAJ

Cameras	GS-1500 2/3-inch Vidicon B/W
	GS-2500 2/3-inch Vidicon B/W with Viewfinder
	NU-1003 Color

Magnavox Video Systems, 1700 Magnavox Way, Fort Wayne, IN 46804

Camera	CV 400 1-Tube NTSC Color Hand-Held

Panasonic Video Systems, Div. of Matsushita Electric Corporation of America, PO Box 3980, Grand Central Station, New York, NY 10017

VTRs	NV-3082/WV 3082 Portapak 1/2-inch B/W EIAJ-1 (VTR is color-capable with color adaptor NVA 610)
	NV-3020 VTR 1/2-inch B/W EIAJ-1
	NV-3020 SD VTR 1/2-inch B/W EIAJ-1 Editing
	NV-3120 VTR 1/2-inch Color and B/W EIAJ
	NV-3130 VTR 1/2-inch Color and B/W EIAJ Editing
	NV-8020 VTR 1/2-inch B/W Time Lapse
	NV-504 VTR 1-inch Color and B/W
Cameras	WV-241P 2/3-inch Vidicon B/W
	WV-341P 2/3-inch Vidicon B/W with Viewfinder
	WV-2100P 2-Tube NTSC Color
	WV-8200P 2-Tube NTSC Color with Viewfinder

Sanyo Electric Company, Communications Products, 1200 West Artesia Boulevard, Compton, CA 90220

VTRs	VTR 1200 VTR 1/2-inch B/W EIAJ-1 Slow Motion and Time Lapse
	VTC 7100E Portapak 1/2-inch B/W EIAJ-1

Cameras		VC 500 2/3-inch Vidicon B/W Hand-Held
		VC 1150 2/3-inch Vidicon B/W
		VCM 2000 2/3-inch Vidicon B/W with Viewfinder

Sony Corporation of America, 9 West 57th Street, New York, NY 10019

VTRs		AV/AVC 3400 Portapak 1/2-inch B/W EIAJ-1
		AV 3600 VTR 1/2-inch B/W EIAJ-1
		AV 3650 VTR 1/2-inch B/W EIAJ-1 Editing
		AV 8600 VTR 1/2-inch Color and B/W EIAJ
		UV 340 VTR 1-inch Color and B/W Editing
Cameras		AVC 3200 2/3-inch Vidicon B/W
		AVC 3200DX 2/3-inch Vidicon B/W with Viewfinder
		AVC 3210 2/3-inch Vidicon B/W with 2:1 Interlace
		DX 5000B 2-Tube NTSC Color

Technisphere Corporation, 215 East 27th Street, New York, NY 10016

VTRs		TC 3130 VTR 1/2-inch Color and B/W EIAJ Editing (Panasonic NV3130 with modifications)

SWITCHERS AND SPECIAL EFFECTS GENERATORS

Concord Communications Systems

TCP-2 3-Camera Switcher/SEG Random Interlace Sync
TCP-15 5-Camera Switcher/SEG 2:1 Interlace Sync

Dynair Electronics Inc., 6360 Federal Boulevard, San Diego, CA 92114

SE 70 A-(R) 3-Camera Switcher/SEG External Sync with Key and Mat Color and B/W
VS 152A 6-Input 3-Bus Switcher/SEG with Vertical Interval Switching Color and B/W

GBC Closed-Circuit TV Corporation, 74 Fifth Avenue, New York, NY 10011

MEA 5100 4-Input Switcher/Fader 2:1 Interlace Sync
MEA 7300 6-Input Switcher/Fader 2:1 Interlace Sync with Key and Mat Color and B/W

Panasonic Video Systems

WJ-540P 5-Input Switcher/SEG 2:1 Interlace Sync
WJ-545P 5-Input Switcher/SEG 2:1 Interlace Sync with Genlock
WJ-5000P 5-Input Switcher/SEG with Vertical Interval Switching Color and B/W

Shintron Company Inc., 144 Rogers Street, Cambridge, MA 02142

366 4-Input Switcher/SEG with Vertical Interval Switching
370 4-Input Switcher/SEG with Vertical Interval Switching Built-in Colorizer

Sony Corporation of America

SEG-1 4-Input Switcher/SEG 2:1 Interlace Sync
SEG-2 6-Input Switcher/SEG 2:1 Interlace Sync with Key
SEG 600 6-Input Switcher/SEG 2:1 Interlace Sync with Key and Mat Color and B/W

Viscount Industries Ltd., 105 East 69th Avenue, Vancouver, BC, Canada

1120 Switcher/SEG Color and B/W
7V3 Switcher/SEG Color and B/W with Key and Mat

MONITORS/TVS

Apeco Video Systems, Div. of Apeco Corporation, 2100 West Dempster Ave., Evanston, ILL 60204

Audiotronics Corporation

Concord Communications Systems

GBC Closed-Circuit TV Corporation

General Electric Company (Conrac), PO Box 1122-104, Building 7, Electronics Park, Syracuse, NY 13201

Hitachi Shibaden Corporation of America

JVC Industries Inc.

Magnavox Video Systems

Motorola Communications and Electronics Inc., 4545 West August Boulevard, Chicago, ILL 60651

Panasonic Video Systems

RCA, Front and Cooper Streets, Camden, NJ 08102

Sanyo Electric Company

SC Electronics (Setchell-Carlson), Subsidiary of Audiotronics Corporation

Sony Corporation of America

VIDEO PROJECTORS

Amphicon Systems Inc., 1 Graphic Place, Moonachie, NJ 07074

  200 A and 270 B/W
  Amphicolor 1000 Color

General Electric Company

  PJ-500 Color
  PJ-700 B/W

Kalart-Victor, Plainville, CN 06062

  Telebeam B/W

Sony Corporation of America

  VPP-2000 Color and B/W
  VPS-500 Screen

AUDIO EQUIPMENT

AKG distributed by North American Philips Corporation, 100 East 42nd Street, New York, NY 10017

Altec Lansing Corporation, 1515 South Manchester Avenue, Anaheim, CA 92803

Audiotronics Corporation

Bogen Corporation, 100 South Van Brunt Street, Englewood, NJ 07631

ElectroVoice Inc., 600 Cecil Street, Buchanan, MI 49107

Shure Bros. Inc., 222 Hartrey Avenue, Evanston, ILL 60204

Sony Superscope, 8150 Vineland Boulevard, Sun Valley, CA 91352

LIGHTS

Berkey-Colortran, 25-20 Brooklyn-Queens Expressway West, Woodside, NY 11377

Smith-Victor, Griffin, IN 46319

MISCELLANEOUS MANUFACTURERS and EQUIPMENT DISTRIBUTORS

Consolidated Video Systems Inc., 3300 Edward Avenue, Santa Clara, CA 95051

Philips Broadcast Equipment Corporation, subsidiary of NORELCO, 1 Philips Parkway, Montvale, NJ 07645

Vicon Industries Inc., 130 Central Avenue, Farmingdale, NY 11735

Video Components Inc., 601 Main Street, Spring Valley, NY 10977

SOME MAJOR LENS MANUFACTURERS

Angenieux (A)
Apeco (Ap)
Bausch and Lomb (B&L)
Berthiot (B)
Birns and Sawyer (B&S)
Canon (C)
Century Precision Optics (CPO)
Cosmicar (Co)
Eastman (Es)
Elgeet (El)
Karl Heitz (KH)
Kern Paillard (KP)
Kilfitt (K)
Panasonic (Pa)
Rank-Taylor-Hobson (RTH)
Schneider (Sch)
Sony (So)
Tamron (Ta)
Vicon (Vi)
3M Wollensak (3M)
Zeiss (Z)
Zoomar (Zo)

SOME AUXILLARY LENSES

(from Spiratone, 135-06 Northern Boulevard, Flushing, NY, 11453)

180º Fisheye: provides a 180º circular image.

Curvatar: doubles the angle of coverage of any lens.

Multiple imagers: provides 3 or 5 concentric images, or 3 parallel.

Variable Macrovar: allows for extreme close-up zooming.

Vignetar: provides vignette of soft edges around a sharp center image.

SAMPLING OF LENSES (16mm C-mounts)

Focal Length	f/stop	Horizontal Viewing Angle	Manufacturer
4.5mm	f/2	88º	(Co)
5.7mm	f/1.8	80º	(KH)
6.5mm	f/1.9		(CPO)
8mm	f/1.5		(El)
10mm	f/1.8	55º	(A)(S)
15mm	f/1.3	35º	(A)
25mm	f/0.95	25º	(A)
25mm	f/1.4		(A)(El)(Es) (3M)
50mm	f/1.4	10º	(KP)
75mm	f/1.4	5º	(CPO)
85mm	f/2		(Z)
100mm	f/1.8	5º	(CPO)
300mm	f/5		(B&L)
500mm	f/5		(B&S)
1000mm	f/4.5		(B&S)

Zooms

9.5mm–95mm	f/2.2		(A)
11.5mm–90mm	f/2.1		(C)
12mm–120mm	f/2.2		(A)
12.5mm–50mm	f/1.8		(Vi)(So)
12.5mm–75mm	f/2		(Z)
16mm–86mm	f/2.5		(KP)
20mm–80mm	f/1.8		(El)
35mm–140mm	f/2.2		(A)

ANNOTATED BIBLIOGRAPHY

American Radio Relay League. *The Radio Amateur's Handbook*. Newnington, Conn.: The American Radio Relay League, 46th ed., 1969.

Though written for amateur radio operators, this book provides a hands-on approach to constructing and using electric circuits.

American Society of Cinematographers. *American Cinematographer Manual*. Hollywood, Cal.: American Society of Cinematographers, 1966.

Specifically intended for filmmaking, it is, however, a useful addition to any library of audio/visual technique and technology.

Beiser, Germaine and Arthur. *Physics For Everybody*. New York: E.P. Dutton & Co., Inc., (Paperback), 1960.

Easy reading for an understanding of basic physics.

Fink and Lutyens. *The Physics of Television*. Garden City, N.Y.: Doubleday & Co., Inc., Anchor Books, 1960.

A well-done introduction to TV, from physics to TV set.

Grob, Bernard. *Basic Television*. New York: McGraw-Hill, Inc., 1964.

Written primarily for educating TV service technicians, with a thorough introduction to the circuits of the TV camera and receiver, but not the VTR.

Lipton, Lenny. *Independent Filmmaking*, revised edition. San Francisco: Straight Arrow Books, 1973.

Similar to the *American Cinematographer Manual*, but written for the independents. Good discussion of independent film technology which can be of use to videomakers as well.

Shure, A. *Basic Television*, Vol. I. New York: John F. Rider, 1958.

A sort of comic-book version of Grob's book, much less comprehensive in the area of electronics.

Sloan Commission on Cable TV. *On the Cable*. New York: McGraw-Hill, Inc., 1971.

Useful for obtaining an overview of the issues surrounding the reality and potential of cable TV. Because it was written in 1971, it does not incorporate more recent developments.

Vergara, William. *Electronics in Everyday Things*. New York: Barnes & Noble, Inc., 1967.

An introduction to electronics for the lay person. Presented in a question-and-answer format.

Videofreex. *The Spaghetti City Manual*. New York: Praeger Publishers, Inc., 1973.

The first book about videotape recording and maintenance (especially concerning the Sony portapak), by people using the medium.

White, Gordon. *Video Recording*. London: Newnes Butterworths, 1971.

Written by a British electronics engineer, a comprehensive rundown of all video recording systems, oriented mainly toward professional recording.

INDEX

N

National Television Standards Committee, 103
negative image, 121
ni-cads, *see* nickel cadmium batteries
nickel cadmium batteries, 116
nixie tubes, 179
noise, 46
nucleus, 2

O

octave, 73
oersteds of coercivity, 97, 167
Off/Air recording, 160, 168, 170
ohm, 10, 11, 18, 30
Ohm's Law, 12–13, 18, 21
omnidirectional mic, 144
one-hour tape adaptor, 137
op amps, *see* operational amplifier
open-wire line, 118
operational amplifier, 134
optics, 41
optics equipment, 137
oscillator, 27, 31, 73, 94–95, 96, 123–125
oscilloscope, 179–180
overmodulation, 36
oxides, 97

P

PAL, 103
panning, 137, 142
parallel connection, *see* connections
particle energy, 97
particle theory, 19, 30
passive mixer, 114
pedestal control, 124
pedestal height, 128
pentodes, 25
phase, 27, 38, 79–82, 149–150
phase angle, 102, 103, 108, 180
phase modulation, 34, 38, 104
phase shifter, 108
phosphorescence, 40
phosphors, 92, 106
photoflood lamps, 153

photoelectric effect, 39
photon, 5, 7, 32, 39
photon absorption, 42
photosynthesis, 42
picofarads, 21
picture resolution, 176
picture signal, 96
piezoelectric effect, 47
pinch roller, 139
pincushion distortion, 53, 183
pi-network, 65
plano-concave divergent lens, 50
playback-only disc system, 133
plumbicon, 60
PM, *see* phase modulation
polarization, 44
polaroid material, 44
polyester filmbase, 97, 98
polymeric binder, 97, 98
portable mic mixer, 115
portable video system, 38
portapak, 115, 116, 123, 135
portapak-to-monitor cable, 138
potential difference, 2, 10, 19, 25, 29, 94
potential energy, *see* energy, mechanical
power equipment, 136
power loss, 14
power sources, outdoor, 165
pre-amplifier, 114, 165
pre-emphasis, 74
principal focus, 44
prisms, 50
proc amp, *see* processing amplifier
processing amplifier, 124, 169
program bus, 122
proton, 2, 10
pulse, 66
pulse counter demodulation, 74
pulse generator, 66

Q

Q signal, 102, 108
quadrature, 102
quad systems, *see* quadruplex scanning systems
quadruplex scanning systems, 76, 77
quartz lights, *see* halogen lamps
quantum, 28, 39

R

Radio Frequency: amplification, 96, 164; level, 126; modulation, 33, 34, 125, 138, 164; radiation, 171; signal, 188
radio mics, 145
random interlace, 60
random switching, 120
rapid rectilinear lens, 6, 53
real-image convergent lens, 50
receivers, 34: black-and-white, 96; color, 106–107
rechargeable batteries, 117
recording heads, 87, 184
record mode, 140
rectification, 24, 27, 31
red, green, blue signals, 102, 106
reflected light exposure meters, 153
reflection, 42
reflectors, portable, 153
refraction, 43
RGB signals, *see* red, green, blue signals
regulator, 115
relative brightness level, 128
repair, 183–184
resistor, 11–14, 18, 20
resolution, 60
resonant frequency, 23, 30
retrace, 60
RF, *see* Radio Frequency

S

saturation, 100, 102
saturation levels, 130
sawtooth waveform, 95
scan conversion, 163, 167
scanning, 59–60, 76, 94, 133
SECAM, 103
second generation copy, 166
SEG, *see* special effects generator
semi-conductors, n-type and p-type, 29, 31
series connections, *see* connections
service centers, factory *versus* authorized dealers', 181
servo-control, 76, 77
servomechanisms, 48
servos, *see* servomechanisms
servo systems, 79–80, 184
shadow mask, 106, 107
shielded cable, 118
shielded twin-lead line, 118
shooting, 140–142

short circuits, 16–17, 19
shotgun mic, 145, 148
shoulder brace, 137
showing: multi-monitor, 164–165; mobile, 165; video theatre, 165–166; video projection, 166
sidebands, 33
sight, 5
signal amplifier, 124
signal drive circuits, 50, 66
signal frequencies, 181
signal generator, 181
signal loss, 87
signal-to-noise ratio, 46, 74, 112, 133
signal waveform, 179
silver oxide cells, 117
sine wave, 32
sine wave oscillator, 73
single-mic recording, 147–148
single sideband transmission, 33
6-pin connector, *see* din connector
skew, 86, 139, 161
slave tape, 166, 167, 168
slow motion, 89, 133
small-scale integration, 134
soldering, 178–179
soldering iron, 138
solenoid switching, 88–89
solid state, 29
solid-state display, 131
solid-state electronics, 31
sonic sound wave, *see* sound waves
sound, 6: frequency, 45; wavelength, 45
sound dubbing, 150–151
sound equipment, 138, 144–145
sound intensity, 45
sound levels, 139–140
sound monitoring, 143
sound signal, 96
sound system, 110–114
sound waves, 6; infrasonic, 45
speakers, 113; dynamic, 165; electrostatic, 165
special effects generator, 120–122, 163–164
speed of light, 4
spherical aberration, 50, 51
splicing, 158
split-screen images, 120
splitter, 164
square wave oscillator, 73
SSI, *see* small-scale integration
stable operating level, 28